REDTAILS IN THE SUNSET

Darren Moncrieff

REDTAILS IN THE SUNSET

The untold story of the Central Australian Football Club

ABORIGINAL STUDIES PRESS

To Sarah Mary Jones, and Kumantye Palmer
– this is for you both.
DM

First published in 2025
by Aboriginal Studies Press
Reprinted in 2026
© Darren Moncrieff 2025

All rights reserved. No part of this book may be reproduced or transmitted in any form or by any means, electronic or mechanical, including photocopying, recording or by any information storage and retrieval system, without prior permission in writing from the publisher. The *Australian Copyright Act 1968* (the Act) allows a maximum of one chapter or 10 per cent ofthis book, whichever is the greater, to be photocopied by any educational institution for its education purposes provided that the educational institution (or body that administers it) has given a remuneration notice to Copyright Agency Limited (CAL) under the Act.

The story told in this book takes place in Central Australia on the lands of the Arrernte Peoples. The Arrernte cultural knowledge in this book is owned by the Arrernte people of Central Australia. All rights to Indigenous Cultural and Intellectual Property remain with the Indigenous owners of the knowledge and cultural expression and, should you wish to use or publish any ICIP, you will need their permission.

The opinions expressed in this book are the author's own and do not necessarily reflect the view of the Australian Institute of Aboriginal and Torres Strait Islander Studies (AIATSIS) or Aboriginal Studies Press.

Aboriginal and Torres Strait Islander people are respectfully advised that this publication contains names and images of deceased persons and culturally sensitive information.

Every effort has been made to trace and acknowledge copyright holders and obtain necessary permissions for the use of material in this publication. If any source has been inadvertently overlooked,Aboriginal Studies Press will be pleased to make the necessary corrections in future editions.

Aboriginal Studies Press is the publishing arm of the Australian Institute of Aboriginal and Torres Strait Islander Studies, operating on the lands of the Ngunnawal and Ngambri people.

GPO Box 553, Canberra, ACT 2601
Phone: +61 2 6246 1183
Email: asp@aiatsis.gov.au
Web: aiatsis.gov.au/asp

ISBN (pb) 978-0-85575-206-4
(epub) 978-0-85575-262-0
(epdf) 978-0-85575-266-8

Cover design by Upside Creative
Edited by Nadia Johanson and Darby Jones
Text design and typesetting by Upside Creative

Cover photo: Redtails players (from left) Jayden Prior, Tyson Carmody, Caleb Hart, Reggie Smith and Bradley Turner jubilant after defeating Darwin powerhouse club St Mary's by four points in their NTFL Premier League debut match at Traeger Park in Mparntwe/Alice Springs.
(Photo: Justin Brierty / *Centralian Advocate*, Tuesday 9 October 2012)

CONTENTS

AUTHOR'S NOTE

The Australian game of football has been a constant in my life. It was 'love at first kick' from the first game I saw on a grainy, black-and-white TV at my gantharri's house. It was the mid-1970s. I was around six years old and hooked! Ever since, this game — football, footy, Aussie rules footy — has held for me a timeless mystique. It is a game that speaks to me like no other abstract activity can; one that is altogether unique in the world of sport.

As a kid, playing footy was home, a safe space; it held me close and everything in this world made sense. It is this sense of wonderment and closeness that has kept me engaged with this game in all the decades since.

As an Aboriginal man, a sense of justice for my people has informed much of my worldview. And what the Central Australian Football Club — the Redtails — set out to achieve also aligned with those sensibilities.

In that sense, this is more than a football book, more than a sports book. My hope here is that you will gain a greater understanding of the ongoing work being done to help our people — Aboriginal people — overcome disadvantage in this country, as well as an understanding of what this game means to a lot of people in Central Australia. Maybe you'll even develop a new appreciation for football. Hopefully all three. Above all that, my overall hope is that you like what I have written.

DARREN MONCRIEFF,
5 MAY 2025

INTRODUCTION

Take a grassroots football club in the geographical centre of Australia, spin a compass, and take flight toward wherever that needle points. That, essentially, was the objective concocted in Alice Springs by a pair of far-sighted and selfless individuals. Their aim was to achieve the improbable. The dynamic duo of Rob Clarke and Ian McAdam took a grand plan from the dry desert of the Red Centre of the Northern Territory into the blustery world of the tropical Top End at the edge of the Arafura Sea. The brief: begin at Alice Springs, encroach their way northward, and breach the impenetrable walls of Darwin football. It was in Darwin, and in Darwin football, where I first met Rob Clarke.

It was 2012, and I had just returned to the Top End capital in October of that year. I had first left the place in 2003 for the eastern states. I returned to write for Indigenous media and to continue playing football. I was 41 turning 42 — still fit enough to run around; but obviously silly enough to put my body through the rigours of this young man's game when way past AFL draft age. But football and playing football is where I find a certain joy. Me and the Redtails crossed paths in Darwin but not on the football field. We crossed on the pages of my mind when I wrote several articles about the Redtails' attempt to join the Northern Territory Football League during this time. As part of that work, I wanted to document the Redtails on game-day, to see what the hype was all about. I attended some of their games. One was against the Tiwi Bombers. Another against Nightcliff.

For my articles I went straight to the source and spoke with Rob on several occasions, in person and on the phone. I even saw him at the Parap Village Markets once — there he was, proud-as in his Redtails team polo during the hottest hour, under the scorching Darwin sun. I thought, *he's mad!* But also, *here's a man who wears his heart on his team polo!* I also thought that I'd like to buy one of those team polos, but that I wouldn't be wearing it at the hot markets.

Rob was always forthcoming with my calls and my questions, always happy for a yarn. I gained a good insight from his thinking and his words, some of them reproduced in this book. Interestingly, from those initial conversations in 2012 to the many we had had over a decade later for this book, his motivation has stayed the same. It is always about the team with Rob; always about the club, and always about what it could do for Central Australia and the people that live there. Ask him a question about his own hard work and personal sacrifices, and he'd deflect the conversation back to the club.

I don't ever recall meeting Ian McAdam during this time though. Of course, Ian was there, but we never crossed paths or spoke. We eventually did a decade later in Alice Springs. I was researching for this book, and I got to know another selfless individual whose work and concern for Aboriginal youth drives much of his waking life.

Both men understood what football meant to Aboriginal people in their communities. But I don't think Rob Clarke or Ian McAdam could have imagined what was in store for them when they embarked on this journey — the challenges, the roadblocks, the worldly waves they would face during this mighty four-year effort in taking a rag-tag bunch of footy part-timers and community Countrymen head-to-head against their semi-professional city-cousin counterparts. Among the issues they encountered along the way was the 'butterfly effect' from a rising bloc of South Asian nations, a dysfunctional Northern Territory government, a distracted sports minister, a footy chief whose inbox was redlining, and a Red Centre 'jewel' that sat so close yet so agonisingly far.

The buy-in from the local Alice Springs football community and businesses was strong, but convincing the custodians of the game in Darwin was another story. This is that story.

SOMETHING GOOD MUST COME OF THIS

IT is spring and the evening desert air is crisp and clear on an early October night. There is a swarm of people on an open field. An excited hum and an infectious energy resonate across the expanse. Something is brewing. In the middle of this excitement rises a six-foot tall, solidly built, middle-aged white man. He is looking up and carrying a smile as wide as the field behind him.

The man is in a state of utter jubilation, just like the throng around him. His hands are raised. One is clenched in a fist as a gesture of triumph; the other is holding a trophy in mid-salute to persons unseen.

The man is perched atop the shoulders of two people. One is an Aboriginal man, and the other is a white man — necessary distinctions in the context of this shared moment. These two are in their 20s. They are wearing identical outfits, and their beaming smiles light up the Central Australian night. All three men — Black, white and beaming — have shiny medals around their necks. This trio and the people around them are sharing in something special. We are in Alice Springs, and this scene captures a significant moment toward the end of 2012.

The big, happy white man with the triumphant fist and shiny trophy is Rob Clarke — early 40s, local Alice Springs-born self-made business owner, and a third-generation Central Australian whose family arrived in these parts over 80 years ago. Clarke is the President of the Central Australian Football Club which had just recorded a famous victory against the odds. The game they had won was the culmination of a mountain of work by Clarke and a dedicated band of friends, partners, locals and volunteers. The win was a key plank in an ambitious and audacious plan, unlike anything seen in the region before or since.

It was also one part of a multi-layered response to a personal tragedy two years earlier.

***

On a quiet Alice Springs night near the end of 2010, a senseless and needless act of violence took place. Kumantye Palmer was a young man from Amoonguna, a small Aboriginal community with about 50 houses, a short 15-minute drive south-east of the big town. In the early hours of 31 October 2010, on a dimly lit street corner, Kumantye was met by a person known to him. The circumstance of their meeting remains unknown, but in the hands of Kumantye's antagonist was a sharp object. Kumantye was stabbed with that sharp object by his assailant. Kumantye would later succumb to injuries from the stabbing.

He was 21.

This senseless act of violence was an all-too common occurrence among a group of people disproportionate to the general population in this town.

Kumantye Palmer and his people from Amoonguna are mostly Eastern and Central Arrernte speakers and are recognised as the Traditional Owners of the general area of Mparntwe (pronounced M'barnt-wa) — the Arrernte name for where Alice Springs is now located.[1]

ABORIGINAL CULTURAL MOURNING PROTOCOLS

The non-use of deceased persons' first and-or full names, sometimes in perpetuity or for a specific timeframe, is a sign of respect for the living and the dead; the specifics of which may also vary among the hundreds of cultural and language groups across the country. For the Amoonguna community, 'Kumantye' as a reference is culturally acceptable; the young man's family also accepts 'Joshy'. Variations in pronunciation, and therefore in spelling, include 'Kumanjayi', 'Kwementyaye' or 'Kunmanara'.

HIDDEN IN BROAD DAYLIGHT

Central Australia encompasses mostly the southern half of the Northern Territory.[2] It also encompasses parts of far-north South Australia, large tracts of Western Australia's far east, and the far-western reaches of Queensland and New South Wales. At the centre of Central Australia is Alice Springs, a big country town. Central Australia evokes a certain 'romance' and mystery for those who have yet to visit. It is renowned for its breath-taking landscape and the rich history of the languages, law, lore, culture and art of the Arrernte Peoples who have lived in harmony on these timeless lands for thousands of years. But under those deep blue skies and within the picture postcard landscape, a dark side hides in broad daylight.

A 2020 NT Department of Health report titled 'Mortality in the Northern Territory 1967–2014', revealed a shocking array of statistics. It found that injury is by far the leading cause of death for young Aboriginal people in the Northern Territory. It accounted for 68 per cent of deaths in children aged five to 14, and 70 per cent of deaths in young people aged 15 to 24, in the period from 2006 to 2014.[3] As if to underscore the sad and fateful eventuality of these findings, a young man the same age as Kumantye Palmer had met the same fate at a Town Camp in Alice Springs only a few weeks earlier.[4] As coronial inquest followed coronial inquest, and as two large families grappled with the twin afflictions of grief and hopelessness from losing their boys, hopeful change came from an unlikely source.

In Alice Springs, Kumantye played for Rovers Football Club in the Central Australian Football League (CAFL). Football — Aussie rules football — is the number one game for the thousands of Aboriginal people in Central Australia. In football, Kumantye was a bright prospect. At the Rovers Football Club was Rob Clarke. During their time at Rovers, Kumantye and Rob Clarke had formed a close bond. The young man had potential, and Clarke also held some promise for him outside the game.

> *We played A-grade together from about the 2008 season onwards. I was in the ruck, he was a midfielder, so we became close on the field. I used to go pick him up from Amoonguna for training and games and then take him home, or go and get him for club functions. After our games, and during our car trips, we started talking about life and work and I took him to job interviews. Once he called me about some big drama at home, and there was a racial incident in football that we navigated together. So we had that three years together, we became friends like that. (Rob Clarke)*[5]

The day after Kumantye died, Clarke heard the awful news.

> *On that Sunday I think I was going to work and my wife Alecia got the phone call, and I remember I just sat in the car. I didn't know what to say or do. Then I just lost it, lost my emotions. I couldn't believe it. I thought I was doing something good but it obviously wasn't enough.*

Clarke's personal struggle with the grief he carried for Kumantye — even a level of self-blame — would soon turn to frustration, and a growing indignation toward the town he thought he knew.

The newspaper that serviced Alice Springs and Central Australia was the *Centralian Advocate*, a tabloid owned by News Corp (Australia). First published in 1947 (as an independent newspaper), the paper was a bi-weekly read; its publication days were Tuesdays and Fridays.[6] At its peak, the paper claimed an Alice Springs readership of 12,000 of the estimated 25,000 people who called the place home.[7] Nowadays, the *Advocate* is a weekly lift-out in the croc-obsessed ALL-CAPS FRONT PAGE HEADLINE Darwin-based tabloid and News Corp stablemate *NT News*.

In most editions, the *Advocate*'s beat was local goings-on, town council meetings, police reports, crime, yard sales, the housing market, local sport, reality TV 'stars', celebrity goss — the Kardashians probably — lamington drives, bingo days, trivia nights, Rotary meetings and other feel-good fluff. Of the rich and multitudinous layers of Aboriginal knowledge and cultural protocols in an area soaked in these timeless ways, the *Centralian Advocate* was found wanting.

During the 1970s, as First Nations people across the country began asserting themselves mostly in politics and in the land-rights movement, the paper came under increasing fire for its lack of positive reporting on Aboriginal people.[8] In a little-known judgement in the early 1980s, the Supreme Court of the Northern Territory had issued a court order to the editors of the *Advocate* to destroy a particular edition of the newspaper. The paper was found by the court to have breached Aboriginal cultural protocols by printing a photo of a location where someone had died.[9] This was but one of a litany of complaints levelled at the paper over the years.[10] It was into this environment Aboriginal people and allies pushed to establish a voice of their own. The result was the country's first Aboriginal-owned media organisation, the Central Australian Aboriginal Media Association.[11]

But it was the total lack of attention given to the death of Kumantye Palmer by the *Centralian Advocate* and its editors that both astonished and angered the local community. And Rob Clarke. There simply were no reports, no follow-ups, no examination, no celebration, no anything about the life and loss of Kumantye Palmer in the editions following his death. The paper representing the region and claiming a readership of two-thirds of the Alice Springs population basically ignored the passing of yet another young life on its doorstep. Except, that is, for this:

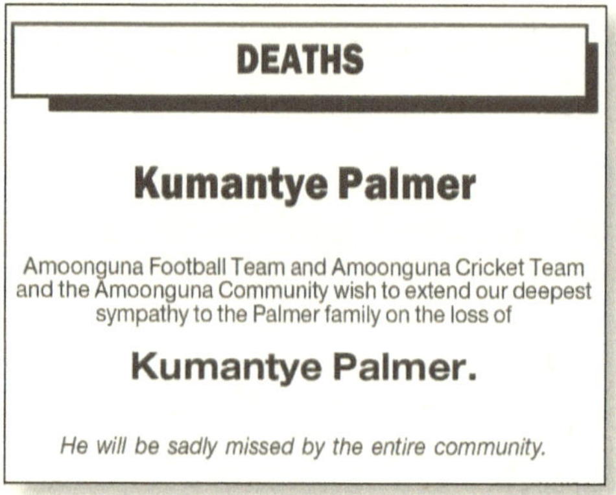
DEATHS

Kumantye Palmer

Amoonguna Football Team and Amoonguna Cricket Team and the Amoonguna Community wish to extend our deepest sympathy to the Palmer family on the loss of

Kumantye Palmer.

He will be sadly missed by the entire community.

This brief but poignant notice was written and paid for by the people of Amoonguna and the community's football and cricket teams in which Kumantye had played. In terms of how much this notice would have cost, judging by its size and rates per line and column-centimetres, around $50; just enough to fit among the fine print of the classified ads section where one can also find great specials on power tools and savings on groceries.[12] It was all the community could afford. And that was the only mention of Kumantye Palmer in the local newspaper in the days and weeks following his tragic death.

It seemed to everyone that as far as the *Centralian Advocate* was concerned, acknowledging Kumantye's life and untimely death was best left to a grieving community, and the money they could spare to buy space in the local paper to pay their respects. The takeaway from this for the local community, and for Rob Clarke, was that there was a growing apathy toward Aboriginal youth in Alice Springs; that there was a passive acceptance of Black loss of life; that the place Rob Clarke's family had called home since the 1940s had apparently resigned itself to just not care. This, for him, was a disquieting and unhappy realisation. 'In any other place in the country, it would get attention,' he said when we revisited these tragic events, 'but to me, it was just like it was a normal thing here.'

As Rob Clarke worked to come to terms with these events in the weeks and months that followed, his mind turned toward a radical concept, something he had pondered over several years earlier, but which had arrived now with a greater sense of urgency. It was an answer to a question with no apparent solution — the question of how people generally, and local media specifically, could simply not care. The idea that was percolating in his mind had its origins in the divergent trajectories of four Central Australian Aboriginal young men. Trajectories that took them far away from home and into the cut-throat world of professional sport.

THEY MIGHT BE GIANTS

If the hard bigotry of prejudice and discrimination is a wall that keeps the marginalised out of the opportunities of the social and economic mainstream, then the soft bigotry of low expectations is a prison. NOEL PEARSON[1]

IN the early years of the 2000s in Alice Springs there was a local junior Aussie rules football team called Northside Power. The coach at Northside Power was Rob Clarke, and the man was in his element: teaching kids the way of the Sherrin (the ball used in Aussie rules named after Melbourne-based saddler Thomas William Sherrin).[2] Clarke's time as Northside Power coach included overseeing the young players' development, and sharing his love and enthusiasm for the Australian game.

Among the many juniors passing through at Northside was a kid with a fair set of skills. Jake Neade was his name. Jake was from a tiny town called Elliott that was an eight-hour, 750 kilometre drive north of Alice Springs.

Elliott's traditional name is Kulumindini, in an area that is the traditional home to the Jingili desert people; the Wambaya people to the east and south-east; the Yangman and Mangarrayi to the north; the Mudbura and Gurindji to the west; and the Warlpiri, Warlmanpa and Warumungu to the south and south-west — all of whom had traditional associations with the Jingili and ceremonial ties to the watered areas around Elliott.[3] Tidy tiny-town Elliott has around 250–300 people, 80–90 houses, a footy oval, a golf course, and a roadhouse that serves the best chips this side of Larrimah. Jake Neade from Elliott showed a lot of potential at Northside Power.

Another youngster showing potential at one of the many other junior football clubs in Alice Springs around this time was Dom Barry. Dom, like Jake, was one of several hundred juniors from Central Australia who were well-versed in the ways of Aussie rules football. Jake and Dom were both rangy in physique and athletic in movement. With the encouragement of their coaches, the pair began to flourish on the field. Later, as they grew, and sought greater opportunities in football and in education, their mentors supported the pair's enrolments at St Patrick's College, an independent Catholic secondary boarding school for boys in far-away Ballarat.

Ballarat's population at the time was edging toward 100,000 people.[4] It is the third largest Victorian city in population behind Melbourne and Geelong. The regional centre is celebrated for the 1851 miners' rebellion against the British administration of the Colony of Victoria, who were set on imposing licence fees upon the workers (essentially a personal tax on workers).[5] The uprising led to bloodshed in which 27 people — mostly rebels — were killed. These events are widely viewed as the beginning of Australia's version of representative democracy, and from which our basic freedoms of speech, the right to vote, and the rights of workers were established.[6]

It was in historic Ballarat that Jake Neade and Dom Barry joined the school's football team. Following standout efforts on the field, the pair won spots in the town's representative team, the North Ballarat Rebels (a name that honours the town's legacy). The Rebels played in the TAC Cup, a quasi-national elite under-18s competition (sponsored by the Traffic Accident Commission in Victoria) where some of the best young footballers were invited to play.[7] The TAC Cup was also where clubs in the professional Australian Football League (AFL) would send their talent scouts. It was here, as a pair of Rebels, that Jake Neade and Dom Barry came to the attention of AFL scouts on the lookout for the Next Big Thing.

Back in Central Australia around the same time, another kid was also on the rise in Alice Springs junior football. Curtly Hampton was in his mid-teens when he, like Jake and Dom, left the familiarity of home and family to pursue his football dreams and further his education. With the support of his family, Curtly enrolled at Immanuel College in Adelaide, a school of the Lutheran religious order, and joined its football team. Curtly's skills were a welcome addition to the school's team and he progressed in leaps and bounds. He won selection in an AIS-AFL Academy side and was a popular choice as captain. The Australian Institute of Sport and AFL joint organisational academy was a football, education and personal development program with a 12-month scholarship attached. Curtly displayed a maturity beyond his years and he captained the youth side with distinction.

GREATER WESTERN SYDNEY ZONE

Around 2011, parts of the Northern Territory were 'zoned' to Greater Western Sydney, or 'GWS'. Nicknamed the 'Giants', GWS was a new club established in Sydney's sprawling west by the AFL Commission. They came into the league in 2012 after a two-year lead-in, progressing from the TAC Cup in 2010, and then the newly established North East Australian Football League (NEAFL) in 2011. The Melbourne-based AFL Commission — the peak body governing Aussie rules football in Australia — was looking to grow the game in New South Wales, so they planted the Giants in the stronghold of rival football code rugby league. The Commission's mission was to spread the

Aussie rules gospel far and wide outside its traditional heartlands. With the Giants strategically placed in Sydney's west, the Aussie rules-loving Northern Territory was 'annexed' as a recruiting zone for the new club.[8]

The Northern Territory enjoys higher Aussie rules player-participation rates per capita than anywhere else in the country, and the Giants needed some of that ready-made talent to complement what they were building.[9] In practical terms, what this annexation meant for the Giants was that the NT's footballers were also theirs, in that the club had first dibs on those players ahead of the other AFL clubs — its 'NT Zone'. How the Commission did this was by way of its annual national draft: a 'lottery' system of player selection where AFL clubs pick promising footballers from a pool of many thousands of young hopefuls from across the country. In the 2011 October–November draft period, GWS dived into the national pool of talent with a pocketful of picks. The Giants were building their inaugural squad ahead of their debut AFL season in 2012. The club was on the lookout for top talent. Despite living and playing in Adelaide at the time, Curtly Hampton's football stocks were tied to the Northern Territory by virtue of his original residency and where he played junior football, and so by extension he was 'tied' to GWS by virtue of the club's NT recruiting zone. The Giants liked what they saw in the athletic and mature 17-year-old and, applying one of their two NT Zone selections, chose Curtly as one of the first crop of players in the national draft. Curtly and the Giants made their senior football debut in round 1 of the 2012 AFL premiership season. The young Central Australian would go on to play 51 games for GWS from 2012 to 2015, and a handful more at the Adelaide Crows in 2016.

In the post-season of 2012, having completed their first season in the AFL, GWS was on the hunt for more talent to build into their promising squad. The club's scouts alerted the Giants to the potential shown by a pair of Rebels from Central Australia now in Ballarat, Jake Neade and Dom Barry, whose football stocks, like Curtly's, were tied to the Northern Territory. While they were not exactly what the club needed at the time, the Giants played the trade game. At the 2012 November draft, GWS used the NT Zone selections it had held in reserve to on-trade the pair in what was a two-pronged deal with rival clubs Port Adelaide and Melbourne. The caveat being that, in exchange, GWS would receive compensatory picks in the draft, as per the convoluted rules at the time. It was a huge gamble. For their part, Port Adelaide and Melbourne were happy to oblige and the clubs accepted the Giants' offers. Over the next six years, from 2013 to 2018, Jake Neade and Dom Barry would build brief but serviceable AFL careers at both clubs, respectively.

THE PROBLEM WITH THIS PATHWAY

The personal drive and success shown by Curtly Hampton, Jake Neade and Dom Barry in navigating their way through foreign environments and into professional AFL football had more to do with individual exceptionalism than chance. And while Rob Clarke felt a personal level of pride in the AFL career of his former Northside Power star Jake Neade, he was bothered by the circular route that Jake, and Dom and Curtly, were compelled to take for their best shot at making it in the big time. What chance, the coach wondered, was there for other kids from Central Australia with just as much football talent as this trailblazing trio but who may have lacked the structural support of family and friends, and the education system? Clarke fully understood the pathways the AFL had in place for young football hopefuls from outside the big cities. This was primarily via the labyrinthine route of national tournaments, the TAC Cup, the draft and zones. But clear football pathways from Central Australia directly *into* the AFL system did not exist for the many talented Jake Neades, Dom Barrys, Curtly Hamptons, and others who were just as talented but lacking the confidence and drive to do what these boys did.

It is also worth remembering the anomalous recruitment in the AFL of 20-year-old Liam Jurrah around this time. Jurrah, from the Central Desert community of Yuendumu, joined AFL club Melbourne. Jurrah, also known by his Warlpiri skin name Jungarrayi, was selected by the Demons at the 2009 AFL pre-season draft. He would play 36 games over four years with the club, including a pre-season exhibition game in China, of all places, where he kicked the winning goal on the final siren in a repurposed stadium filled with bemused locals.[10] Jurrah's introduction into professional football came via a dizzying process involving two AFL clubs, a club in the Victorian Football League (VFL), a couple of games in Darwin with Nightcliff, and an interstate match for the 'Big V' of Victoria[i] all in the space of a couple of months. It was this convoluted manner of Jurrah's AFL recruitment that drove home the need for a better way, more tailored toward the specific needs of Central Australians.[11]

The lack of a direct route from Central Australia into the world of AFL football compelled these four Aboriginal young men to take a giant detour away from the security of their families, Country and all they knew at a young and potentially vulnerable age. Had there been clearly defined and established pathways directly from Central Australia into the AFL, their respective journeys would have been more localised, less uncertain, and with less risk. But this did not exist. Without the Giants' NT Zone allocation, or their own initiative, this young cohort's potential and obvious talent may have never been realised.

In Rob Clarke's mind, this was not ideal. There must be a better way. How about, he pondered, an all-inclusive locally driven semi-professional football club in Central Australia? One where young men could grow and thrive in football while living at home and on Country rather than chancing it elsewhere? A club where young men could develop in football to an acceptable standard that AFL scouts would be negligent to ignore. At its core, Clarke's primary idea was for a localised pathway system for the many talented and likewise ambitious Central Australian young men who could enjoy the luxury of having the AFL come to them; just like it is for their counterparts in the

---

i Victorian representative teams are known colloquially as the 'Big V' by virtue of the 'V' for Victoria, and the team's guernsey design: navy blue with a big white 'V' on the front.

big Australian towns and capital cities. In the wake of his young friend's tragic death, Clarke's thoughts of this solution had only grown.

A SHARED PASSION

It was about this time that another local man was bouncing around several thoughts of his own within this football-life 'vacuum'. His thoughts were about how best to guide the region's troubled youth to realise and expand their prospects in football and beyond.

In 2011, Arrernte and Kija man Ian McAdam was part of the Alice Springs' Clontarf Foundation Academy team. The academy was a youth-based school football program originating out of Western Australia in the late 1990s. McAdam understood that meaningful employment was key to addressing the many issues facing his community. From his own experience, he knew young Countrymen could do much better than what mainstream society generally expected of them. They could overcome the 'soft bigotry of low expectations' and lead productive and purposeful lives, rejecting that real-time, damaging systemic practice articulated first by former U.S. President George W. Bush for African Americans in their country, and later repurposed by Aboriginal academic Noel Pearson for Aboriginal people in ours.[12, 13]

Ian McAdam and Rob Clarke didn't know it at the time but a shared passion for a weekend tradition would bring the two men and their emergent ideas together.

FORKS IN THE ROAD

In Chinese philosophy: Yin & yang were introduced ... around the year 400 BC. Daoism (or Taoism) sees life as a balancing act, with the idea that opposites are needed in order for harmony to exist.

'YIN & YANG IN CHINESE'[1]

TWO central figures emerge at a pivotal moment of this story.

Rob Clarke's grandparents' arrival in Alice Springs in the 1940s would see the family establish roots in Central Australia that would flourish for the next three generations. To get to know Alice Springs-born Rob Clarke is to understand a man's love of football. He is a football jack-of-all-trades: club president, team coach, player, former player, runner, waterboy, stretcher-carrier, tape man, administrator, bus driver, taxi driver and all round go-getter. In many ways, the game of football informs a lot of what one needs to know about Rob Clarke. Outside of football he is a diesel mechanic by trade, running the Fidler & Clarke diesel mechanics workshop in Alice Springs.

Ian McAdam was born in Darwin. As a two-year-old in 1974, he was one of several thousand people evacuated from the Northern Territory capital in the wake of Cyclone Tracy. As a teenager, McAdam moved from Alice Springs to Adelaide, where he later completed an apprenticeship as a carpenter. Apparently he can make a mean kitchen cabinet! McAdam credits his strong work ethic to his parents: legendary stockman Charlie McAdam and his wife, Val Stokes. Around 2005, McAdam left Adelaide to return to Alice Springs. In 2011, he was part of the town's Clontarf Foundation Academy team, based at Yirara College in Alice Springs.

Rob Clarke's style of engagement can endear or enrage those he deals with, particularly on matters he is unapologetically passionate about. In contrast, Ian McAdam exudes the chill exterior of a mellow fellow with a mind as sharp as a tack. Together, their collective energy is like yīnyáng; the ancient Chinese philosophy describing how opposite or even contrary forces can sometimes work together in harmonious collusion. These somewhat contradictory forces would soon discover a commonality and would collude toward a harmonious purpose on a day out at the footy.

McAdam recalls clearly how he and Clarke first met. 'Right there,' he said, 'at those steps.' We're at Traeger Park. McAdam is pointing toward a set of concrete steps rising like a concrete whirlpool into the Bowden McAdam Grandstand in a steady swirl. It's a bright, sunny mid-year day in Alice Springs and the green turf at the vacant venue is soft under our bare feet. The day's topic is those events over a decade ago. The circumstances of the *why* of their informal greeting, however, is long forgotten. Only the *how* is remembered, and that it was during a football game at Traeger Park in the early part of the 2011 Central Australian Football League (CAFL) season.

Not everyone knows everyone in Alice Springs, but in shared interests like football they mostly do. On the day they had met, McAdam and Clarke arrived at Traeger Park only vaguely aware of each other's existence. At a fortuitous moment, they ended that day as new friends with a shared vision for the region's youth. McAdam's summation of that day speaks of a pivotal moment in both their lives, 'It was like a real fork in the road moment, that's what happened here,' he said.

McAdam was enjoying watching the game with people he knew. His recollection of that day was that Clarke was fully in the ear of someone from AFL Central Australia (AFLCA) — an administrative football body in the region. 'We just got talking,' he said. 'Rob talked about how he was hassling AFLCA about being able to use Traeger Park for a [football] rep squad, and I started talking about this youth program I wanted to get going.' As McAdam and Clarke occasionally checked in on the football game playing out before them that day, they listened intently to what each had to say about their respective ideas, mostly in broad terms. McAdam's was a holistic, whole-of-life approach to equip the region's youth with life skills based around employment and study. Clarke's was forming a football club with semi-professional aspirations for the region's young men to play for when they would otherwise be idle. Clarke shared his and McAdam's thinking:

> *Macca had the same thought, to engage young men to do good for themselves, but it wouldn't work without the 'carrot' [football] and the carrot wouldn't be sustainable by itself.*[2]

Finding common ground, the men kept the conversation going well into the weeks and months that followed. At some point along the way, they arrived at a consensus on what could be possible if they joined forces and integrated the best parts of their respective ideas into one.

The rudimentary plan Ian McAdam and Rob Clarke later shook hands on was a football-employment program for the region's youth requiring them to be in work or study or gain the necessary skills to land a job and keep it while in regular training for the game they loved. Young men in the area were falling by the wayside. In 2010, according to the Australian Bureau of Statistics, the

'Aboriginal and Torres Strait Islander prisoner population in the Northern Territory comprised 81% of the total prisoner population'. Digging deeper, in Australia 'there were 7584 prisoners who identified as Aboriginal and Torres Strait Islander at 30 June 2010. This represented just over one quarter (26 per cent) of the total prisoner population, compared with 25 per cent at 30 June 2009. Aboriginal and Torres Strait Islander prisoner numbers increased by 3 per cent between 2009 and 2010'.[3]

In all social markers, Aboriginal youth in their prime years in the Northern Territory were more often incarcerated than they were leading productive lives. This plan, McAdam and Clarke hoped, would go some way toward addressing those issues.

The productive dialogue and exchange of ideas energised both men. Instinctively, they knew something special was brewing. Both men were, and are, well-known and well-connected in Central Australia and they would call on these connections to take their idea from mere concept to something tangible.

But why football? Why land on a particular sport to facilitate change in such complex social issues? What can football do that social work, PhDs, government policies, royal commissions and their recommendations cannot? To help answer these questions it is important to first understand where Aussie rules football sits within the broad collective of Aboriginal people, and in regions like Central Australia.

NEARLY FORKED

There are more than a few curiosities to life in the Northern Territory — good-ways. There's a little game people here play called 'Two Degrees of Separation'. It simply goes like this: when meeting someone new, name-drop a few souls and chances are, you will find common ground in someone you both know. With such a relatively small population the little game's strike-rate is exceptionally high.

There's also a cryptic saying in the Territory that goes like this: these walls have ears. It means be mindful of what you say and to whom you say it — word can, and does, get around. Perhaps a new game Territorians could play is the 'Guess Who Heard What I Just Said?' game.

One day late in 2011, a curious exchange between Rob Clarke and Tony Frawley took place at Traeger Park. Unbeknownst to Clarke, a boardroom power play was underway within Northern Territory football. The Alice Springs administrative body AFL Central Australia (AFLCA) had oversight of football in the region within a several-hundred-kilometre radius of town. AFLCA had its own board of directors overseeing the organisation's duties. But the Darwin administrative body AFL Northern Territory (AFLNT) sought governance of all football in the Territory. This power struggle would play out over several weeks.

The occasion this day was the local finals of the 2011 CAFL season at Traeger Park. The walls within the Bowden McAdam Grandstand had apparently heard and spoken of the grand plan Rob Clarke and Ian McAdam were brewing because at the game that day, sitting just two degrees away, was Tony Frawley. Tony Frawley was the chief executive of AFLNT and was in year six of a 10-year tenure in the role. He had just arrived in Alice Springs and went straight to the game to talk football business with his AFLCA counterparts.

Apparently, while at the footy, Frawley had become aware of the basic outline of the Clarke–McAdam plan, and this had piqued his interest, if for other reasons. For his part, Clarke was as surprised as anyone that day to learn that his and McAdam's as-yet unrealised plan was now being roped into this football power-play between Darwin and Alice Springs.

> *I remember I passed by Tony Frawley and he basically said, 'If you don't help get this over the line, then we can't help you,' it was along those lines. I didn't know what it was all about, so I just ignored it. (Rob Clarke)*[4]

To decrypt the cryptic, according to Rob Clarke, Tony Frawley was saying that if Darwin had someone in Alice Springs as well-connected as Rob Clarke, then the Darwin takeover of Central Australian football would be that much smoother. Essentially, football's top brass in Darwin needed local support in Alice Springs. Whatever form that was, was anyone's guess.

To add another Territory euphemism, 'whispering walls', indeed.

'JEWEL IN THE CENTRE'

Like an emerald-green gem sitting untouched on a red-desert floor, Traeger Park sits flush in the middle of Australia, its pulse beating to the year-round movement of body and ball.

Organised Aussie rules football has been played at the Alice Springs venue since a field was carved out at the site by men on graders during the Second World War, when the town was a hub of activity for the 'war effort'. The nameless and dirt-filled field was formally christened 'Traeger Park' on 7 October 1961, when Sir Paul Meernaa Caedwalla Hasluck, Minister of State for Territories (1951–1963), cut the ribbon at its official opening.[5]

The venue was named after an interesting fellow, engineer and inventor Alfred Hermann Traeger (1895–1980). Among Traeger's many useful inventions, his main claim to fame was as the developer of the world's first pedal radio, the development of which proved fundamental to the inception of the Royal Flying Doctor Service.[6] No-one can recall if old man Traeger actually played sport on the field bearing his name, but the plaque commemorating the moment was struck in his 66th year.

Traeger Park is nestled within the suburbs to the south of Alice Springs's town centre and straddled by Gap Road on the eastern side and Telegraph Terrace (the town part of the Stuart Highway) on the western side. It sits just three blocks away from the CBD. Traeger Park boasts most of what modern stadiums in Australia enjoy.

The Alice Springs Town Council operates and maintains Traeger Park year-round, keeping the playing surface in tip-top shape — almost carpet-like — despite Alice Springs's average yearly rainfall being a lowly 280 millimetres. Across its lifetime, the venue has played host to various forms of professional sport, primarily football and cricket. While its official capacity is set at 7200 people (seated), in 2007, it was standing room only when a touch over 11,000 souls crammed in for an AFL pre-season game. This remains the highest crowd on record for the venue.[7]

Both the Central Australian Football League and the Alice Springs Cricket Association are headquartered at Traeger Park.

Around the ground are what locals call 'Trees of Knowledge' — these are gnarled trunks and branches of storied old-timers that have seen life come and go like the breeze that passes through them.

The dimensions of the playing surface are approximately 168 metres in length, and 132 metres in width. By comparison, the Melbourne Cricket Ground, the iconic 'MCG', measures 174m long and 149 metres wide.[8, 9] The football goalposts follow the nationally standardised north-south direction. Four light-towers flank the arena and their lux capacity allows for night games and for those games to be televised. The Ted Hayes Scoreboard with manually movable numbers and letters sits on the north-eastern side of the ground. Nowadays it is neighboured by an electronic scoreboard full of pixelated beauty during play.

On the western side of the venue, sitting grandly in stately fashion, is the impressive 225-seat Bowden McAdam Grandstand, named after the late Michael Bowden, and Gilbert McAdam (older brother of Ian). Originally called the Ted Hayes Grandstand, the Bowden McAdam Grandstand honours two influential Central Australian figures. Michael Bowden played for Richmond in the Victorian Football League (VFL) from 1967–1971 and won a premiership with the Tigers in 1969. Post-VFL, he moved to Central Australia where he is remembered fondly for his work in support and advocacy for Aboriginal people in remote communities. His legacy in the Northern Territory lives on through his children and their families. Gilbert McAdam, older brother of Ian McAdam, carved out a productive career in football with St Kilda and Brisbane in the AFL from 1989 to 1996 and later as a public figure and advocate for his people. The grandstand comes with media and corporate boxes, and retractable seats at a comfortable angle, providing fans with elevated, clear and uninterrupted views of the playing arena.[10]

The view south from the field, however, is what sets this venue apart from any other in this country. From ground level, two kilometres away, rising quietly above the native gums and solar-clad rooftops is the Tjoritja, a stunning part of the lengthy West MacDonnell Ranges National Park. Its viewable shape is in the form of the Dreamtime Yeperenye — the caterpillar — the story the Arrernte people tell in their altyerre (the Arrernte way to tell their stories).[11] The Tjoritja sits in grand silence, resting now after completing its journey; its final form sculptured by time immeasurable in human years. In geological terms, it is a compacted series of bare quartzite and sandstone parallel ridges rising as a plateau estimated at 600 metres (2000 feet) above sea level. It extends to the east and west of Alice Springs and is around 400 kilometres in total length.[12] The old overland telegraph line was built across it in 1872. These days, telecommunication towers can be seen from the ground.

Thus completes the picture of Traeger Park — the premier sports venue in Central Australia. Proud locals call it the 'Jewel in the Centre'.

ADAPTING TO COLONISATION

Aboriginal peoples have used sport as a self-determination tool to offset the impacts of colonisation, racism, structural violence and structural inequalities...

SHEPPARD, RYNNE, AND WILLIS[1]

WHEN the British drove a flagpole into the ground at a sheltered cove on the eastern side of this large island-continent it was like a symbolic stake driven into the hearts of the original inhabitants. The quintessential British act took place at a location that the original occupants, the Gadigal people of the Eora Nation, called Warrane. It was done on what the European Gregorian calendar said was the 26th of January 1788 CE. This wasn't the first visit from the 'people from far away'— the berewalgal — just that this time the berewalgal stayed. And this time, the berewalgal made this place their business.[2] And so with a wave of the hand and a colourful flag, the irreducible sovereignty of the Gadigal people and of the countless other Nations also living on these lands was summarily dismissed. The number of people living on this continent at that time was estimated at around 750,000 in more than 250–300 autonomous groups with their own distinct languages, traditions, cultural practices, ceremonies, lore and law.[3]

Undeterred and generally unbothered to find out, the berewalgal established what they called the Colony of New South Wales. To the Gadigal's growing unease, a steady flow of more and more berewalgal continued arriving by boat at Warrane. The Gadigal people and their Countrymen would soon learn the berewalgal called themselves 'British' — British berewalgal. And what the British berewalgal were doing was a totally British berewalgal thing to do. And, in the eyes of the British berewalgal, it was their god-given imperial right to do whatever the hell they wanted.

After a time, British imperialism's dirty co-conspirator — colonialism — was fully unleashed. Colonialism's overarching purpose is to seize control of a sovereign nation's resources while dividing and subjugating that nations' people by all and any means necessary. It is a practice that defines the 'white way'. Olde Worlde European powers had carved up large tracts of Africa, the Americas, South-East Asia and the many islands of the world's oceans into manageable chunks, aided by sizeable sentries armed with an array of weapons they once only used on themselves.[4] The goal was the promised wealth that could be extracted from the New World, seizing the people already living there and the earthly resources beneath their feet.

This system of governance so foreign in its ways was forcibly imposed upon the Gadigal with strange and mysterious fighting sticks that could drop a man dead from a great distance, and on great, unknown beasts that neighed to their masters' commands. At the end of those pointed rifles, on poisoned blankets, restricted movement and unimaginable cruelty, the dispossession of land, language and culture was the unholy trifecta the British sought and thoroughly achieved in what could easily be described as an orgy of destruction, so ferocious in its near annihilation of this land's First Nations peoples and their cultures. The genocide of entire clans and bands of Aboriginal people was, from the perspective of the British and their descendants, at least, an unfortunate by-product of 'manifest destiny'; a military and religio-social concept which defined the British-American incursion into the lives and lands of Native Americans around the same time.[5]

APPROPRIATION OF MARN-GROOK

Fast-forward 80 years. The colonialists — now well and truly entrenched on this land as settlers and squatters, firstborns and born-to-rulers — saw an opportunity to appropriate more of traditional Aboriginal culture for the purpose of entertainment. Namely, the numerous ball games First Nations peoples had developed and enjoyed for several thousand years. For Aboriginal people these were more than games. This was ceremony, a celebration of life and tradition they were desperate to hold onto in the face of real-time physical and cultural genocide.[6] One Aboriginal traditional ballgame caught the settlers' eyes.

The Djab Wurrung clan of the Gariwerd lands of the broader Gunditjmara Nation lived unbothered for thousands of years in an area the British once called the Port Phillip District (1836–1851). When they weren't hunting and gathering and enjoying the life they had known since forever, the Djab Wurrung had a ball-kicking game they called 'marn-grook'.[7] Translated to 'game of ball', marn-grook was played by two large groups of people gathered in a loose collection opposite to each other. The object of attention in this game was a soft, durable, round-ish object made of opossum skin, called a 'mumark'. The mumark was grabbed by whoever could get it, kicked up into the air, and leapt at with hands reaching high and in great numbers. Marn-grook was ceremonial in that there was prestige attached to the participants.

In 1889, anthropologist Alfred Howitt wrote about this game and variations of it among the different groups in the area:

> *This game of ball-playing was also practised among the Kurnai, the Wolgal [Tumut river people], the Wotjoballuk as well as by the Woiworung, and was probably known to most tribes of south-eastern Australia. The Kurnai made the ball from the scrotum of an "old man kangaroo", the Woiworung made it of tightly rolled up pieces of possum skin. It was called by them "mangurt". In this tribe the two divisions, Bunjil and Waa, played on opposite sides. The Wotjoballuk also played this game, with Krokitch on one side and Gamutch on the other. The mangurt was sent as a token of friendship from one to another.*[8]

Among the Port Phillip District squattocracy was the Wills family who had settled in a place they called 'Lexington' on the lands of the Djab Wurrung. The family patriarch was Horatio Wills who had a kid called Tom Wills.[9] In 1861, Horatio Wills and 18 others were killed on the Cullin-la-ringo Plains in Central Queensland by Aboriginal people as a payback killing for one of their own.[10] This is reportedly one of the largest massacres of white people by Aboriginal people in this land's blood-drenched history. Tom Wills was with his father's expedition, but he and a handful of others were away on horseback getting supplies when it happened. The resultant payback of the payback saw around 370 of the Gayiri people murdered, an indiscriminate slaughter that nearly wiped out an entire people. In a massive development, a 2021 report about this event hinted at Tom Wills's involvement in these killings.[11]

From the age of five, Tom formed close bonds with the resident Aboriginal families and reportedly grew familiar with their language, customs and games. And marn-grook. At the age of 14, Tom was sent away to England to be educated at the Rugby School where he developed as an excellent all-rounder in the English game of cricket, as well as an early form of rugby football. This rugby game was part of a broader movement called 'muscular

Christianity'. This movement originated in England in the mid-19th century and took root among the British upper classes. It held to the beliefs of patriotic duty, discipline, self-sacrifice, masculinity and the moral and physical beauty of athleticism; sport was a key tenet of this overall philosophy.

Back in the district, now the Colony of Victoria (1851–1901) and with a new city they called 'Melbourne', after six years away, Tom Wills was back home and excelling at several sports, including cricket. This cricket game was a sport fiercely contested between the colonies of New South Wales and Victoria. A lateral thinker, Wills was a prolific letter writer to the colony's newspapers, and in 1858 a publication called *Bell's Life* published one of his letters. In the old-timey language of the day, Wills put forward the need for the colony's cricket players to keep in shape in the off-season (winter), 'lest their sporting prowess be found wanting when cricket resumed in the summer'. Recalling his time in England playing a rudimentary form of early rugby football, the answer in Wills's mind was a winter-time game, a new sport.

He wrote the following:

> *Now that cricket has been put aside for some few months to come, and cricketers have assumed somewhat of the chrysalis nature (for a time only 'tis true), but at length will again burst forth in all their varied hues, rather than allow this state of torpor to creep over them, and stifle their new supple limbs, why can they not, I say, form a foot-ball club, and form a committee of three or more to draw up a code of laws? If a club of this sort were got up, it would be of vast benefit to any cricket-ground to be trampled upon, and would make the turf quite firm and durable; besides which it would keep those who are inclined to become stout from having their joints encased in useless superabundant flesh.*[12]

A response came about two weeks later in the form of what became known as 'kickabout games'. These games were played with an odd-shaped ball and a loose collection of rules made up as they went along. While nothing formal apparently came of these games, the seeds were planted. A year later, in 1859, Tom Wills, together with William Hammersley, James Thompson and Thomas Smith, published a series of rules for a new foot-ball game with the original goal in mind, keeping cricket players active and in shape during their off-season, the winter.

On 17 May 1859, with the publication of the *10 Rules of the Melbourne Football Club* document, a new foot-ball game was thus codified.[13] The game that evolved from these rules not coincidentally drew from some of the key elements of marn-grook, but this remains in fierce dispute.[14] Like a new-born baby, this game would remain blissfully ignorant of the furore its own birth would cause. This 'child' of the colony would grow rapidly as a popular recreational pastime in Melbourne.

In 2008, the AFL Commission published what it holds as its official history of Aussie rules football in this country, *The Australian Game of Football — Since 1858*. Inside, the late historian Gillian Hibbins (1936–2022), formally rejects marn-grook as an influence of the modern game.

> *There is no mention of Aboriginal football by Wills in letters or in the two cricket guides he edited. On the contrary, there is much evidence to show that Wills, in fact, favoured Rugby School, as set out in the preceding text.*[15]

The AFL's formal position on marn-grook was met with equal parts support and incredulity. Among the incredulous was academic, author and historian Jim Poulter who took the Commission and some of his peers to task in a 6930-word rebuttal. Poulter, speaking with Mike Sexton on ABC Radio in 2008, said:

> *If Tom Wills had said, 'Hey, we should have a game of our own, more like the football that Blackfellas play' it would have killed it stone dead before it was even born.* [16]

Backtrack a few years from the game's codification in 1859 to 1851, when the discovery of gold in the northern regions of the district precipitated a mad rush of people from Melbourne. The subsequent rush for gold — the 'gold rush' — lasted years and an exodus from the south saw thousands of people surge north and west in search of the valuable mineral. They also took this new football game with them from Melbourne into the regions and new towns that were popping up. Organised football later sprouted throughout these new settlements, some with teams, names and uniforms, and an ever-evolving set of rules.

And so as sacred sites became mine sites and gold became generational wealth, football remained. This fast-paced game took on a life all its own. It became massively popular across the mostly southern and western regions of the now-federated states of what came to be called *Australia*. The game today is now a major sport and a multi-billion-dollar industry with millions of followers.[17]

Despite all of what they'd lost, despite their wholesale exclusion from the colonialists' new cities and towns and the wealth accumulated from resources extracted from their sacred and ancestral lands, Aboriginal people adapted to some of this change; literally for their own survival. Some of them also became good at this football game. Football would provide these men and a growing band of their Countrymen with a sliver of acceptance, an acknowledgment of their humanity that the white man's law dared not entertain.

By the 1930s — around 70 years after its codification in 1859 — this new football game would become thoroughly interwoven into the fabric of life in the new cities and towns that dotted the rapidly changing, mostly 'southern' Australian landscape. It also became the football of choice in the Northern Territory.

From 1863 to 1911, the Northern Territory was administered from the 'free' colony of South Australia. In fact, broadly from around Alice Springs and northwards to the shores of the Arafura Sea, this large tract of land's original designation was the 'Northern Territory of South Australia'. Football — informally 'Aussie rules' football now — was the main game in South Australia, and as South Australians provided the bulk of government employees and labourers in Darwin and in Central Australia, they brought this football with them.[18]

Before the outbreak of the Second World War in 1939, Alice Springs's white population was reportedly around 950 people.[19] During that war this number swelled to around 8000, as the place transformed from a convenient trade-route stop-off into a strategic military hub and administrative centre for the war effort.[20] Following the end of the war in 1945, the town's population settled at less than 2000 people.[21] Informal games of football were played in Alice Springs by the various army divisions stationed there during the war. Formalised sport was introduced a year later when a handful of Aussie rules games were organised between the resident townsfolk. One of those games included a team referred to as 'locals', presumably a team of Aboriginal men, but that is not definitive. One individual behind the formation of early football in Alice Springs was Mick Costello, a local man who was educated in Adelaide and played football there. He also served overseas during the war. According to local history, Costello was an Aboriginal man from the Arrernte people, so it was entirely possible Aboriginal people were playing this new game in Central Australia earlier than the recorded instances suggest.

Following a break in the hot summer months, organised football returned to Central Australia and in July 1947 a game was played between two teams called the Allied Works Council and the Half-Caste Boys which — as that now discredited eugenics-inspired designation alludes to — was a team of young Aboriginal men. This game was won by the Aboriginal team and in that side Henry Peckham[i] and an 'M' Goodhall were named best players.[22]

A week later, encouraged by growing local interest, a new football body was formed to facilitate these games, called the Central Australian Football Association (CAFA). Among the first clubs formed to play in the new football association was Pioneer Football Club, a club with a rich Aboriginal history since its inception. Pioneer Football Club is the region's most successful club. To date (early in 2025) they have won 33 senior men's premierships since their inception in 1947, or a flag every 1.8 years; in that time they have played in 55 grand finals, or a grand final every 1.9 years.[23] In time, the CAFA — later the Central Australian Football League (CAFL) — would become the premier football competition in the region. In the more than 75 years since, it spawned several more clubs and today the Federal, West, South Alice Springs and Rovers football clubs join Pioneer as league mainstays. The CAFL would also produce a steady stream of incredibly talented footballers. In *The Centre of Australian Football — 25 Years (1997–2022) of AFL in Central Australia*, author and match-day commentator Randall 'Stan' Coombe details firsthand accounts of notable footballers from the region, their exploits on the field, and their legacy.[24]

In the years and decades since the game's origin-story in the centre of this country, the appeal of Aussie rules football had spread to the numerous Aboriginal communities around Alice Springs and the outer reaches of Central Australia. As Djirribal woman and academic Lee Sheppard points out, organised sport generally provided Aboriginal people a cultural offset — a reset, even — of the traditional ways and games they knew and played before the white man arrived.[25] Additionally, researcher Gary Osmond makes the general argument that, '[Football] has been appropriated by Aboriginal people for their own purposes.'[26]

---

i Henry Peckham was regarded as Central Australia's greatest footballer. He had a brief stint in South Australia where he was lauded for his tough and skilful play. He later returned home and dominated in local football.

With solid support from individuals like Ted Egan, football teams and competitions popped up like wild saltbush throughout Central Australia, including across Anmatjere Country and in communities like Ltyentye Apurte, Ntaria, Papunya and Yuendumu. Some of those community teams would later join the CAFL in Alice Springs. In time, football would become the indisputable number one sport in those communities, which remains true to this day.

One can only imagine how marn-grook of the Djab Wurrung people — and purlja of the Warlpiri people — would have evolved with Aboriginal autonomy and without white interruption, but that is a thought lost to history. What we do know is what Aussie rules football has come to mean to the Djab Wurrung of the Gariwerd today, and to the Aṉangu, Arrernte, Luritja, Pintupi, and Warlpiri people of the Central Desert where it is played like ceremony. Football, in some of these parts, is held in delicate balance with traditional practice and modern progress, as noted in *Aboriginal Rules*, a film about a Warlpiri footy team:

> *The culture might be 40,000 years old but the rules have changed, and football is the new Dreaming that holds the balance in young men's lives. A new version of an old ceremony has emerged in the remote community of Yuendumu. It's called football. And it's definitely more than a game.*[27]

As observers and partakers of the modern game and as local men, Rob Clarke and Ian McAdam understood that the rules of this new game of football were now written in the red sands of the Central Desert. They wanted to tap into this rich vein of football engagement as a vehicle for their shared vision. Clarke himself would write, echoing sentiments expressed by the Warlpiri:

AFL football sits alongside Aboriginal culture in terms of how important it is to young Indigenous men. It is played 12 months of the year in most communities in Central Australia and not surprisingly the most popular and influential males in the communities are footballers. We will use their passion for football to engage them in our program... to build confidence and self-esteem. We don't have to reinvent the wheel, this 'carrot' already exists. Young men would do anything to play at a high level and represent their region.[28]

BUILDING A BLUEPRINT

It is quite unique to win two flags in six days. To give something back to the Territory is fantastic. This is very special for me.

ANDREW MCLEOD (TWO-TIME AFL AND NT THUNDER PREMIERSHIP PLAYER, ON NT THUNDER'S HISTORIC PREMIERSHIP DOUBLE)[1]

IAN McAdam's fork-in-the road moment with Rob Clarke spurred him into action. McAdam was burning the midnight oil at Clontarf and at home, developing a basic outline for his part of the plan. The focus was on young people in the 18–25 age bracket. It would be geared toward this group's mental and physical health, wellbeing, education, numeracy and literacy, and awareness of alcohol and tobacco use. Employment prospects for this cohort would be sharpened with job-ready mentoring, life-skills training, work experience, and a direct pathway to employment. It would also incorporate an important personal development element focused on leadership, language and culture.

Essentially, the plan was aimed at engaging young men in a supportive and intensive environment. McAdam knew where to take this. 'I hit Congress up for a meeting,' he said.

'Congress' is the Alice Springs-based Central Australian Aboriginal Congress (CAAC), the largest community-controlled health organisation in the Northern Territory. Formed more than 50 years ago, Congress is an institution. It is an agent for support and advocacy primarily around health.[2] Of their first meeting, McAdam said, 'I talked to them about the Good Sports program [but that] I still wanted to do this program, but within a sporting club context'.

With health and general wellbeing forming part of Congress' charter, and football a key plank of the Clarke–McAdam vision, McAdam knew Congress would be somewhat receptive. He was specific about what their overall vision was, and what it was not. Still, it took some convincing. 'Congress is Congress and their thing is health,' he said. He had his work cut out.

> *It took a while to get their head around what I was saying. I was basically saying,* Don't leave sport behind. If we're going to do this thing, let's flip it around and add football to it. This was more than just sport.
>
> *I said to them that this wasn't just about football, that's been done, it didn't need to be done again. The talent is there but that talent is failing to stay there because the ability to find a job, find a house, to go interstate, to negotiate these things, it's just not there. So we did that and that was basically the start, and this footy program was the major reason why. (Ian McAdam)*[3]

Congress saw merit in the proposal as it complemented part of its own overall strategy. They found the money and McAdam was granted two positions to build his plan. He had a foot in the door at Congress and was halfway out the other at Clontarf. He soon engaged with the Desert Peoples Centre (DPC), an organisation in the business of education and training. It was a strategic pairing. The joint venture saw the program come under the umbrella of the DPC's Tjaiya Rratja – Right Tracks program.

> *When we decided to do this we knew that if locals were going to support us, we must support them and we did that by basically creating this program from the bottom up. (Ian McAdam)*

Right Tracks supports sports clubs to provide a positive, functional, inclusive and sustainable environment for their members. Recognising the huge role that sport plays in the development of healthy individuals and communities Right Tracks aims to strengthen the link between sport and community health outcomes.

Partnering with existing and new sporting clubs the Right Tracks program includes:

- Health Education
- Leadership
- High Performance Program
- Club Development
- Employment Support
- Goodsports Program
- Health Checks
- Coach Development
- Skills Development[4]

The Right Tracks program works because it utilises and builds upon the sense of identity, belonging, purpose and inspiration that comes from association with sporting clubs. Sport is a powerful environment to connect children, men and women with vital information, skills and strategies to push for inclusive, equitable, healthy and safe sporting spaces for everyone.

Positive thinking, goal-setting and resilience to challenges is incorporated throughout all Right Tracks activities and particularly in sport training. Sporting clubs play a big role in supporting vulnerable members of the community through ongoing social and emotional challenges, including mental health, suicide and domestic violence. Right Tracks acknowledges that clubs are not just places to play sport but can be like a second family — providing identity, social support, networks and role models.

To further support local sports clubs, they are entitled to up to $500 of sporting gear from Intersport Alice Springs once their members have completed health checks. Right Tracks staff are knowledgeable, committed and respected community members. The Right Tracks program is designed and led by locals, for locals. Health is viewed holistically, and social determinants of health are tackled.

'SHOW ME THE MONEY!'

AS Ian McAdam busied himself moulding his part of the vision into shape, Rob Clarke got busy building the football side of his. In spite of Clarke's many experiences working in and with football clubs, starting one from scratch with such lofty aims was a new experience and a massive undertaking. Clarke is the founder and owner of Fidler & Clarke, a mechanical repair and parts shop servicing mostly the pastoral and trade industries. His connections to the local business community run deep. To them he took the message that he was establishing a regular-season regional representative football club where players were required to be engaged in work, study or both.

Neither Clarke nor McAdam could do this on their own, however, or from their own pockets, no matter how generous each of them felt they could be. Financial investment from the business sector would underpin the program's first crucial steps. And so, locking in sponsors was a critical component to this overall plan. For his first shot, Clarke aimed at a corporate big hitter that was a somewhat contentious choice — Santos, an Australian-owned energy company, which counts its yearly revenue in the billions.

LAND RICH, DIRT POOR

In 1976, federal parliament passed the *Aboriginal Land Rights (Northern Territory) Act 1976 (Cth) (ARLA). It was the first legislation of its kind, giving Aboriginal and Torres Strait Islander peoples the right to claim Country where traditional ownership could be proven.*[1] It predated Mabo by 20 years. Presently, under ALRA Northern Territory (NT), Aboriginal peoples have '... inalienable freehold title to 50 per cent of the NT and, through the High Court's 2008 Blue Mud Bay decision, about 85 per cent of the NT coastline'.[2]

The paradox, though, is that under this legislation, Aboriginal home ownership on traditional lands is ambiguous. The land granted ownership under ALRA is held in a Trust, which means the community and/or Traditional Owner (TO) claimant group collectively owns the land or lands, and not any one individual. This means that individuals who wish to build and own their own homes on their lands cannot do so, nor can they use it as equity. This has often led to communities and TOs being described as 'land rich but dirt poor'.[3] This scenario leaves remote communities and individuals who don't have spare change for their sports programs with an ongoing dilemma, to which there is no ready answer, only a suite of complex solutions. It is into this void that corporations enter with outside capital, often willing to fund individuals, entire sports carnivals or sports teams. Stepping into this space in recent years has been Rio Tinto, partnering with the AFL and the West Australian Football Commission for its *Footy Means Business youth football program.*[4] Rio Tinto, of course, was the mining giant that in 2020 destroyed 46,000-year-old rock shelters with rock art of significant cultural importance at Juukan Gorge in WA's Pilbara region.[5]

WHAT IS SANTOS?

Enter: Sandman, err Santos, the Australian-owned mining giant founded in 1954.[6] Santos's core business, like its fellow players in the resources sector, is, essentially, digging up Country. The multi-billion-dollar organisation is headquartered in Adelaide, and it is Australia's second-largest independent oil and gas producer, and one of the largest in the Asia-Pacific region. In 2018, its yearly revenue was estimated at US$3.66 billion (roughly A$5.1 billion), with an underlying net profit after tax of US$727 million (roughly A$1.04 billion).[7] Given the right circumstances, this big multinational would leap at an opportunity to brand First Nations sport, which Clarke had calculated correctly.

'Santos' is an acronym of the organisation's official name, South Australian Northern Territory Oil Search. 'Santos' is a Spanish word that means 'saints' or 'holy', but Santos's activities could be viewed as anything but saintly.[8] Over the past decade-and-a-bit Santos's presence has become ubiquitous in Indigenous sport as a major sponsorship partner. It obviously has the money to sponsor Indigenous sport but its involvement in this space is a divisive topic within the community, given how the company has obtained its wealth.[9] Santos doesn't help itself either.

As early as the first decade of the 2000s Santos's place within Indigenous sport was seen as inappropriate. The much-derided 'Greenies' and 'tree-huggers' were among the early mobilisers against the mining giant placing itself as major sponsor of community events and Indigenous sport. In 2015, in an open letter, Frack Free NT Alliance denounced Santos's sponsorship of the popular Darwin Festival (while the Alliance committed $10,000 as a kick-along for festival organisers to find an alternative).[10]

Santos, it seemed, liked to hedge its bets. In a particularly egregious move in 2014, it partnered with the Queensland Police Service in a sponsorship arrangement that saw the organisation's logo printed on police cars.[11] Seeing police and their vehicles with wraparound Santos decals at clashes with protesters at environmentally and culturally sensitive sites is to see a dystopian version of the future.[12] Do we really need a state apparatus actively working to crush its own people at the behest of a multibillion-dollar, multinational corporation?

In April 2023, Santos received a public rebuke from Ngarrindjeri-Kaurna Elder Uncle Major 'Moogy' Sumner for using his images in promotional materials at their annual general meeting (AGM) in Adelaide. Uncle's face was shown with the words *One Future* superimposed over it in a video at the AGM. And he wasn't happy, saying:

> *I have written to the CEO of Santos today to ask that my image be removed from their promotional materials immediately. I also ask that Santos apologise for their use of my image without my consent. I have never given permission to Santos to use my image.*
>
> *Santos have used images of Aboriginal people, including mine, in their promotional materials to give the impression that we consent to the destructive fossil fuels projects that they are carrying out on Aboriginal land.*
>
> *It is disrespectful that Santos used my image without ever seeking my consent. It is disrespectful that they continue to plan destructive coal, gas and fracking projects on Aboriginal land without the consent of Traditional Owners and Custodians...*
>
> *I would like to make it clear that I stand with the Gomeroi people, Tiwi Islanders and all Aboriginal Traditional Owners and Custodians who are fighting to protect their country from Santos projects. Our future is not in destructive fossil fuel projects. The future we want is one where our Country is protected and our voices are heard. Traditional Owners*

> *and Custodians should have the right to say no to mining projects on their lands by companies like Santos.*[13]

To their credit, Santos removed Uncle's image and a few days later formally apologised.[14]

Rob Clarke was not oblivious to facts like these, but the man had a vision and his immediate concern was that the vision needed dollars. He approached the organisation with his grand plan and the mining giant was more than happy to support the new program as a major sponsor.[15] The Mammon of Saint Santos would do for now.

Other organisations to jump on board as sponsor-partners included Ingkerreke Commercial, a localised building and construction company, Centrecorp Foundation, and Asbuild NT, among others. A suite of smaller organisations hearing the good word followed suit and clamoured for inclusion.

INDEPENDENCE DAY

While busy securing sponsorship, Rob Clarke was also fine-tuning what the new football club would look like. He had a vision for how it would operate and the parameters he set for it were clear from the beginning. It was important to get this part right.

Clarke knew who was who in local football and how the game in Central Australia operated. The mainstay clubs of local football were Federal, Rovers and Pioneer and they were established in 1947, alongside the CAFA-CAFL. West Alice Springs came later, in 1968, and South Alice Springs (formerly Amoonguna) around the same time.[16] Pioneer and South have rich, local family traditions going back to their foundations. West and Federal generally attract the blue-collar set; Rovers is a mix of all four. The new football club forming in Rob Clarke's mind needed to be separate from these and operate entirely independent from the primary football competitions these clubs operate in: the CAFL, and the Barkly Australian Football League (BAFL) in

Tennant Creek (a seven-hour drive north on the Stuart Highway), and the Community Cup competition. The CAFL had 15 to 20 teams across A-grade, reserves and a thriving under-18s. The Community Cup involved teams from Papunya, Yuendumu, Mt Allen and Ltyentye Apurte, among others, and had a fluctuating number of teams in any given season. The BAFL A-grade comprised six teams plus a junior division. It was imperative this new club create an identity separate from all of these.

The plan, then, was to present the club as a clean slate with zero connection and/or association to the AFLCA, any of the clubs in the CAFL or the BAFL, nor to any of the community clubs in the region, but one that was truly representative of all the above. And that was the decision Rob Clarke and Ian McAdam arrived at — the club as a standalone entity. The men knew the local families and their feuds, some that lasted years, layers of which added to already complex matters that were never really resolved. Theirs was a vision of community unity via football. While not necessarily *the* answer, in their minds, a football club that could encourage unity was *an* answer.

Given the scope of this plan, and the immense size of the region, the new club's reach would be *huge*; a 4WD-testing, horizon-bending 600-kilometre trek out from Alice Springs huge. Lucky Toyota was a sponsor.[i] But perhaps the most left-field decision was the next.

WHEN AND WHERE WILL THEY PLAY?

Rob Clarke and Ian McAdam wanted the new football club to become a sort of *destination* club for the region's young men at a time when they wouldn't otherwise have much to do. In Central Australia, that time was the summer months, the local football off-season, hot time in the desert when *no-one* here plays footy. This was a gamble.

---

i Toyota actually wasn't a sponsor.

Summer in Central Australia can be particularly harsh. The average daily high temperature during the summer is a desert-dry 32°C. In January alone, the average high temperature is a sun-stinging 35°C with a night-time low of 22°C. In other words, nightmare conditions for visitors softened by temperate southern climes. But for hardy locals, it was just another Tuesday.

The decision, then — as left-field as it comes — was a strategic one.

Backtrack a few years to 2008 and the AFLNT Board was engaged in an ambitious plan to take Northern Territory football to the clouds. AFLNT wanted a team from the NT to play southern-states football. Frawley and former football great Michael Long took this idea abroad.

Michael Long is a universally recognised Tiwi football great, having carved out an exceptional career in the AFL with premierships and a Norm Smith Medal at Essendon. In 2004, his spontaneous decision to trek on foot from Melbourne to Canberra to highlight the plight of Indigenous people made national and international news. It forced the conservative Coalition Federal Government into action, although that proved to be tokenistic. Long's feat on foot is symbolically repeated each year in the form of The Long Walk at various locations around the country.[17]

The plan Long, Frawley and AFLNT had was for a football team that would represent the iconic black, white and ochre of the Northern Territory somewhere else in Australia. It was audacious.

On separate occasions, Frawley and Long held court with the West Australian and South Australian Football Commissions. Their pitch was for the NT to join either the WAFL in Perth or the SANFL in Adelaide. Despite early enthusiasm and positive noises, the Sandgropers (West Aussies) and Croweaters (South Aussies) were tough nuts to crack. They were super-protective of their respective leagues. They shared in a combined 200-plus years of football evolution and growth. Their respective competitions were institutions with long-standing traditions, rivalries and cultures that played significant roles in forming the blueprint of football in their states and in this country. Although the West Australians' level of interest was greater than that of their South Australian counterparts, the idea on either side of the Nullarbor was quietly shelved.

Long and Frawley returned to the Top End to regroup when, suddenly, out from the Big Pineapple emerged AFL Queensland (AFLQ) with a 'vacancy' in its premier competition, the Queensland Australian Football League (QAFL). This was timely, for several reasons. The AFLQ in Brisbane had the backing of the AFL Commission in Melbourne eager to spread the Aussie rules football gospel further into the Sunshine State. A potential Queensland-Northern Territory alliance could prove advantageous for the AFL, for football in Queensland and, by extension, the Northern Territorians. Sort of like a Qantas 2.0, but it's football, not flying. Queensland and Northern Territory Aerial Services (Ltd) originally provided vital connections for the people of western Queensland. The 'NT' in Qantas represented their ambition to fly overseas via Darwin as the main aerial port of entry at the time.[18]

The AFL could see what a Northern Territory team operating in the eastern states could do for Aussie rules in a place where rugby league and Wally Lewis is king. Long, Frawley and the AFLNT's plan to take Territory football abroad was a neat fit with this overall big picture. So when the Queenslanders shouted a round of XXXX at the Pineapple Hotel, several punt kicks from the Gabba, the timing was perfect. Subsequently, in 2008, the Northern Territory Football Club (NTFC) was formed and granted a licence to join the QAFL the following year. The new team — playing as 'NT Thunder' — hit the ground running. The Territory's flagship team would go on to win premierships in 2011 and 2015.

What Rob Clarke and Ian McAdam sought to do in Central Australia aligned with the strategy of NT Thunder. The 'Thunder' was flying the Territory colours as a rep team in the Eastern States, chasing premierships in the home of cane toads and rugby league. Thunder played in the QAFL from 2009 to 10, and in the QAFL's successor, the North East Australian Football

League (NEAFL) from 2011. The club comprised some of the best available football talent in the Northern Territory, with a few ring-ins. Most Thunder players came from the Darwin-based Northern Territory Football League (NTFL), some from Alice Springs, Katherine and Tennant Creek, and a few exiles from interstate. Home games were mostly played in Darwin at Marrara Oval with a handful in Alice Springs at Traeger Park.

Essentially, Thunder was a winter-time regular-season football club in the business of chasing premierships and winning them. In September 2011, the club claimed a historic double when they won the NEAFL Northern Conference grand final, against Morningside, and then the 2011 NEAFL premiership in the Northern-Eastern cross-conference grand final, against Ainslie from Canberra, a week later. The victory over Ainslie was played and won in Alice Springs, at Traeger Park. For a short time, from 2011 to 2013, Thunder also played in the invitation-only midweek pay-TV League Championship Cup, or 'Foxtel Cup'. This was where leading football clubs from the state and territory leagues played off against each other as curtain-raisers to the AFL, or sometimes as standalone games. For example, Swan Districts from the WAFL could be playing against Southport from the QAFL; this was much in the mould of the old pre-season Escort Cup from the 1970s that involved the top teams from the WAFL, SANFL, VFL and sometimes Tasmania. Thunder played in all three seasons of the experimental play-off tournament. In real terms, NT representative football chanced upon a winning formula and the crew from Alice Springs wanted some of what was brewing.

Rob Clarke and Ian McAdam felt they could leverage the growing goodwill NT Thunder was generating from the game's powerbrokers in Darwin and emulate the club's on-field model in Central Australia. Their plan was to build on what the Thunder was doing and provide the Central Australian region's footballers a representative platform of their own. 'Their presence was advantageous to us,' Clarke said. 'It was a stepping stone for our players to build into that pathway, so it made sense.' The men soon arrived at a consensus on what they wanted to do with this thing. The club would:

1. represent Central Australia,
2. be a regular-season football team,
3. play during the summer months, and
4. vie for premierships in an established club competition.

Now in possession of a blueprint for their plan, the pair needed somewhere to take this, somewhere to play. While the carrot may have been football, the lure was representing Country. This dynamic duo had grand plans and aimed high, but how high, and to where? The answer was in the skies, and beyond the desert horizon.

IRRARNTE, FLY HIGH

The club Rob Clarke and Ian McAdam were building presented a blank canvas. It needed a name, a nickname, a mascot and team colours. Given the club would potentially represent an entire region, it needed catch-all, inclusive names and terms that covered the bases.

The Northern Territory Football Club (NTFC) provided inspiration. The NTFC's objectives aligned with the Clarke–McAdam vision. Clarke had a part-time role with the Thunder as its Alice Springs-based part-time southern division coach, guiding the team's Central Australian players. He was a proud man looking on when they won the NEAFL premiership at Traeger Park in September of 2011.

In name, the NTFC represented the entire Northern Territory in a faraway league. And so, with aspirations aligned to that of the NTFC, the name for the new club the duo arrived at was an inspired choice: Central Australian Football Club (CAFC) — original, on-point, name-perfect. Trademarks and registered copyrights soon followed. The CAFC's core objective was to provide a club where young Aboriginal men could thrive, so a mascot with traditional ties would be most fitting.

Fans love to identify with a team via its colours, logos and mascots; the general trend of sports teams is mostly centred around animals. In Central Australia, there were enough native animals for Clarke and McAdam to choose from, but it took a bit of homework because the region's football clubs had that market mostly cornered.

The iconic kangaroo was taken as a mascot by the Ali Curung and South Alice Springs football clubs. Eagles, those magnificent birds of prey, were represented by the Papunya, Pioneer and Janapurlalki football clubs; the eagles' big-sky rival, hawks, were the preferred choice for the Elliot Football Club, while Warlpiri at Yuendumu celebrated the magpie as their team's mascot. The eventual choice came from a fortuitous moment, Clarke said:

> *I was at the Alice Springs Show and just trying to think up a mascot or a nickname. Then I saw this great painting — it was of red-tail black cockatoos, and it looked beautiful. On the way home I rang Macca and I told him, 'Redtails!'; he said, 'What!?' then hung up on me. A day later, he rang back and said, 'Alright then, let's do it.' But I said, 'Too late, I already am.'*[19]

In the Arrernte language of the area, the red-tailed black cockatoo is irrarnte. This bird is one of about 44 species in the cockatoo family. It is a regular sight in the blue skies enveloping the Central Australian landscape. Irrarnte is totem in local lore and holds significance for the region's Aboriginal people. And, as these things go, it was an original and inspired choice for a sports team.

Striking: The Redtails' guernsey the players wore across the two-year, two-season NTFL Premier League trial period in 2012 and 2013. The striking design of a red-tailed black cockatoo in the centre is complemented by the stunning transition of colours that depict the Central Australian sunset. The red-tail image was designed by the multi-talented Rob Clarke, CAFC co-founder and club president. (Digital re-creation: Jack Wallace 2025)

The club colours would also reflect that of the irrarnte: red and black, with white and a touch of desert-ochre yellow. With this colour scheme, the original sleeveless player-issue guernsey was a refreshing departure from the standard football guernseys. The colours were in understated tones and shaped within the contours of the playing strip: the ochre-yellow formed into frontal downward arches over the shoulders and pectorals; down the side were black panels and the centre was white. In this centre space was the unmistakable image of the male red-tailed black cockatoo, wings up, red tail feathers in full view, and an unmistakable head turned to his right. The NTFL logo was on the top-right chest and on the opposite to that was sponsor Centrecorp's logo. The AFLNT logo, to make it official, was centred between these. Player numbers featured across the back and above that was perhaps the best touch: 'CAFL Est. 1947' — a nod to the game's foundation and history in Central Australia. The material was new-age, light and extremely comfortable. Subsequent re-issues of the playing strips followed this design that also had sponsor logos on the back. The club polo shirts followed this standard, but with sleeves and a collar.

Thus, the Right Tracks Program (Tjaiya Rratja) / Central Australian Football Club Redtails was born. The club had a name, the program had a name, the team had colours, and the players and supporters had something to wear. The pieces of the puzzle were coming together.

BIG SKY COUNTRY

THE football club without a game and only a name called Alice Springs home. But where and what is Alice Springs? The full story of settler colonial history in this country can be found elsewhere, and apart from a shallow dive into the dark past earlier this book ain't it.[1] But here are the bare facts.

The town of Alice Springs is located roughly in the geographical centre of the continent now called *Australia*. The town's coordinates are 23°41'50.93" S and 133°53'1.03" E which, hmm, from memory, means it is exactly 1496 kilometres south of Darwin, exactly 1534 kilometres north of Adelaide, and exactly 38 kilometres shy of being truly equidistant between the two.

Alice Springs is the Northern Territory's third largest centre behind Darwin and Palmerston. The town was first called 'Stuart' until 1933 when it changed its name to that of a nearby waterhole named after Alice Todd, wife of Charles Todd, who drove much of the new settlement's establishment from around 1870. The area the town sits on was/is called Mparntwe, a name given by the Arrernte People, the original and traditional owners of the area. The town's unique location under endless blue skies, ascending from the rich, red pindan sands of the Central Desert gives rise to the romantic notion of Alice Springs as the 'beating heart of the Red Centre'. The 2016 Census by the Australian Bureau of Statistics revealed Alice Springs as a relatively young town with a median age of 35 from a population of 24,753 people, 17.6 per cent of whom are Aboriginal and/or Torres Strait Islander.[2]

The people who populate this remarkable place are a cosmopolitan mix of Traditional Owners, adventurers and wanderers; dreamers and social workers; Countrymen, missionaries and fugitives; born-and-breds, blow-ins and transplants.

As one can expect from a large regional centre, Alice Springs has all the mod cons of 'Big Town' Australia. This includes an administrative hub, town council, a glasshouse Supreme Court — within which one mustn't throw stones — private housing, public housing, backpacker accommodation, suburbs, a CBD, vibrant murals, shopping centres, food courts, juice bars, cool cafés, sippy lattes, all the takeaways, nightlife, funky clubs, dodgy pubs, Tinder probably, the franchises, 24-hour servos, suburban supermarkets, a casino, an 18-hole rolling-green golf course, a modern aquatic centre, schools, libraries, media, Wi-Fi, all the trades, private industry, a cemetery, light industrial areas, traffic lights, intersections, roundabouts, footpaths, public transport, taxis, hire cars, rail, sealed roads, dirt tracks, bookshops, op-shops, traditional and contemporary art centres, festivals of all the arts, museums, an airport, a public hospital, the service industries, and a dry riverbed running through the middle of it all. A little-known fact about Alice Springs is that it is the only Australian town closest in proximity to every beach in the country — true story.

Alice Springs is also the regional and administrative hub for Central Australia making it a sweet spot for businesses seeking greater bang for their buck. Strategically, this was perfect for the Central Australian Football Club.

In legislative terms, Alice Springs is tied to Darwin. In commercial terms, it is tied to neither Darwin nor Adelaide; again, this was advantageous for the Redtails.

Rob Clarke and Ian McAdam had the rare luxury of choosing which direction they could take the Redtails. They weren't constrained by rusted-on football traditions, nor was there any regional biases. This club was built from scratch. There were viable football options north and south of Alice Springs. To understand that choice, it is important to first understand the hierarchy of Aussie rules football in this country, and what that hierarchy looked like around 2011–2012, the time of the CAFC's formation.

***

Officially 'Australian Football' — colloquially Australian rules, Australian rules football, Aussie rules, Aussie rules football — the home-grown game has several layers of competition with varying standards in how it is played. These range from national level über-professionalism; state- and territory-level semi-professionalism; and amateur-level part-timers in the country, parks and out bush. These layers are designated into tiers, with 'Tier 1' sitting at the top, and this is where we begin:

TIER 1

- Australian Football League (AFL) – national, professional, 17–18 clubs[i]

TIER 2

- North East Australian Football League (NEAFL) – playing out of Queensland, New South Wales, Northern Territory and the Australian Capital Territory, part-time, semi-professional, 10 clubs[ii]
    - South Australian National Football League (SANFL) – based in Adelaide, semi-professional, 8 clubs

---

i In 2011, Gold Coast Football Club joined the AFL as the league's 17th club; in 2012, Greater Western Sydney Football Club joined the AFL as the league's 18th club. In 2023, the AFL Commission granted a provisional licence to Tasmania to become the league's 19th club.

ii The NEAFL was disbanded in 2020. Some of its former clubs joined an expanded VFL in 2021 and 2022.

- Tasmanian State League (TSL) – statewide, semi-professional, 10 clubs
- Victorian Football League (VFL) – based in Melbourne, semi-professional, 13 clubs
- West Australian Football League (WAFL) – based in Perth, semi-professional, 9 clubs

TIER 3

- Northern Territory Football League (NTFL) – based in Darwin, semi-professional, 8 clubs[iii]

Tier 1 football was obviously unsuitable for the Central Australians. The AFL competition is the highest level of football in the country; its players are full-time dedicated professionals with an army of coaches and support staff behind them. The game is also backed by big corporate industry and enjoys ongoing multi-billion-dollar broadcast rights deals. The game on the field is at a world-class level, equal in those terms to the other major world sports. Central Australians who have cracked the big-time modern-era AFL include the Bowden brothers, Joel (Richmond), Patrick (Western Bulldogs, Richmond) and Sean (Richmond); Fred Campbell (St Kilda, Sydney); Matt Campbell (North Melbourne); Richard Cole (Collingwood, Essendon); Adrian McAdam (North Melbourne) and Greg McAdam (St Kilda), who are Ian's older brothers; Gibson Turner (Richmond); Darryl White (Brisbane); Darryl Wintle (Adelaide); Tom Logan (Brisbane, Port Adelaide); Liam Patrick (Gold Coast); Lachlan Ross (Essendon) and the quartet of Jake Neade (Port Adelaide), Dom Barry (Melbourne, Port Adelaide), Curtly Hampton (GWS, Adelaide) and Liam Jurrah (Melbourne) whom we met earlier. For the start-up Redtails, the AFL was simply out of the question.

iii The NTFL has since been elevated to Tier 2 status.

The Tier 2 football leagues were somewhat optionable for the CAFC, but there were several caveats.

The NEAFL was a recent construct. It was a hybridised mishmash of 17 south-east Queensland, metro Sydney and Canberran football clubs — anyway, NT Thunder was there first.

The VFL was firmly set with its clubs and histories. It was also a 'feeder' league into the AFL system, therefore rather complicated — plus it was too cold.

The Tasmanian State League? And the WAFL? They might as well be in other countries.

The SANFL in Adelaide was a familiar place for Central Australian footballers and fans. For the Redtails, this great southern league loomed large. In the late 1970s and early 1980s, several Central Australians made quite the impact in the SANFL, like Greg McAdam (Ian McAdam's brother), Les Turner and Lance White at North Adelaide. And Gilbert McAdam (Ian and Greg's brother) who was the first — and is still the only — Aboriginal man to win the Magarey Medal, the SANFL's fairest-and-best award when he played for Central District in 1989. The SANFL was certainly an option, given its proximity to Alice Springs. But again, given the early experimental nature of the CAFC the proposition could not be a serious consideration at this time.

That left the Darwin-based Tier 3 NTFL. This was the most realistic option.

Darwin and Alice Springs share political, civil and familial links going back decades. For example, if you were to poke around both places long enough, family Mob or an 'expat' from either end will inevitably pop up out of somewhere. Despite a perceived political disconnect from city-state Darwin that sometimes frustrates the Central Australians, the many shared social, sporting and cultural histories run deep. Darwin is home away from home for a lot of Central Australians.

If anything else was to tilt the decision northward it was the timing of the respective football seasons. This was a critical point in the overall purpose of the CAFC. Football in Central Australia is played from around April-May through to September, the 'traditional' football months. But in the Top End, the NTFL season runs from October through to March, during the summer months, a historical quirk that has worked well for over 100 years. In practical terms, what this means is that as ecstatic Central Australian footballers raise their premiership trophies and medals in triumph in September, Top End footballers are only just preparing to kick their first ball in anger in October. The alternate seasons of the CAFL and NTFL dovetail nicely into each other.

A push north by the Redtails would also remove any *competition* with the established local leagues for players — the region's young men in their football prime years. A push into northern summertime football would complement the local leagues and their players by providing a productive outlet for this cohort. This was the reasoning behind Rob Clarke's decision for the club to become a summertime destination for local footballers, an astute decision in the context of the big picture.

Just like NT Thunder, the premierships that would provide local validation lay elsewhere, and for the desert-based Central Australian Football Club this was in the tropics, in Darwin, and in the semi-professional senior men's Premier League division of the NTFL.

In just a short time, Rob Clarke and Ian McAdam had built the foundations of a club that would draw the various local football tribes together. They now had the means to draw two larger tribes together — one whose heart beats in the bush, the other whose heart beats to the rhythm of the tropics in the northernmost city of the country.

But was Darwin ready? Was Darwin football ready? Was anyone there ready for Alice Springs? What would the established clubs there think? There is resistance to change, even in football. And in Darwin football, any change to the status quo meant a perceived threat — on the field, and the bottom line.

MERE FORMALITIES

On 20 July 2012, Rob Clarke and Ian McAdam took formal steps to make things official, registering the club with the Australian Securities Investment Commission as *Central Australian Football Club Incorporated.* From there, a board of directors was assembled. The board comprised a mix of working professionals, local people passionate about their community, astute business folk and, by practical necessity, family members close to the Redtails. The Redtails' first board members were Jake Clarke (Rob's son) as Club Secretary; Alecia Clarke (Rob's wife, Jake's mum) as Treasurer; Rob Clarke as President; Ian McAdam as Vice-President; and, as committee members, Paul Ah Chee (Director at Alice Springs Desert Park), Paul Graham (owner construction manager at Asbuild NT), Karl Hampton (former NT Sports Minister, father of former Giants player, Curtly Hampton), Harold Howard (Central Land Council) and Craig Reid (Managing Director at Red Centre Technology Partners).

The Redtails bandwagon also welcomed its first No. 1 ticket-holder: Wayne Kraft — owner of the Overlanders Steakhouse with the best cuts in town. A gregarious character, 'Krafty' loves his footy like he loves his steak — heaps! He said:

> *Out of the blue I received a call from Rob Clarke, asking me if I would consider accepting the Redtails' No. 1 ticket-holder honour. My response was* Yes, of course! *not really knowing what my obligations and financial expectations of that support might be, [but] I was honoured. It was probably the greatest honour to have ever been bestowed upon me by a country mile. The club's committee covered the whole gamut*

of both Aboriginal and whitefellas; I was deeply honoured. We dared to dream! It's a clichéd statement, but you have to get out there and have a crack.[3]

FOOTBALL'S SEISMIC SHIFTS

FOOTBALL in the Northern Territory's Top End had undergone significant change and substantial growth around the time of the Central Australian Football Club's formation in 2011–12. Gone was the singular view and insular idea of what the game in Darwin ought to look like; in its place was a forward-looking entity that catered to a diverse and assertive community. The CAFC decided this was where they wanted in. It is central to the club's story.

In 2005, the South Melbourne-transplanted-to-Sydney Swans had just broken a 72-year premiership drought after defeating West Coast in an epic AFL grand final. And earlier that year, Tony Frawley had just undergone a transplant himself — from footy-mad Melbourne to madland Darwin as Chief Executive of AFLNT. It was a role he would have been mad not to take up. He was a man for the times, and not actually mad.

Tony Frawley was from the Frawley clan whose association with the game spanned generations. His brother, the late Danny Frawley, played more than 250 senior games in the VFL–AFL and in representative football. His uncle was former Collingwood player Des Tuddenham who played during the

1960s and 1970s. His cousin, Paul Tuddenham, played around 40 games for Collingwood in the late 1980s. Tony's nephew James Frawley is a celebrated AFL footballer and premiership player of the 2010s.

***

One of the earliest 'submissions' to cross Tony Frawley's shiny new desk as the fresh exec at AFLNT was the persistent talk he kept hearing about the push for the Tiwi Islands to join the NTFL senior men's competition.

Up to that point, the NTFL hadn't changed its look since the late 1980s. That was when Southern Districts emerged from the sprawling rural area outside of Darwin just beyond the 'Berrimah Line' to become the league's seventh team in 1987.[1] That same year, Katherine Kangaroos, based in Katherine 320 kilometres south of Darwin, became the league's eighth team. But the team's 640-kilometre seven-hour roadtrip with a football match occasionally breaking out had become unsustainable. After just two years, they withdrew from the NTFL at the end of the 1988–89 season. For near-on 20 years thereafter, the senior men's NTFL competition operated as an odd-numbered league with a problematic bye.[i] The 'submission' that piqued Tony Frawley's early interest would address this problem. It was coming from the Tiwi people of the Tiwi Islands, 80km north of Darwin in the Arafura Sea.

Tiwis have long played Aussie rules football. On the islands, they have their own competition — the Tiwi Islands Football League, then played during the summer wet season. Over the decades, Tiwi footballers have lit up the game and excited the crowds in Darwin, the southern states, and increasingly in the AFL and AFLW. The Tiwis' popularity among fans in Darwin extended across the various teams and grades. But the islanders wanted a club of their own. Luckily for them, they had an ally in football's new bossman.

'When I got there,' Frawley said, 'everyone was talking about, *a Tiwi team this, a Tiwi team that*. So I said, *Well, why don't we put one in!*'

---

i From 1989–2005, the NTFL was made up of Darwin Buffaloes, Nightcliff, Palmerston (North Darwin until 1996), Southern Districts, St Mary's, Wanderers and Waratah.

Frawley, the Tiwis, and a small army of support staff got to work.

> *With the Tiwi proposal, the club presidents voted for a seven-week trial period. The players would be drawn from the other NTFL clubs so the trial period would be a bit easier [on the existing clubs] in that respect. (Tony Frawley)*[2]

At the time, many of the best Tiwi footballers were playing throughout the NTFL's seven existing clubs, and a lot of them were key to their respective teams' success. Among a host of players was 2005–06 premiership forward Ephrem Tipungwuti with the Darwin Buffaloes; big-bodied Adam Kerinaiua who came off the interchange bench to win a premiership at St Mary's in the 2004–05 season; and James Scrymgour who would win a flag with Wanderers in the 2010–11 decider.

The trial period suggested by Frawley would do two things:

1. alleviate teething problems for the fledgling Tiwi team, and
2. help the existing clubs adjust without some of their Tiwi stars.

The trial period would take place in rounds 1–7, during October and November of the 2006–07 season.

A side called the 'Super Tiwis' was assembled and fixtured in to play each of the seven teams once over a seven-week period. The idea was to see how the islanders fared on the field, and to see evidence of structural support off it, in terms of a Board, committee, club members, sponsorship and fan support.

Any lingering doubts as to a standalone Tiwi team's competitiveness on the mainland was dispelled in the most emphatic fashion. The islanders brought with them their dynamic brand of one-touch football, where playing-on is the rule rather than the exception, and where chaotic unpredictability was exciting and highly effective. The Super Tiwis won all but one of those trial games and most of those victories were by significant margins. They also won an extra post-season trial game against that season's premiers, Southern Districts. Super, indeed.

The Tiwis upheld their end of the bargain, showcasing their capabilities as a standalone team. The players and their fans brought with them a new noise, a tangible energy, and a positive vibe to Top End football. They filled in the blanks the competition didn't know it needed filling.

Early in 2007, the AFLNT Board granted the Tiwis a Premier League licence to join the competition on a permanent basis as the eighth senior men's team in the NTFL. In a short time, the Tiwis would be winning finals and grand finals.

The Tiwis' inclusion in the NTFL was significant on two fronts. It was the first time that an Aboriginal-led football club-organisation had joined a major Australian state or territory-level competition, and it showed that if and when presented with a solid case Frawley and co. weren't closed off to the idea of outsiders wanting in. Taking retrospective notes on both points (particularly the second), were the Central Australians.

Having breached the once-impenetrable eastern seaboard with the NT Thunder, NT football's quest for world domination was only just beginning.

FOOTY AGREEMENTS IN THE TOP END

From around 2009, AFLNT initiated peace talks with Darwin football's final hold-out, the super-niche Top End Australian Football Association (TEAFA). The TEAFA played during the summer wet season, in sort of direct competition with the NTFL that played during the same time. TEAFA was its own football eco-system with a handful of clubs and players who played for the fun of it. Led by local luminaries such as the tireless Bill Gear, TEAFA was originally NTFL 'C Grade' from 1979 to 1981. In 1982 it became the Northern Territory Football Association (NTFA) before its third and final name-change to TEAFA in 2000. TEAFA had what the AFLNT and its clubs wanted — successful club brands, fan bases, human capital and people in football who loved the game. They also had the resources that went with them, like time, money, expertise. Perhaps the best way to explain TEAFA was that it was to the NTFL what the Victorian Football Association (VFA) was to the Victorian Football League (VFL) from 1897 up until the 1990s — a rival football competition with less resources but finding its niche with a distinct identity, teams, history and culture.

The AFLNT and TEAFA talks landed on a peaceful resolution at a special general meeting in April 2010 when the TEAFA Board effectively voted itself out of existence. Everything it had was shifted to AFLNT. Its clubs, players, key personnel and brands were wholly absorbed into the NTFL. With the now former TEAFA clubs under the control of AFLNT, the governing body expanded the NTFL to tiered grades to accommodate the newcomers — Premier League, and Divisions 1 and 2.[3]

A year after the TEAFA takeover, AFLNT's talks with the board of AFL Central Australia (AFLCA) finally bore fruit. AFLCA, which governed football in Central Australia, had seen 13 general managers come and go over a 12-year period. In September 2011, after several months of back-and-forth negotiation — which included the day Rob Clarke and Tony Frawley crossed paths at Traeger Park — AFLNT announced its takeover was complete. In a public statement, AFLNT said it would, 'assume control of AFLCA following a special general meeting by the AFLCA Board which will be passing a resolution that would hand governance of AFLCA to AFLNT'.[4]

***

Women's football was also beginning to make its presence felt around this time. Footy for women in the Territory was largely self-organised by a handful of passionate individuals. An NT women's team — the Kites — received a much-needed boost when the AFL Women's National Championships was held in Darwin in 2003.[5] Buoyed by the Kites' highest finish at these championships (third) the women's game rose steadily from sideline curiosity to serious football and with its own senior Women's Premier League competition inside a decade.

In 2011, planning began for a wholesale facelift at Marrara Oval where there was an underutilised space behind the goals at the McMillans Road end, or to the left of screen if you're watching from home. For two decades, football in the Territory was administered from a collection of poky offices deep inside the bowels of the Maurice Rioli Grandstand, named after the late, great football icon from the Tiwi Islands. If AFLNT wanted to facilitate this bold new era of its own making it needed to get with the times, man. The plan was to build a modern, state-of-the-art administrative centre that would house the Board, key personnel and guests in a suite of spacious offices, function rooms, plus accommodation with a mini-museum and a base for its new team, NT Thunder. Frawley and former AFL great Michael Long teamed up (again) and with another blueprint they sounded out the late Simon Crean, then Labor Federal Minister for Regional Development. Crean was receptive to the plan. Costings for the centre were projected to be upward of $15 million.

In July 2012, AFLNT announced it had secured the capital required for the large-scale project. Most of the money had come from Federal Labor, the NT Government and the AFL Commission in Melbourne. Among that total also was $3.5 million from the Aboriginals Benefit Account (the ABA).[6] The ABA is a special account for Aboriginal people and was established under the *Aboriginal Land Rights (Northern Territory) Act 1976*. The ABA receives monies from the Commonwealth based on the value of royalties generated from mining on Aboriginal land in the NT.[7] Construction began shortly thereafter and in 2015 the final coat of paint was applied to football's new headquarters, the Michael Long Learning & Leadership Centre (MLLLC), named in honour of another great man of NT football.[8]

In just a few short years, football in the Top End had undergone significant and transformative change. The shift was seismic. Before us now stood a drastically altered football landscape. In the period from 2007 to

2011, the AFLNT Executive had engineered the creation and transition of 20 senior teams, and several thousand players across 89 clubs in 10 senior, senior reserves, women's and junior divisions all under the umbrella of the Northern Territory Football League. This was a phenomenal achievement. It may have taken several decades but football's kingmakers had yielded to the game's changing face and rising powerbase. Its tectonic plates had shifted with the times.

Observing all these goings-on with wide-eyed wonderment was the gang from Alice Springs. The Central Australians wanted in on this progressive and expansive environment. If ever there was a good time to get in on what was brewing in the Top End, this was it.

FOOTY ADMIN IN THE TOP END

Up until 2001 'Northern Territory Football League' was both the name for the Darwin-based competition *and* the game's administration. But in that same year, the game's administration was rebranded to AFL Northern Territory (AFLNT) while Northern Territory Football League was retained as the name for the on-field senior men's competition (see Appendix 4).

AFLNT is headquartered at Marrara Oval, interchangeably known as 'Football Park', 'Marrara Stadium' and, to the corporates, 'TIO Stadium' (stemming from a long-term commercial arrangement with the former NT government-owned Territory Insurance Organisation which was controversially sold off by the Adam Giles CLP Government in 2014.[9]) Marrara Oval was built during the Steve Hatton-Marshall Perron era of the Country Liberal Party (1987–1994) and was opened in 1991.

Darwin football in the olden days was played on the Esplanade, where the Cenotaph is, at the edge of the city overlooking Darwin harbour. Later, it moved to Gardens Oval in the leafy suburb of Gardens. But population growth necessitated a shift.

Marrara Oval is located within Darwin's sprawling sporting precinct in the suburb of Marrara, straddling McMillans Road, one of the city's main arterials, and Darwin International Airport. It is the Northern Territory's premier sports venue. It hosts the entire NTFL season from October through to March, AFL and NRL pre-season and premiership matches and, on occasion, international cricket.

Marrara Oval's official capacity is 15,000 people (5000 seated) but on 7 February 2003, 17,500 people crammed into the venue (mostly within the standing-room only outer sections) to watch the long-awaited return of football's 'All-Stars' representative match. The team, formally called the ATSIC Aboriginal All-Stars, played against AFL club Carlton in front of this record-breaking crowd (a record that stands to this day).

In 2017, 13,500 people packed in at the venue to watch the Rugby League World Cup quarter-final between Australia and Samoa.

In cricket, two Tests have been played at the ground: Australia v Bangladesh in 2003, and Australia v Sri Lanka in 2004, plus four one-day internationals involving Australia and Bangladesh. Each of these games, however, achieved less than satisfactory attendance figures.[10]

The first iteration of an 'NTFL' took place around the years 1916–17. It was a tumultuous beginning to say the least, blighted by nepotism, ineptitude, and cold-hearted racism.[11]

Another major sport necessitated the NTFL to be played during the summer months, the only major Australian state or territory football competition to do so. Cricket, using the same ovals as football, if played in its 'traditional' summer months, is impractical in the Top End due to the constant rains that ruin pitches. And football, if played in its traditional winter months, is impractical in the Top End due to the rock-hard surfaces that ruin knees.[12] The Territory's sporting pioneers more than 100 years ago were left with the only viable option and that was to flip the seasons around — football in the summer-wet, cricket in the winter dry.

THE 'CODE WARS' – A CONDENSED HISTORY

What really distinguishes Australia is that among our four football codes there's this equilibrium in terms of contestation for the hearts and minds between consumers, [but] they all interact with some level of interest between them.

DR HUNTER FUJAK ON THE BACK STORY PODCAST[1]

AUSTRALIANS are a progressive bunch, and we stand unique in the world in matters of sport. We are openly bi-codal. We will march in the streets (to the stadiums) in all the colours of the rainbow and be mighty proud of it. Australia has four professional football codes with a population of around 28 million people; that's roughly the same numbers as North Korea, only that the socially and politically challenged North Korea knows only soccer. Our landmass is roughly comparable to that of the United States's 48 contiguous states, but that country's population of around 330 million eclipses ours 13 times over.

The socially gregarious United States only wants to know American football — or gridiron — over which the multi-billion-dollar National Football League (NFL) reigns supreme.

Nowhere else in the world is there a country comparable in population, landmass or any other measure that sustains four professional football codes to the extent we do here. The football codes that command so much of our loyalties and weekend attention are Aussie rules, rugby league, rugby union and soccer, administered by the Australian Football League (AFL), the National Rugby League (NRL), Super Rugby (SR) and the A-Leagues (AL) respectively. Even with this sporting 'multi-codalism', there exist long-held divisions between Australians and our games — geographical, and ideological.

Victoria, Tasmania, South Australia and Western Australia long ago took to Aussie rules football; Victoria, of course, being the birthplace of the Australian game.[2]

New South Wales and Queensland embraced the imported English game of rugby union from the late 1800s, and later, that game's dynamic northern England off-shoot, rugby league (established in England in 1895) from 1908.[3]

A diaspora of migrant Europeans who have so enriched the Australian story have largely held on to the soccer of their original homelands. The spread and local ownership of soccer in Australia has had the welcome by-product of our national teams, the Socceroos and Matildas, regularly qualifying for FIFA World Cups and the Olympics.

In the Northern Territory and Australian Capital Territory there is an openness to all the footballs where a happy cross-code pollination takes place, but this is the exception rather than the rule

Into this complex bi-codal disorder the AFL and NRL competitions command the lion's share of attention with billions in broadcast rights and millions of bums on seats that the quasi-international Super Rugby and A-Leagues can only dream about.[4] If we dive deeper still, there is even more divergence: a 'southern states AFL vs. northern states NRL' divide marked by the mythical *Barassi Line*. The Barassi Line — an old-timey term coined in the late 1970s and named after VFL great, the late Ronald Dale Barassi — is a playful take on what was known as the Brisbane Line, a controversial post-war allegation levelled at the Menzies-Fadden federal governments of the 1940s and 1950s. The alleged plan for such a line was to separate the northern portion of Australia, beginning at Brisbane, which would be surrendered to the Japanese should things go pear-shaped in the Second World War. Yes, really.[5]

In theory, football's Barassi Line begins from the point where the borders of north-east Victoria and the NSW south coast meet, from which it runs north-west diagonally up into the NT, ending at the Territory capital, Darwin. If you look at the Barassi Line on a map, to the left of the line is where Aussie rules rules, and to the right is where rugby league is king. In reality, the Barassi Line is a construct of the earlier football-culture code wars, the most recent outbreak of which was not that long ago.

'WAR OF ATTRITION'

Around 2004–05, the Australian Rugby League Commission (ARL) began the process of installing a new (and 16th) team in the NRL competition, based in the heavily populated Gold Coast region of south-east Queensland.[6] The Gold Coast is a competitive sports market and the rise and demise of several national league teams in the region has proven challenging for sports administrators, partially due to a diverse and often transient population (see Appendix 5). There are indeed diehard rugby league fans and transplanted southerners stuck on Aussie rules on the Gold Coast, but outnumbering them are the sun-worshippers, beach babes, gym bros and meter maids who couldn't care less about stupid footy — both of them. Nevertheless, in 2007, the NRL's newest team, the Gold Coast Titans, played their first season in the national competition. Closing in on their 20th year, the Titans are carving out a solid share of the Gold Coast market from their purpose-built base at Robina Stadium.

Around this time, the AFL Commission in Melbourne sought to establish more of a foothold in NSW and Queensland, deep inside 'enemy territory' on the other side of the mythical Barassi Line. Their reasoning was that Australia's first and third most populous states having just two AFL teams between them (the Sydney Swans and Brisbane Lions) wasn't enough. Super-ironically, both those teams are historical transplants from Victoria.[i] Perhaps the AFL was wishing to capitalise on the Lions' astonishing 'three-peat' of premierships in 2001, 2002 and 2003, and the Swans' breakthrough 2005 premiership. Expansion into these 'markets' would be a value-add to the all-important broadcast-rights deals and go some way toward winning the hearts and minds of the next generation. In 2008, the AFL Commission won support from the 16 existing clubs to establish two new teams — one on the Gold Coast, the other in western Sydney.

In 2011, after a two-year lead-in via the TAC Cup and the VFL, the Gold Coast Suns played their first season in the big league. From their base at Carrara Stadium, the Suns, like the Titans, have carved out a niche market (with steady numbers) on the Gold Coast.[7] The Suns' inception, however, sparked an early sortie in the 'code wars'. Upper management at the Titans vowed their club would actively work to maintain their No. 1 mantle in the region.[8] Clive Palmer, too, had it in for the new AFL club. The real-estate mining magnate and one-time politician had earlier secured an A-League licence for a team called Gold Coast United in 2008. In that same year, when the consortium behind the Suns (GC17) presented its bid for an AFL licence, Palmer could barely hide his disdain for the homegrown game:

---

i The South Melbourne Football Club was relocated to Sydney in 1982. The name-change to Sydney Swans came in 1983-84. The Brisbane Bears was a hastily formed outfit created to play in the 1987 VFL season along with the West Coast Eagles that same year.

It looks like it's fallen on its face a bit. I don't know how much substance there is to it. I don't know if there's a need for an AFL club here on the Coast, I don't know if they can fit in. I do know, though, that ourselves and the Titans fulfil a community need.[9]

In 2012, after just three seasons, Palmer and United were shown a red card by Football Federation Australia. The A-League is yet to return to the region. Happily, the Titans and the Suns have gotten along amicably since, with the clubs' social media-comms teams sharing messages and Millennial memes of encouragement and support at crucial junctures of their respective seasons.

Like the Suns, the AFL's new Sydney team, Greater Western Sydney Football Club — the Giants — had a two-year lead-in via the TAC Cup and VFL before entering the AFL in 2012. The Giants were confronted with plenty of local hostility, led by towering figures in rugby league like Phil 'Gus' Gould, who once famously threatened to walk off the set of the (NRL) *Sunday Footy Show* if AFL dared be mentioned. The audacity! In just their eighth season, the Giants played off in the 2019 AFL grand final. Gus, reportedly, has the AFL and the Giants still on mute. Bless.

The AFL was not altogether blameless in these affairs. During the formative days of the Suns and Giants, a lit match was held above this code-war tinderbox. Backed by an AFL Commission in Melbourne armed with a 'war chest' filled with billions in broadcast-rights dollars, a plan was hatched to actively poach big-name NRL players to play for the two new teams, presumably to fast-track promotion of the game in these new markets. Such a switch from the 'man's game' to 'aerial ping-pong' was seen as sacrilegious, blasphemous and downright treasonous. This was the source of Gould's TV 'tanty', the Titans' early worries, and Palmer's curious insecurities. The reasoning behind the AFL's poaching plan was to create a sustained level of publicity for the two new clubs in 'hostile' markets with daily headlines, increased mentions on air and in print, and greater TV coverage. The AFL committed to playing the long game.

Two young NRL players were separately identified to make the switch to the AFL: Karmichael Hunt and Israel Folau, both supremely gifted athletes and footballers. Hunt was a Brisbane Broncos 2006 NRL premiership star at key-position fullback. Folau was a super-athletic, try-scoring phenom with NRL giants Melbourne Storm from 2007 to 2008 and the Broncos from 2009 to 2010. Both represented the Queensland Maroons in State of Origin and the Australian Kangaroos. This pair was sounded out by the AFL.

The AFL got their wish, and the pair would later accept lucrative contracts, to make the code switch. Conservative reports suggest that the Hunt and Folau contracts were worth around $2 million,[10] which put more than a few rusted-on AFL fans offside because they believed that the spots on the Suns and Giants playing lists ought to be reserved for those who had grown up with Aussie rules and who dreamed of one day playing in the AFL.[11] Hunt's 2010 contract with Gold Coast was initially for two years with a clause for two more, which he enacted. He played four seasons and 44 games with the Suns that included kicking a stunning 60-metre goal on the run (against Geelong) and living out every kid's dream of kicking the winning goal after the final siren (against Richmond, in Cairns). Hunt left AFL football to play rugby union in Super Rugby with the Queensland Reds and NSW Waratahs. Such was this guy's incredible skillset, he later won selection with the Wallabies, where he played in six Tests. In 2021, Hunt made a brief return to the NRL and reunited with the Broncos for one season.

In late 2010, Folau signed with the Giants for two seasons. Unlike his fellow convert, however, Folau's stint in the AFL was largely forgettable.[12] He left the Giants and the AFL in 2013 after just 13 games. Folau, like Hunt, crossed over to rugby union. The men were mates and former Broncos teammates and there was a happy reunion when Folau joined Hunt at the Waratahs and later at the Wallabies where he played in 73 Tests. Folau later returned to rugby league and joined Catalan Dragons in the English Super League.

As these two extraordinary athletes grappled with the Sherrin, form-fitting shorts and no sleeves they also felt the sting of ostracism from the wider football community. Online discussion forums had become big in the early 2000s. *Big Footy* (Aussie rules) and *League Unlimited* (rugby league) were the go-to platforms of the day. If you were unfortunate to spend even half a minute perusing any of the hundreds of threads on both platforms, the abuse for simply being a fan of a specific football code would leave you shaking your head. Tabloid print and TV media mined forum content from towering intellects such as *NumptyBum76* and *Ya_Mum_*. Back page newspaper articles leading with terms like 'AFL invasion' would lead the day's discussion, often riding on the back of the progress Hunt and Folau were making.[13] These forums weren't always mindless cesspits of abuse; there was also some decent content to read. As time moved on, Numpty and co. grew up or could see that a happy football coexistence could totally be a thing.

The Hunt-Folau experiment landed with mixed results. It certainly raised the profile of the AFL in the northern markets and gave much-needed publicity to the two expansion teams during their infancy in 'non-heartland' areas. It is highly unlikely the exercise will be repeated, though, and we may never again see talented footballers making such high-profile switches from one incredibly dynamic football code to another. That will be our collective loss.

***

The code wars were bolstered in 2010 when Football Federation Australia (previously Soccer Australia) pointed a crooked finger at the AFL Commission for undermining its bid to host the mid-year 2022 FIFA World Cup.[14] An Australian mid-year World Cup would severely impact both the AFL and NRL seasons due to FIFA's need for the best stadiums in the country, whose stipulations require any playing surface be clear of all 'content' a minimum of four weeks before use.

The AFL's staunch defence of its contractual obligations to its myriad stakeholders led to a string of daily headlines and columnists denouncing the home-grown football code for denying the world game its long-awaited time in the Aussie winter-sun. But for all that white noise, no-one needed to worry. Australia's bid for the World Cup received just one vote, and a personal invite to a Senate inquiry to explain exactly what FFA did with the $40 million in government money it was given for the bid.[15] In the end, the 2022 World Cup bid was won by that global football superpower, Qatar, which became the first host nation in the history of the World Cup to bow out at the first stage (and without winning a game).

Fuelling much of this code-war rhetoric was News Ltd, the worldwide multi-platform media organisation that appeared in the crosshairs of The Greens, which sought a royal commission into the organisation's divisive practices.[16] News Ltd had shareholdings in several NRL clubs and owns pay-TV's Fox Sports channel. The NRL had long bowed to the demands of its masters at News which — together with Channel 9 — largely dictates how the season ought to look to maximise its investment, e.g. the meme-worthy 'name a more iconic duo than Brisbane Broncos and Friday Night Football' exists for a reason. In contrast, the AFL was, and remains, largely a free-to-air sport, and is generally unshackled from the influence of News, with just a quarter of its games exclusive to pay-TV. But the take-up of pay-TV in Australia is low and News is desperate for content to drive subscriptions. It sees more AFL content as key to this. But it knows from previous experience the AFL won't budge on its approximate 75:25 FTA-pay-TV split. Employing the age-old bait-and-switch method to divide, the media giant and its stable of daily tabloids and teams of writers drum up sensational headlines and negative narratives about the home-grown game in the northern states to downplay its value.

Rather than celebrating what is unique to this country, News's tactics have the effect of dividing and confusing a population that would rather live peacefully and enjoy their football of whatever persuasion.

In practice, this bi-codal life, this cross-pollination of football has enriched us as a nation.

PUTTING THE HARD WORD ON DARWIN

LIKE biggest mob spinifex on a windswept claypan, talk of a new football club spread quickly across Central Australia. The buy-in was strong. Sign-on day was gonna be huge.

Throughout much of 2011 and early 2012, the idea of a locally driven representative team captured the imagination of the region's footballers. The lure might have been a job via the Right Tracks program, but the bait was playing football for Country and playing in Darwin.

While Darwin's 2011 coup of Central Australian football had zero bearing on the Redtails, it did give Tony Frawley and co. a closer look at the new kids in town. The grand plan that the Territory football's chief had only heard about had now grown into a tangible reality. Frawley and Rob Clarke held several talks in person and on the phone over many weeks in 2011 and the early part of 2012, in which Clarke made clear the club's ambitious ploy to play in Darwin. But there was pushback. 'We approached AFLNT with our plan,' Clarke said. But the reaction he received was an assumption that they had no players and no competitive history to help their case. He was told to come back with more than just a question. Clarke asked if they'd entertain his proposal. And they told him that if he got the money together, they would.

> *I reckon late in 2011, I asked them again and it was Yes, no, no, yes. I went looking everywhere for money and the reaction was good. We ended up with about three hundred members — that was a big drive — and about 12 businesses came on board, so it was a good buy-in locally. We ended up with $75,000 in the bank.*[1]

Although Darwin saw merit in the concept, the club's potential place in the Premier League would come with a raft of conditions. Darwin's primary concern was brand protection. They were worried that the CAFC's presence could negatively impact the integrity of football in Alice Springs (specifically the CAFL) as well as that of the Territory's flagship football vessel, NT Thunder (the Northern Territory Football Club).

Darwin's first concern was understandable. The CAFL would mark its 65th year in 2012. It is a local institution. As the vast majority of the Redtails players would come from the CAFL, Frawley's concern was player burnout and what that could do to the CAFL generally.

Darwin's second concern was rather odd. A month earlier, Thunder had won the 2011 NEAFL premiership in front of a big crowd at Traeger Park. The rep team was also building on its presence in Central Australia, drawing players from the region, some of them among the Thunder's best performers. Anything that would draw resources and attention away from the Thunder or, worse, usurp Thunder's position as primary flagbearer of NT football would not be looked upon favourably. Darwin's concerns here were misplaced. The CAFC Redtails would be playing in the summertime, opposite to the winter-time Thunder. There would be no clash of resources.

Clarke's case for the Redtails' admission into the NTFL was compelling. Locals were jumping on board. Volunteers were lining up. The region's footballers were keen. The business community was reaching for change, and the ubiquitous team polo shirt was all the rage around town. Then there came a breakthrough.

> *Today the key stakeholders of the Central Australia [sic] Football Club (CAFC) presented to AFL Northern Territory and AFL Central Australia executive a proposal to enter a team into the NTFL in the future.*
>
> *The aims of the new Club are two fold:*
>
> 1. *To provide greater football opportunities for CA players*
> 2. *Engage, mentor and support young men in CA into meaningful programs into the community*
>
> *From day one the philosophy is that players involved will have to be working, training or studying in order to be allowed to play.*
>
> *The proposed CAFC has entered into a joint venture with Tjaiya Rratja – Right Tracks (under the umbrella of the Desert People Centre) which is a program used to attract and retain young Aboriginal males in meaningful activities like schooling, training and apprenticeships.*
>
> *The new Club will be provided with an opportunity to play a number of trial games in Darwin in the NTFL at the beginning of season 2012/13 with the possibility of some of these games being played in Alice Springs.*
>
> *AFLNT CEO Tony Frawley welcomes the application and advises that this is a true indication of AFLNT's strategy and vision for representative football across the NT.*
>
> *"The advent of the Central Australian Football Club means that the AFLNT's strategy of having representative teams*

> *from all parts of the Territory to make up the NTFL will be close to reality.*
>
> *"It follows on from the formation of Wadeye Magic and Katherine Hawks. It has always been our aim to have a 12 team NTFL and this team enables us to achieve this."*
>
> *Rob Clarke from the CAFC steering committee says this is a unique opportunity to make the NTFL a truly representative competition.*
>
> *"In the event of the Central Australian Football Club entering the NTFL this will create a combined interest and following for all Centralian people and an amazing opportunity for young Centralians to become more engaged within the community and display their football prowess in a State based league. This combined with the Right-Tracks program will have a positive effect on the whole Centralian community."*
>
> *AFLNT were very clear that with advent of the new Club that the current structure of Central Australian football and NT Thunder is not impacted on, which includes protection of current revenues and programs. The concept must be financially viable in both the short and long term and improve the structure of football in the whole of NT.*[2]

This, in effect, was an agreement in principle only, and an official-unofficial memorandum of understanding (MoU) between AFLNT and CAFC. An MoU falls somewhere between a written contract and a handshake deal. It provided the club's stakeholders in Alice Springs and football's administration in Darwin a clear understanding of the overall plan, and the expectations from each camp. Happily, for the Central Australians, it held exactly what they were after: a proposal for the Redtails' inclusion in the NTFL.

Where Darwin and Alice Springs did see eye-to-eye was in the opportunities football afforded to young men in the region, those within the

18–25 age group, and how this would be tied to meaningful opportunities in employment and study. This was the bread-and-butter mix of the Right Tracks element of the Redtails football program. And a grown-up version of the Clontarf Foundation that required school-aged youth in its academies to maintain high attendance rates in the classroom to partake in its football programs.

In the statement, AFLNT also revealed its ultimate long-term plan: to grow the Premier League from the existing eight teams to 12 teams. Expanding beyond Darwin to become a true and proper *Northern Territory-wide* football league was an idea kicked around the park over many years in the Top End.

The Katherine Football Club's short-lived sojourn into Darwin in the 1980s was the only other serious shot at true expansion beyond the Berrimah Line (technically, NTFL club Southern Districts lies around 21 kilometres south of this mythical line). The Kangaroos enjoyed a measure of success in Darwin, but it was short-lived according to football historians David Lee and Michael Barfoot.

> *Prior to establishing its own competition in 1988–89, Katherine competed as a club in the NT Football Association, winning Premierships in the inaugural 1982–83 season and 1984–85. The Katherine club then joined the NTFL Reserves competition, winning the 1985–86 and 1986–87 Premierships. It was accepted into the NTFL League competition in the 1987–88 season and finished bottom of the ladder.*[3]

The Katherine team lasted just two seasons in the top-flight in Darwin after which the idea was largely put on the backburner. However, the Tiwi Bombers' inclusion in the Premier League and subsequent success on the football field gave Darwin hope that another regional club in the top-flight was a possibility.

Anthony Venes was the general manager of community football at the AFLNT from 2010 to 2016. He said the push for expansion during his time in Territory football was high on the Darwin agenda. AFLNT's invitation to the CAFC in October 2011 opened the door for the Redtails to be one of those expansion clubs.

> *In my time at AFLNT under Tony Frawley, there was a strong push to expand the NTFL by encouraging regional participation. The [Katherine-based under-18] Big River Hawks, it was hoped, would find a way to increase its funding reserves and consider a senior side, at least in Division 1. We had remote programs running that brought community players into Darwin to play for NTFL clubs. Wadeye Magic had a stint in Division 1 as a result of the remote area program. Other regions requested to put a team into one of the senior competitions — Division 1 or Division 2. Funding was the biggest hurdle on pretty much every occasion. (Anthony Venes)*[4]

The Executive's big-picture vision was now in the public domain and the CAFC was sitting pretty in the box seat. The club arrived out of the blue and right on cue. The precedent set by the Tiwis five years earlier was the one to follow. Anthony Venes said:

> *We got the Tiwis in; when we started to talk to them [Redtails] we based a lot of those plans on what we had already done.*[5]

The Central Australians had a year to get things right. Following the invitation, the new club held a series of Q&A meetings in Alice Springs with local stakeholders, football officials, players and the general public, including former Pioneer coach, John Glasson:

> *I was happy with how it went, they answered questions to the best of their knowledge that they have at this stage. My main concern was playing outside the normal season when*

the local clubs usually have a bit of a rest before starting their pre-season but it's like other issues, when the issue arises it will be further looked at. From what I've heard, Tony Frawley from AFLNT wants a Central Australian side to make it an entire NTFL, and it is going to gain a lot more momentum.[6]

Captain of Rovers Football Club Luke Farrows was one of many local footballers in Alice Springs keen to get a look in at the Redtails. He spoke on what the presence of a local team aiming for NTFL inclusion would have on local footballers:

I think a lot of local players would train harder because it is a reachable goal. I would be proud if one day I was able to look back and say that I played for Central Australia.[7]

WILL THEY, OR WON'T THEY?

Still not entirely sold on the idea, months later, AFLNT took steps to placate Redtails' management. While not a concrete guarantee, AFLNT granted the Central Australians a provisional licence with a raft of conditions. In guarded tones, Darwin wrote:

AFLNT's proposed NTFL expansion strategy will take its next carefully planned step with the ... newly formed Central Australian Football Club ... being granted a provisional NTFL licence which will allow [the] club to play a four-game trial series in the upcoming 2012/13 TIO NTFL Season.

According to AFLNT CEO Tony Frawley, "the proposed entry of the Central Australian Football Club into the NTFL promises to be as exciting as the entry of the Tiwi Bombers and the Wadeye Magic into the league. The Central Australian Football Club has been formed to give the town of Alice

> *Springs the opportunity to be represented at the highest level and while we are excited about the prospect of an Alice team competing in the NTFL, full entry into the league will be contingent on a number of strict criteria being met during and after the trial period. We feel that four games will give [the Redtails] an idea of the challenges that lie ahead as they seek to gain full entry into the Premier League.*
>
> *"We will sit down ... after the trial period and conduct a full review to assess the success of the trial and what [the Redtails] need to do to take the next all-important step toward full entry. We expect the existing NTFL clubs to be supportive of the trial as an expanded league will bring multiple benefits for all the existing premier league clubs. We will be working closely with the club presidents to ensure this is the case."*[8]

The tension was palpable. The weeks that followed were a nervous wait.

'It was just a few weeks prior to the start of the [2012–13 NTFL] season; we were holding our breath the whole time,' Rob Clarke said.[9]

THE RUMBLINGS OF THEIR DISCONTENT

The progress the Central Australians were making toward Darwin wasn't going unnoticed. Rumblings of discontent were stirring in the Top End. The noise of civil unrest within clubland had threatened to derail the Redtails' progress. The Premier League clubs in Darwin reside in a crowded sporting marketplace where the city's dollars can only go so far. Some were not at all happy with this Redtails malarkey. Maybe they saw CAFC as a financial threat. Perhaps the world did end at the Berrimah Line after all. Anthony Venes confirmed as much but said those conditions for the Redtails' inclusion — notably, having dibs on some of the players — would help smooth the waters.

As far as the existing NTFL clubs were concerned there were mixed feelings about having these outer-lying teams participate. Some put their hand up, others not so much. If I remember correctly, we provided NTFL clubs with the ability to select Redtails players after their trial, which provided extra incentive to embrace the concept.[10]

Footy's bossman Tony Frawley was in the Redtails' corner. He had had an outsider's view of Darwin football. He said he worked hard to convince the NTFL clubs of the merits of bringing the Redtails in.

They saw the NTFL as a Darwin-based competition but I never saw it that way. I wanted to see more of the regional and remote teams in. The development of football elsewhere, the development of footy in Central Australia and the opportunity for Central Australian players to play in a good level of competition, that was the point of view we had.[11]

Even so, as the chief executive, the final decision wasn't his. That sat with the board. Eight drawn-out weeks later, Darwin said this:

The 2012–13 NTFL season will commence on Saturday, 6 October 2012 after the fixture was ratified at the AFLNT board meeting on Monday night. The Central Australian Redtails will enter the NTFL on a four-week trial from rounds 1-4 with the Redtails hosting the first-ever NTFL match at Traeger Park in round 1 against St Mary's Football Club who will travel to the Red Centre to test the best of what Central Australia has to offer.[12]

This was the break the Redtails were after. It was exactly what they wanted. It validated everything the new club set out to achieve more than 12 months earlier. All involved could finally breathe. 'Once we proved we could fund what we wanted to do, we got the OK; we got the go-ahead,' Clarke said.

The dream Rob Clarke and Ian McAdam envisioned just over 12 months earlier was one step closer to reality. They had a date with Top End football. They wouldn't miss it for the world. And, despite what Hollywood tried to tell us of the ancient Mayans, 2012 would be the year.

BYE-BYE BYE

Bubblegum-pop boy band NSYNC swooned their way into the hearts of the young and impressionable when they crooned *Bye Bye Bye* in the year 2000. The song was from the band's third studio album *No Strings Attached,* and it topped the charts worldwide, including Australia's — revealing a disturbing lack of musical taste in this country, apparently!

On an altogether different note, the Redtails' imminent inclusion in the Premier League meant the return of the problematic 'bye' — a round of games during the regular season in which a team sits out due to not having an opponent. It's not that byes can't work, just given the NTFL's small pool of teams, a bye in the middle of a team's good run of form can blunt momentum, particularly around finals.

The league had earlier eliminated the near-quarter-century-old bye with the arrival of the Tiwi Bombers as the even-numbered eighth team in 2007. But the bye was back because the Redtails were now the uneven numbered ninth team. There was a neat and convenient solution to this, and it came in the form of Darwin club, Banks Bulldogs, as the 10th team.

Banks was the TEAFA powerhouse club turned NTFL aspirant. This well-resourced, super-organised outfit had the administrative nous arguably superior to some of their 100-year-old peers in the Premier League. The Bulldogs were invited into the Premier League alongside the Redtails to play their own trial games. It was a chance for further validation and a welcome test for player and club alike.

Ten teams — bye-bye to the bye.

The scores and results from the Redtails' and Banks Bulldogs' respective trial games would count for their Premier League opponents in the form of ladder position, in the win-loss column, in percentages for-and-against, and with premiership points. The triallists' scores, points, and ladder positions would also be included but more as an exercise in record-keeping. How competitive they could be mattered more. Unfortunately, an opportunity was missed where the league had failed to schedule a game between the Redtails and Banks.

The newcomers had a month to make a point by kicking goals in the new-look 10-team Premier League.

The contrast in their respective draws, however, could not have been starker.

The Redtails' draw was chock-full of Top End powerhouse clubs, while Banks' opponents had finished the previous season way down the league ladder. But if football credibility is what the Redtails wanted — and it was — then this was a path the team ought to take.

The breakdown for the Redtails' trial games was thus:

- three of their four opponents had played off in the previous two grand finals
- two opponents had won the previous two grand finals, and
- one opponent was the league's reigning premier.

Meanwhile, Banks' opponents had finished the previous season on the ladder in:

- third
- fifth
- sixth, and
- eighth.

NTFL PREMIER LEAGUE DRAW

REDTAILS:

Round 1 vs. St Mary's at Traeger Park, Alice Springs

Round 2 vs. Palmerston at Cazalys Arena, Palmerston

Round 3 vs. Tiwi Bombers at Marrara Oval, Darwin

Round 4 vs. Nightcliff at Marrara Oval, Darwin[i]

BANKS BULLDOGS:

Round 1 vs. Waratah at Gardens Oval, Darwin

Round 2 vs. Wanderers at Gardens Oval, Darwin

Round 3 vs. Southern Districts at Marrara Oval, Darwin

Round 4 vs. Darwin Buffaloes at Gardens Oval, Darwin[ii]

HOME & AWAY

The happy afterglow following the CAFC's admission for a trial period, however, was somewhat dampened. Despite assurances in August of 'the possibility of some of [the Redtails'] games being played in Alice Springs', it wasn't unreasonable to expect that at least half of the new club's games could be played at home, but this was not to be. Only one of those games was scheduled for Traeger Park.

An Alice Springs team playing Premier League football away from home makes no sense. The Redtails' location meant regular travel would always form part of their Top End plans, but to deny the home-grown club a meaningful local presence would undo much of what they set out to achieve, which was a visible, local presence and the engagement it can provide. Consecutive weekly travel would also impact the players. Not all of them were from Alice Springs

i Redtails opponents' ladder positions: St Mary's – 4th (also premiers in 2010–11; Palmerston – 7th; Tiwi Bombers – premiers in 2011–12; Nightcliff – grand finalists in 2011–12.

ii Banks Bulldogs opponents' ladder positions in 2011–12: Waratah – 5th; Wanderers – 3rd; Southern Districts – 6th; Darwin Buffaloes – 8th.

so there was road travel measured in hours. Ominously, this issue would play out later for the club.

Flying within the Northern Territory doesn't come cheap. The smaller airlines with their fleet of light aircraft make a motza flying around the regions. For example, a return flight from Darwin to the Tiwi Islands costs upward of $360 per person. For perspective, one can fly return from the Gold Coast to Melbourne from around $150. The options available for the 3000-kilometre Alice Springs–Darwin return trip were limited to Qantas. Flying an entire football team and support staff up and down the Territory was estimated at $30,000 per trip. The CAFC's flights were covered by AFLNT, which was generous and appreciated by the Redtails camp, but this would have been a point of contention by the Darwin clubs. *If* playing just one game in Alice Springs was a specific condition imposed upon the Redtails by the Darwin clubs, then it was short-sighted; if it was a condition imposed by AFLNT, then it was a failure to look at the bigger picture. As with most things, the truth sits somewhere in the middle. A wise, old soul once told this writer: 'There are three sides to every story — yours, theirs, and the truth.'[13]

Costs, coin, and factions within the football fraternity was an early tell as to what the Redtails would be up against. Rumblings were being felt close to home, too.

KEY PERSONNEL

THROUGHOUT much of the 2012 CAFL season, the new team was front-and-centre in the minds of the region's football community, in Alice Springs and out bush. It was an end-of-season goal that gained momentum as the year progressed through the cool, dry desert winter months. And with a potential start date on the horizon, the search began for someone to coach the side.

The net was cast far and wide with some of the applicants coming from outside the Northern Territory. Centralian Shaun Cusack, a former champion player with South Alice Springs Football Club and one-time coach and premiership player in the NTFL, put his hand up for the top job. Cusack, like Ian McAdam, worked with the region's youth at Alice Springs's Clontarf Foundation Academy. He had a solid body of work in this space. Cusack is a man strong on community leadership, a value shared by McAdam and Rob Clarke. The CAFC was on the cusp of football legitimacy, and they needed someone to take them there, someone who knew the lay of the land. He was successful with his application a few weeks out from the 2012-13 Top End season.

Clarke also revealed a suite of additional sponsors for the new venture. Included was Centrecorp Foundation, an organisation in support of disadvantaged Aboriginal young people; Red Centre Technologies (an IT company); the National Australia Bank; and Clarke's own Fidler & Clarke business. Combined with Santos, AsBuild NT, and Ingkerreke Commercial, the club's coffers rose from $75,000 to $100,000 in total. Things were tracking well for the Right Tracks Redtails.

'GOOD NUMBERS, REAL BUY-IN'

While mindful of unnecessarily imposing itself upon local football, and waiting on word from Darwin, the Redtails held intermittent training sessions throughout much of 2012. Players who were keen on taking their football further but had no interest in joining NT Thunder or were otherwise overlooked by the NT club, had an open invitation to train with the Redtails. As local teams thinned out during the region's finals series in August, the players at Redtails training sessions increased.

Coach Cusack bedded down a program for the incoming raft of players of varying sizes, strengths and abilities who would make up the new team. He was interested to see how his philosophy on how best to play the game fared in the new-look Premier League, this time with players with whom he was familiar. Shaun Cusack reflected on those times over a decade later:

> *It was just a good feeling to be involved. It was very exciting when we got the approval to play those four games. I had a feeling we would do pretty well. We had really good numbers trying out for the club, up to 60 players at training. There was a real buy-in from the local players, a good feeling around the concept and players were keen to play in the NTFL. We didn't have to work too hard to get players to training; they wanted to be there. To get that buy-in from the players was amazing — the community, everyone was behind it. For us it was a special opportunity to go out and represent Central Australia.*[1]

TOP SAINT, RISING COWBOY

Seasoned football watchers sat up and took notice of a pair of youngsters flexing their prodigious talent in the 2011 season of the Central Australian Football League.

That year, the CAFL expanded to eight teams. Three teams from surrounding Aboriginal communities joined the five established clubs in Alice Springs. One of those community teams was the Anmatjere Cowboys. Anmatjere is the name for Ti-Tree, the surrounding communities and smaller outstations, which include Pmara Jutunta, Nturiya and Wilora.

At the Cowboys was a strapping young lad called Daniel Stafford making his mark as a solid forward. The youngster earned praise for his bustle in the air and hustle on the ground. Coupled with his sizeable frame and a safe pair of hands, Stafford struck a formidable presence on the field, even this early playing against men. Certainly, the CAFL awards voting panel took notice. The teenager was judged as the best young talent among a strong group of contenders and was a popular winner of the 2011 CAFL Rising Star award for his outstanding efforts that year.

Downfield and 80 kilometres from Alice Springs at Santa Teresa, Darren Young was having a standout season with his team, the Ltyentye Apurte Saints. The Saints nowadays play on a grassed surface with AFL-issue goalposts that are the tallest structures in Santa Teresa; taller even than the large, white, metal Christian cross bolted into the picturesque range that overlooks the small community. The posts were part of a refurbishment of the community's football oval. In June 2022, the oval was the NT winner of the AFL's Community Facilities award.[2] Before all that, however, the playing surface was a dustbowl. But it was on that same dustbowl where a young Darren Young learnt his craft and emerged as one of Central Australia's best footballers. In 2011, Young won the coveted Minahan Medal, the CAFL's fairest-and-best award.[3]

The timing of this pair's emergence would prove fortuitous for the local game. Young was perfecting his craft as a tap-ruckman while Stafford was growing in stature as a strong presence in the forward-line. They were exactly the type of players an astute coach could build a new side around.

BORN TO RUN

The amount of people in New York City was 38 times that of the Northern Territory's entire population at the end of the first decade of the 2000s: 8.1 million people[4] in the Big Apple that dwarfed the NT's 211,000.

But running those mean New York streets and the Bronx and Queens was a group of Aboriginal young men from Central Australia. Running, that is, in a marathon; the 42.2 kilometres New York City Marathon in polar-opposite conditions to home — the freezing cold of a North American winter.

Charlie Maher, Caleb Hart and Reggie Smith played football at the South Alice Springs Football Club from a young age. In 2010, Maher and Hart were part of the first intake of the newly established Indigenous Marathon Project (IMP) by celebrated Australian marathoner, Olympian and two-time Commonwealth Games gold medallist, Rob de Castella.[5] The IMP's goal was a health, education, wellbeing and long-distance-running program for Aboriginal and Torres Strait Islander young people, with the famed marathon its final destination. Maher and Hart were joined by Juan Darwin, from Maningrida, and Joseph Davies, from Kununurra, to become the first Aboriginal men in history to complete the iconic race.

Their results:

- Charlie Maher – Official time: 3:32:41; Place overall: 5,620th (of 44,976)
- Caleb Hart – Official time: 5:01:28; Place overall: 34,995th
- Juan Darwin – Official time: 4:50:34; Place overall: 32,106th
- Joseph Davies – Official time: 3:54:12; Place overall: 12,178th[6]

In 2011, Smith — back home in Central Australia after a stint playing football in Victoria — heard good things about the IMP from his footy mates. Inspired, he signed up, this time with a dozen others from around the country. Smith tackled the marathon with aplomb and he, too, completed the course.[7]

This trio's journey from the middle of Australia to one of the most celebrated world cities had as a postscript a memorable reunion on the football field, and for a greater cause much closer to home.

REDTAILS' FIRST 22

THE horde that rocked up to football training in the lead-up to the Redtails' first game in early October 2012 was a sight to see. The local season had ended four weeks earlier, on 8 September. Gracing the training track was a mix of town and country footballers from the region's disparate clubs, all of whom had played throughout the 2012 season. It was an open invitation. The Redtails could literally field three teams with the squad that had assembled.

The tough job of culling the 60-strong training group down to its best 22 fell to the selection committee, led by coach Shaun Cusack. In football, cutting players is a thankless task. Only rejection in a relationship comes close to what a footballer feels when overlooked for selection — it stings! But the selectors' job was to pick a team best suited for the task at hand, while reminding the others their time would come.

Reflecting the buy-in from the local football community, the majority of the first team came from South Alice Springs Football Club with five players. Federal and Pioneer each provided four players. Rovers had three, while community clubs Anmatjere Cowboys — from which came the 2011

Rising Star Daniel Stafford — and Western Aranda supplied two each. Darren Young, the 2011 Minahan Medallist, was the sole representative from Ltyentye Apurte, and Gibson Turner had yet to sign-on locally after having just returned from Melbourne after a stint in the AFL with Richmond. In addition, there were three world-marathon runners — Caleb Hart, Charlie Maher and Reggie Smith. In total, seven clubs were represented by the Redtails ahead of the first game. The only local club without a representative was Wests.

THE REDTAILS' HISTORIC FIRST 22 (AND THE CLUB'S PLAYER BIOS):

FORWARD-LINE

Daniel Stafford — Impressive key forward player

Jasper Wheeler — Skilful goal-scorer

Charlie Maher — Captain for all four games, extremely quick with huge motor

HALF-FORWARDS

Thomas Gorey — High-scoring forward with a reliable kick

Ryan Mallard — On-field leader who stands up in big moments

Bradley McMasters — Quick forward who can turn a game around instantaneously

CENTRES

Reggie Smith — Specialist wingman who can be dangerous up forward

Abe Ankers — Great contested ball-winner and provides options up forward

Swaine Hill — Solid defender

HALF-BACKS

Baydon Ngalkin — Classy rebounding defender

Paul Campbell — Explosive utility player who can move the ball from backline to forward with ease

Shane Dixon — Extremely reliable backman who shuts down key opposition forwards

BACKLINE

Jack Abrey — Good tagging backman with an effective spoil

Jayden Prior — Strong backman who can shut down big opposition forwards

Tyson Carmody — Reliable backman

RUCKS

Darren Young — Skilful ruckman who can create options up forward

Gibson Turner — Explosive forward who kicks goals from any angle

Gareth Remfrey — Vice-captain for all four games 2012–13 trial period, huge heart and great all-round skills

INTERCHANGE

Luke Adams — Creative player with silky skills

Caleb Hart — Reliable backman who hits contests hard

G. Jack Miller Jnr. (dec.) — High-jumping ruckman and dangerous up forward[i]

Bradley Turner — Specialist wingman with amazing foot skills

---

i G. Jack Miller Jnr. died in March 2015 from heart failure after footy training in Cairns. He was 27. How his name appears here is an ongoing request from his family.

Redtails family: Redtails full-back Jayden Prior with partner Christa Lingen and son Arjay in a promotional shoot at Traeger Park in Alice Springs ahead of the team's historic first NTFL Premier League game against St Mary's. (Photo: Kevin Prior Centralian Advocate, Tuesday 2 October 2012)

A WORTHY FOE

Anticipation was at an all-time high. The Redtails' first opponent in this historic clash was St Mary's — the Saints. Perhaps the most storied club in Northern Territory football, St Mary's entered the NTFL in 1952. Their original formation in post-war Australia was a welcoming place for Aboriginal people and Tiwi islanders. The Saints jumped at the chance to travel to Alice Springs to play the Redtails. By 2012, the club had won 28 premierships since its inception 60 years earlier: that's a flag every 2.1 years.[1] St Mary's, the feared

'Green Machine', presented the Redtails with a grand challenge. As of 2025, St Mary's Football Club has won 34 NTFL (senior men's) premierships since their inception in 1952; a flag every 1.8 years.[2]

Although treading new ground as representative footballers — some literally for the first time — the 44 footballers weren't complete strangers. Several of the Central Australians had played in the Premier League in Darwin, and were either teammates, former teammates or opponents of some of the Saints players. St Mary's were well-known to local football fans, too. One of them, Henry Labastida, was a former Wests player in the CAFL who tied with Rovers' Kenny Morton for the 2007 Minahan Medal. Labastida was back home in familiar surrounds, but this time in a Saints jumper. Locals regularly tuning into ABC Darwin's weekly football broadcasts could name most of the St Mary's players — the Lohdes, the Longs, the MacFarlanes, the Riolis, the Vallejos, the Wilsons, et al: Saints stalwarts, premiership players, Chaney medallists, Nichols medallists, standard-bearers of Territory football.

Early predictions that the Saints would roll the Redtails by a hefty margin made the rounds. Long-time St Mary's clubman and former club President Vic Ludwig even made a bet, telling everyone within earshot that he would *walk* back to Darwin if the Saints didn't win by more than four goals. Such faith. On paper, sure, the teams looked lop-sided in the visitors' favour — seasoned semi-pros from the city against journeymen and part-time footballers from the desert. Except that games aren't played on paper.

TELEVISING THE REVOLUTION

TRAEGER Park looked a treat for its NTFL debut. The Saturday night game was scheduled for a 7 pm start. The sun had since disappeared behind the Bowden McAdam Grandstand and the early evening air was fresh with the smell of spring. A buzz was building. The oval's surface was freshly cut, watered and green. All the line markings were in order, the goalposts were padded. The scoreboard attendants inside the Ted Hayes Scoreboard had all the numbers and the letters at the ready — REDTAILS v VISITORS. The four light-towers were turned on at the earliest sign of dusk. Fans were building in the stands; some had driven in and parked their cars near the southern-side goalposts. Others found a grassy spot on the outer eastern side, near a Tree of Knowledge, or behind the other goals, ready to cheer on their hometown heroes. Club officials in team polos flitted about doing whatever club officials in team polos do.

League officials from Darwin and Alice Springs cast an expectant eye on proceedings from their lofty vantage points in the grandstand. The players appeared out from near the changerooms, one-by-one, some in pairs. Some looked tense, others relaxed, talking, joking, a nervous laugh here, a playful bump there, a few with headphones on, absorbed in music or in worlds of their own making. Tangible excitement hung in the air. Alice Springs had seen nothing like it.

In his pre-game address, coach Shaun Cusack spoke to the players on what this moment meant for them as local men, as community members, as footballers, and as a team. His belief in them was strong. The players were only four weeks out from the end of their local season, and he knew they could draw on that seasoned match-conditioning to run the game out. He told them if they were ahead or within a kick or two at the breaks, they had more of a chance to win. In contrast, St Mary's were in their first real hit-out after several weeks of pre-season training under the hot, Darwin tropical sun, perhaps with some new faces, maybe trying out new structures, most likely with a few cobwebs to clear out ahead of the upcoming 2012–13 NTFL season. If anything, this and a home-ground advantage for the Redtails shortened the odds toward an upset. Cusack was certainly happy to have the Saints first up, if for other reasons.

> *They are, arguably, the best side in the Top End, and for a very long time, so we were pretty excited to have the opportunity to play St Mary's. To have them first up at home was amazing. (Shaun Cusack)*[1]

Two sports-broadcast legends and a recent AFL retiree prepared to call the game from the commentary box on radio for 783 ABC Alice Springs, 105.7 ABC Darwin, and in-sync with an online livestream across the Northern Territory. They were Randall 'Stan' Coombe, long-time local, regular match-day commentator and author, a man in possession of an encyclopaedic knowledge of Central Australian football; Charlie King, the 'king' of Territory sport, a man whose voice could melt butter in a cold fridge; and Matt Campbell, an Arrernte man who won the 2009 Polly Farmer Medal for best-on-ground for the AFL's Indigenous All-Stars, and who enjoyed an 82-game career in the AFL for North Melbourne.

Anticipation in the box was palpable. Coombe introduced the night with the gravitas it deserved, cognisant of sporting history about to unfold and with a sense of occasion. In a flick, like a true pro, he switched his attention to the task at hand. The quotes that follow are a direct transcript from the commentary box.

> *It's Stan Coombe and Matt Campbell with you on ABC Radio right around the Territory — 105.7 in Darwin, 783 in Alice Springs. And you're with us for some history. The Redtails, the Central Australian Football Club Redtails, versus the might of St Mary's. NTFL action at Traeger Park for the very first time. Matt, we were just touching on, on the side earlier on; it virtually is a representative side from Central Australia, and unlike past representative sides, what I really like is the fact we got a fair contingent of blokes from the bush in this team as well. Enormous talent out in our bush communities and it's great to see it starting to filter into our representative sides as well.*

Campbell, a local man with several seasons as a professional footballer behind him, kept true to his roots, fully engaged with his local community and in touch with what the Redtails were doing:

> *Yeah, I think the way the competition is set up now with those bush teams coming in, we're bringing them into the comp and exposing them to opportunities. The boys were really excited at training on Thursday night; the excitement was unbelievable. They're all ready to go, ready to make a bit of history tonight.*

Coombe was drawn by something that caught his eye:

> *The local football supporters, they're starting to come in in their droves at the moment. It wasn't looking too good at the start of the broadcast but have a look around Traeger Park now and it's starting to fill out real quickly. I tell you what, if all the close family members of each and every one of these Redtails players was here, it'd be packed to the rafters because they are certainly representing some real big families out there, some real big football families.*
>
> *Campbell: It's a good turnout and hopefully it's a cracker game and the [Redtails] boys put up a good fight.*
>
> *Coombe: Those blokes from the bush, it's great to see them in. I reckon we can expect some excitement tonight. This St Mary's team, Matt, we all know here in Alice Springs, we all follow NTFL football from a distance, and quite often we have a lot of blokes go up and play in it — this is a club that everyone looks at, they're the measuring stick of NTFL footy. I tell you what, they're not gonna come down and hand the game over to Central Australia.*
>
> *Campbell: Oh no way. I think Central Australia has got a lot to prove and St Mary's know that and they know that they're the powerhouse club and they've gotta stamp their authority.*[2]

***

Before a game can begin, a coin toss is held in the middle of the field to determine which team can decide the end they want to kick to. Several factors will inform a captain which way is best: a strong breeze, a late afternoon sun, forecast rain, rising temperatures, dew. This is an early October night game. There is no breeze. The sun has gone. The air is dry. Conditions are perfect, so there is no advantage to winning the toss, but the coin toss is football convention.

The opposing captains, the Redtails' Charlie Maher and St Mary's Peter MacFarlane, meet in the middle. They shake hands and greet the umpires. The coin lands right for MacFarlane and he points north, to the left of screen if you're watching from home. The commentators chime in:

> *Coombe: It looks like the Central Australian side will be kicking to what we call 'The Gap' end of the ground [south]. The teams are heading to their positions and we're nearly ready for the first-ever NTFL football action in Alice Springs.*
>
> *King: We're not that far away, history about to be made when they bounce the ball down in the middle. 'Stan' Coombe to get it away here at Traeger Park...*[3]

As the 36 players take their respective positions on the field, eight more take their seats on the interchange benches. The expectant crowd around the ground and in the Bowden McAdam Grandstand is filled with excitable energy.

The umpire at the centre-circle raises the object of everyone's desire with one hand — an oval-shaped 'Kangaroo Brand' ball handmade from cowhide. The ball, a Sherrin, is shiny and new, and yellow for night-time visibility. With his other hand the umpire blows his whistle. The timekeepers respond and press a button that sounds out the noise of a toneless, one-note siren. The game can begin.

With both hands this time, the umpire raises the ball higher above his head, each hand with a tight grasp at its corners. He begins a steady lean forward over the centre-circle, slowly bringing the ball forward over his bending back and lowering head; he could almost kiss the ground now. In an instant, and with a sharp flick of his wrists, he brings the ball down fast past his still-lowered head and in a silent act of non-personal violence pounds it into the turf whereupon the unseen laws of physics of pressured-air encased in leather go to work. The ball bounces up, straight, and the two ruckmen to the umpire's left and right time their run to leap for this. As they do their bodies crash into one another, both are determined to get to it first, but neither gains an advantage. A hand each reaches the Sherrin at the same moment in a tangled mess of fingers and palms like a mistimed clap.

The ball tumbles about, its bounce a mystery due to its oval shape. Bodies fly everywhere in the hunt for it. It pings around like a pinball on steroids. It is hectic. It is chaotic. The Redtails somehow scramble it forward through Gareth Remfrey. His teammate Darren Young wins a free kick and quickly boots it long and high in the direction of Daniel Stafford, his eyes only for the ball. But floating in like a night-time butterfly is the Redtails' Thomas Gorey, who takes a spectacular and brave mark, backing sideways-blind into an incoming pack. And the crowd goes wild…

All this inside a minute — 0.54 seconds exactly. Gorey is 25 metres out from the big sticks at the Gap Road end to the right of screen. One for trivia buffs: remember the name, because Thomas Gorey kicks the Redtails' first-ever goal. He is swamped by ecstatic teammates as the home crowd voices its approval with cheers, claps, car horns, banging on signage on the fence that rings the field and on whatever is nearest beside them. The Redtails make the perfect start, a fairytale beginning for a fairytale team. But fairytales don't always have to have fairytale endings, as the diminutive Lord Farquaad from Duloc found out.

The game, the players, the fans settle now into a familiar rhythm. A sway and a flow of skill, brute force and nuance, where movement of body and ball follows the time-worn patterns of a game played out over untold thousands of times for more than 160 years. In this game, the skills are clean and crisp. The players' attention to detail is laser sharp. It is high-level football. It is everything and more of what makes this game so great. St Mary's feel out the Redtails and find a rhythm, get their heads around the dimensions of a foreign field and adjust to the dryer-than-home local conditions. They click into gear like the well-oiled

Green Machine they're renowned to be. Old heads Justin Wilson and Peter MacFarlane lead by example; their teammates joining now in lock-and-step. MacFarlane kicks the Saints' first goal six minutes in and another just before quarter-time. Author, commentator, all-round footy fan 'Stan' Coombe, taking in the enormity of what is before him, pauses during a break in play to say:

> *NTFL action from Traeger Park... sounds fantastic saying that. Traeger Park, the centre of Australian football, [it] certainly is tonight. Big crowd here to watch the CAFC Redtails in their NTFL debut.*[4]

King agrees. Both men have seen and called thousands of hours of Territory football but what they're seeing tonight isn't something they've experienced before or thought they ever would. And it is a thought that can be seen in the many faces at the game, in the game, and around the ground. The crowd is buzzing. The teams provide a quality contest as the minutes and quarters tick by.

The Redtails are holding their own. Coach Cusack's pre-game instructions are followed to a tee. They are hard at the contest and skilful at their disposal. Their tactical ploy is to play on when favourable and provide overlap for the quick-ball receive. Baydon Ngalkin, Luke Adams and Gareth Remfrey provide good run-and-carry, sometimes a bounce, always strong at the contest. Shane Dixon across half-back reads the play like a book in a library, thwarting the Saints at nearly every contest that comes his way. Darren Young belies his size and gathers ground-level balls at will. Daniel Stafford reminds us of his talent and takes the mark-of-the-day (night) when he goes for a climb on another Daniel's (Daniel Hill's) broad shoulders right in front of goal. Our Daniel kicks truly and the fans' reaction has the foundations of the Bowen McAdam Grandstand shaking. The building threatens to collapse with everyone in it moments later when Gibson Turner gathers the ball inside the centre-square, kicks from just inside the line and pumps his fist as it skids through for a remarkable goal. Pandemonium ensues.

The Saints are up for the challenge, however. They've seen this before. They often prey on excited teams jumping out to a lead only for inexperience to be their undoing. Despite their string of success, the Saints are no strangers to adversity. Tiwi man Shannon Rioli provides an early look into a career that will be spoken of for a long time to come; the youngster tonight puts himself in the right spot and kicks a ripper goal that lifts his team. The visitors slowly take the crowd out of the game. They wrest back the lead at half-time.

St Mary's carry that first-half energy into the third quarter, booting 4.4 to 2.3 to lead by 21 points at the final break; in times past an almost insurmountable total but in the modern game, it is nothing. Coach Cusack shows why he's held in high regard. He is in his element. He makes several tactical switches. One is to bring G. Jack Miller into the ruck in tandem with Young. It's an inspired early move. The final quarter begins. Dixon's link-up play with Ryan Mallard and Remfrey is exquisite. In one instance, Remfrey wins the ball at half-forward and nails a long-range shot on goal, his second, and it pegs back the lead after which the Redtails win it forward at the restart. Miller kicks a goal; a minute later so does Maher. Soon after, Mallard nails his first major to put the home side in front for the first time this term. They're on a roll and up by four points now.

Turner, who has been superb in the middle, gets the ball, finds space and drills home his second goal to extend the Redtails' lead to 10 points. St Mary's teams never surrender. As if on cue, they win the ball and push it forward. Wilson somehow manages to get the ball close to goal and kicks the Saints' first major for the quarter and the margin is back to four points. Now there's less than a straight kick in it. The game is approaching red-time. The fans are riding every possession, every split-second decision, every act. It's now or never. The Saints make a play and get the ball moving from defence into attack. The path to goal, via the outer wing, looks clear. They take that option... but it's the man of the moment, Shane Dixon who, in this very moment, steps up and steps in to take a game-saving intercept mark, thwarting the Saints' last-gasp push toward goal and certain victory. The final siren sounds and his is the final act to an incredible game of football. The crowd is beside itself.

The scoreboard tells us the Redtails win it by four — 13.10 (88) to 12.12 (84).[i] In the excitement that follows, Redtails pair Daniel Stafford and Jayden Prior grab a surprised and extremely happy Rob Clarke and put him on their large shoulders; he has a trophy in his hand and a smile as wide as the desert expanse that surrounds them.

---

i The defeat was St Mary's only blemish in the 2012–13 season. The Saints charged through the remainder of the season undefeated toward a 29th senior flag, defeating the Tiwi Bombers in the grand final. Technically, this was a 'trial' match for the opponents which, in pure terms of a football season, shouldn't count, but this is a conversation best left to club and league historians.

A HAPPY AFTERGLOW

A COLLECTIVE sense of relief and euphoria settled upon the Redtails following their first-game triumph over one of the great teams of the modern era, from coach, player, team official, fan, the town of Alice Springs, the region, a boundary-side mascot (had there been one), a semi-naked male streaker (you had to be there)… all justifiably proud of their new team's thrilling win. And rumour has it that Saints stalwart Vic Ludwig was later observed boarding the Qantas flight back to Darwin under a very large hat (this may or may not be true).

The Redtails' familiarity with each other, the ground, local conditions and a supportive and vocal home crowd, estimated at between 1500 and 2000 people, proved to be advantageous.[1] St Mary's, accustomed to at least some crowd support in Darwin even as the away side, were on their own in Alice Springs. They may be held in high regard by the knowledgeable and neutral football fan but in the heat of the contest and against a local side the Saints were on their own. A universal quality that St Mary's football teams do elicit, however, is respect, and plenty of it. There are opponents in football you don't second-guess. Sure, run at them, play them at their own game, but never lose

Triumphant: Central Australia Football Club co-founder and club president Rob Clarke is chaired from the field in triumphant jubilation by Redtails players Daniel Stafford (left) and Jayden Prior. The Redtails had just defeated Top End powerhouse club St Mary's in front of a big home crowd at Traeger Park in Alice Springs in Round 1 of the 2012-13 NTFL Premier League season (Saturday 6 October 2012). Clarke is holding the No More Cup — the NT football 'No More' campaign seeks to eliminate the scourge of family and domestic violence. (Photo: Justin Brierty Centralian Advocate, Tuesday 9 October 2012)

sight of what a team and an opponent standing before you are capable of, particularly one like this. Respect, also, yourself. And respect the game. In other words, prepare yourself to play this game at a level that respects the process. The Central Australian and St Mary's football clubs did just that. And not just because this was a thrilling finish but because, as a collective, they prepared for key moments in this game that put them both in the best position to provide an honest and honourable contest. The grandstand-finish was just the cherry on top. Redtails coach Shaun Cusack was certainly happy:

> *Before the game we spoke about the opportunity we have here. It was the first game of the four-game trial, so I reminded them about what an opportunity they have to step up at this level and in front of their families and local community. We had just come off the (CAFL) season so I knew the players had run in their legs. It was just a matter of maintaining the pressure, that effort for four quarters, playing together as a team and sticking to the game-plan. The crowd got right behind them; by the end they were very loud and that helped the players.*[2]

Ryan Mallard was one of a handful of experienced, mature-age footballers who played for the Redtails. The clever centre half-forward played in the team's only long-sleeve jumper, made especially for his brother, Brisbane Lions' long-sleeved AFL triple-premiership star Darryl White, who joined the Redtails from the beginning but was unable to play due to injury. Mallard spoke of the feeling within the team following the historic first game.

> *We had a great opportunity to represent our region under the Redtails banner, which was a new format. The group that came together, we all know each other's talents. We just banded together to create the best team environment and gelled to beat St Mary's. It was just a great feeling having come together so quickly and to pull off an unbelievable win. No-one expected us to win.*[3]

Coombe's observation mid-match during the Redtails' first game was an unguarded moment that spoke to the overall sense of what everyone felt that night.

> *The Redtails got most of the best players in the region, it was pretty close to a full-strength Central Australian rep side, that 2012 side. The thought of it really happening, that*

> *night, the win... it was a good game of footy. We don't always see that sort of standard here; it was definitely a jump up from (local) club footy. Winning it was great, too, especially against St Mary's, they are the best team.*[4]

TAKEN WAY TOO SOON

G. Jack Miller Jnr played football for Pioneer in Alice Springs, the club his father, Geoffrey Snr, played at. The young Miller was an athletic footballer and a premiership player at the Eagles. Miller played five games total for the Redtails in their first and second trial period — three in 2012–13 (rounds 1, 2 and 4) and two in 2013–14 (rounds 2 and 4).

In the Redtails' first game against St Mary's, his move into the ruck in the third quarter was a turning point. The Saints had pulled away and coach Shaun Cusack sensed a shift in the ruck clearances in favour of the Saints, so he put Miller on the ball. The tactical ploy was a masterstroke. It had an immediate impact upon the contest. Miller's ruckwork and goal in the third quarter began a Redtails surge from which they would eventually win.

In 2015, with his young family, Miller moved to far north Queensland, to Cairns. He was recruited to play football for Centrals Trinity in the growing league there. Moments after completing his second training session with the Bulldogs in mid-March of that year, he collapsed in the clubrooms. Despite the efforts of his new friends and teammates, and paramedics quickly on the scene, he could not be revived. G. Jack Miller's untimely death was from suspected heart failure. The young man is remembered by family and friends as having a generous nature and kind heart, and as a determined and complete athlete. He was 27.

The following tribute from the Pioneer Football Club appeared in the *Centralian Advocate* on 27 March 2015:

The Pioneer Football Club, committee, members, supporters and players are mourning the sudden passing of one of our talented young players.

It was always exciting to watch him play the game he loved so much, and was so passionate about.

When he put on the Green and Gold we always expected exciting things, either an awesome 'screamer' of a mark or booming goal which contributed to many of the club's wins.

Off the field, he was a true gentleman with a caring heart who loved his family very much. We're definitely going to miss you in the Green and Gold, but our memories will be with us all forever.

Our hearts and prayers go out to his partner Jana and his children, parents Kerrie and Geoff (Snr.), brothers and sisters, and to all the Miller, LeRossignol, and extended families.'[5]

Rest in Peace, G. Jack Miller Jnr (1987–2015).

POSITIONAL PLAY

For the uninitiated, what exactly does an Aussie rules football team do and what does a game look like? Despite the apparent chaos, there is method to the madness.

Firstly, there is no off-side rule, as in soccer, nor a 'knock-on' rule, as in the rugbies; this allows for a 360° game and continuous play. There are 18 official positions on the oval which means there are 36 players on the field at any one time, and all 36 of them can move anywhere they want, but generally time their movements strategically, and positionally, to their strengths and to maximise their team's chances of winning.

The game is built around five primary key-positions. In relatable terms this is referred to as the 'spine'. Picture an imaginary line running through the middle of the ground, end to end from goalpost to goalpost — like a spine —

punctuated by a centre-square in the middle with two 50-metre arcs either side of that, wrapping-in their respective goalposts. Like a human spine, a team's spine must be strong and provide structural support for the moving parts connected to it. The spine — football's key positions — consist of a full-forward (near the attacking team's goalposts), centre half-forward (at the attacking team's line at the centre-square), ruck (in the middle of the centre-square), centre half-back (at the defensive team's line at the centre-square) and full-back (guarding the defensive team's goals). For the opposing team, reverse these positions, i.e. a full-back will stand a full-forward, a centre half-back will stand a centre half-forward, etc.

Those who make up the spine, the key-position players — the KPPs— are a team's specialists. They are the stars of the show; they are the game-changers, the crowd-pleasers, the highlight reel-ers, the wicked scene-stealers. If AC/DC's Bon Scott had ever written a song about football, this would be it.[i]

Around the spine, around the KPPs, are the multiple moving parts that complete the body of a football team. In the centre-square, at the feet of the ruckman, is the centreman, rover and ruck-rover; their job is to win the ball from the ruck contest.

Either side of full-forward are the forward-pockets, their role is to offer options in attack and 'crumb' the packs for the loose ball. Up from the pockets are the half-forward flanks who provide outside run and loosely-based 'pincer movements' like in war when a centralised attack is simultaneously supported from left and right — something like that. Up from them are the wingers located either side of the centre-square and these are the 'whippets' with leg-speed to cover the vast space that an oval-shaped field provides. A kick into space ahead of a speedy winger is one of football's true delights; recall for a moment legendary commentator Sandy Roberts's iconic call in football's era-defining 1992 AFL grand final as West Coast wingman Peter Matera 'sets sail

i A reference to 'Rocker', written by former AC/DC frontman Bon Scott for the band's second studio album, *T.N.T.* (1975).

for home!' on the way to the Eagles' historic first premiership. Peter Matera was named on a wing in the 1904–2005 AFL Indigenous Team of the Century.[6]

Down the defensive end from the wingers are the half-back flankers and the back-pockets. This quartet forms the nuts and bolts of the back-six from where blood is spilt and premierships are built. These players have an innate sense of the game and their understanding of the patterns and shapes unfolding ahead of them is second nature. It is no secret some of the best coaches in the business grow up in the game playing as defenders.

And that, in a nutshell, is football.

ROCK ON, REDTAILS!

Adam Thompson moved to Central Australia around 2010 and it was there that the Aussie rock 'n' roll icon had a happy reunion with an old mate, Redtails co-founder Ian McAdam. A lifetime or two earlier, Thompson's ascension as a bona fide rocker continued a long and storied tradition in Australian music. Thompson is the lead singer of Chocolate Starfish. With a commanding stage presence drawn from the core of his being, Thompson joined his contemporaries like Jimmy Barnes of Cold Chisel fame, Michael Hutchence of INXS and The Angels' Doc Neeson as icons of Aussie rock.

Thompson completed the sights and sounds of Chocolate Starfish with a unique set of vocals, stage antics second to none, and a shiny bald head that helped push a rock-revival during mid-90s peak-grunge. The group's 1994 self-titled debut studio album spawned several hits including opener 'Four Letter Word', 'All Over Me', 'Mountain' and a cover of 'You're So Vain'. The disc rocketed up the Australian charts and toward certified gold and platinum status with sales pushing close to 100,000 copies. It peaked at number two on the charts and won an ARIA for Most Popular Album of 1994.[7]

In 'Mountain' — a lyrically-powerful and moving five-minute power-ballad — Thompson agonises over a difficult choice between life and love at home or a lifelong career-dream elsewhere; the tune strikes a perfect chord for those with souls on the mend or already broken hearts.

In the intervening years, Thompson spoke much about social responsibility as a major driver in what he does, in and outside of music. He later formed MusoMagic, a program designed to engage with people of diverse backgrounds and life experiences.[8]

Thompson took MusoMagic to Central Australia to film a TV series called *Outback Tracks*. This was around the time of the Redtails' formation, and around the same time team management was looking for a club song the boys could sing after a win, as is football custom. This prompted Ian McAdam to go searching for the Mountain man somewhere out in the desert. And he found him, as Thompson recalled:

> *'Macca' had shown me these lyrics, they weren't set to a tune, more a stream of consciousness, and he said,* You reckon you can put these to a melody and a tune toward an anthem? *We looked at them, went back and forth, tidied them up, made a composition and put it all together at Sun FM studios, the commercial radio station there.*[9]

The result was a one-minute rocker on identity, loyalty and resolve that rises in a crescendo toward a foot-stomping finale.

> *Rock will always be my influence, of course, but I remember we put some didgeridoo to it, and I know that's not traditional to the Central Australian sound, but it provided a good angle; we put clapsticks in it, too. Creating an anthem is not easy; it had to be accessible as well as making sure Ian's lyrics came to life. (Adam Thompson)*

This most unlikely union between Aussie rock royalty and Central Australian football shared in an unforgettable moment when the Redtails won that historic first game at Traeger Park. Thompson was present when the pumped-up players and club officials fresh from a stunning victory linked arms and launched into the new anthem with gusto in a mix of song and sweaty embrace. He remembers it well.

> *To be part of that Central Australian football culture was a cool thing. You don't plan for these things to take shape; music transcends all cultures and all nations, and it's great when something creative comes together and with the passion of winning that game they got something to celebrate it with; it was a great feeling. (Adam Thompson)*

Thompson is no stranger to football, he himself once an ace on the field: 'I grew up on Yorta Yorta country, in Shepparton [and] I was best-on-ground in the under-18s grand final for the Mooroopna Cats!'

REDTAILS' CLUB SONG

Centralians are coming!
Centralians are coming!
Centralians are coming!
You've got a red… tail!
Stand up!
Walk alongside of me.
You've got a red… tail!
Proud and true,
You're a part of the family.
We're the red-black-and-white Centralian might,
Redtails through and through.
We'd give it all we've got to win, we're the mighty cockatoos,
We'd give it all we've got to win, we're the mighty cockatoos,
We'd give it all we've got to win, we're the mighty cockatoooos.
Redtails!

SCORES ON THE BOARD

HIGH on endorphins after defeating the powerhouse might of St Mary's in front of a raucous home crowd, the Redtails landed at Darwin International with confidence heading into their round 2 match against Palmerston. Palmerston, the growing satellite city 30 kilometres south from Darwin via Tiger Brennan Drive and/or the Stuart Highway, is home to the Magpies who enjoyed a glorious run in the early 2000s but nothing much since. This was a Saturday night game.

Selectors made six changes for the game at the Magpies' home ground, Cazalys Arena. The Central Australians acquitted themselves well. After an even start, the visitors clicked into gear and dominated. In the second quarter, they kicked seven goals to one, from which the Magpies never recovered. Daniel Stafford booted six goals, Gibson Turner put in a superb performance from the middle, while Jayden Prior marshalled the team's defence with aplomb in the Redtails' workmanlike 36-point win.

In a game that by rights should have been played in Alice Springs, seven days later the Redtails stepped onto Darwin's Marrara Oval for the first time. Top End football's 'spiritual home' had seen almost a quarter-century of football. In that time were finals and grand finals, epics and disasters, all part of football lore, like when in 1994 the ATSIC Aboriginal All-Stars took on AFL club Collingwood and won[1]; when grief-stricken Southern Districts, led by football great Michael McLean as coach[2], finally brought the premiership trophy to Freds Pass, in honour of young teammate Mark McCasker, who had died way before his time just weeks earlier[3]; and when the freshly minted Fremantle Football Club played its first game in the preseason of 1995 against the NT Buffaloes.[4] Now, it was the Central Australians' turn to add another entry to Top End football folklore at Marrara.

On the horizon in ominous formation appeared the Tiwi Bombers who, like their mascot, were (figuratively) flying. Seven months prior in March, the Tiwis claimed a historic maiden NTFL premiership after defeating Nightcliff in the 2011–12 season grand final. The Tiwis' rise as a force in the Premier League was sweet vindication of one of Tony Frawley's first acts as chief of Territory football. The 2011–12 grand final was the Tiwis' second such appearance since their inclusion in the Premier League. The first came in the 2009–10 season-decider, in just their third season, when they fell short to St Mary's.[5]

The Bombers presented to the Redtails what and where they wanted to be: a semi-professional football club populated by Countrymen with a national profile in the big league, playing in grand finals and winning premierships. This was the aspiration that informed the Central Australians from day one. It was also when coach Cusack's men felt the sting of defeat for the first time. They did themselves no favours with wild inaccuracy, registering 0.7 in the first quarter alone. The Tiwis fielded the bulk of their premiership stars. The Central Australians, never to go down without a fight, bravely clawed back a 41-point deficit at half-time but were 23 points in arrears at full-time.

Incoming: A pack forms under the incoming ball in Round 3 of the 2012–13 NTFL Premier League game between the Redtails and Tiwi Bombers at Marrara Oval in Darwin on Saturday 20 October 2012. The Tiwis defeated the Central Australians by 23 points. This was the Redtails' third game of their first trial period in the Premier League, and their first and only loss in 2012. (Photo: Brad Fleet / Sunday Territorian, Sunday 21 October 2012)

The Redtails' fourth and final match came against Nightcliff, the team vanquished by the Tiwis in the March grand final. Nightcliff, the Tigers, seemed destined to remain 'forever the bridesmaid, never the bride' — an old-timey football saying in which a team plays in grand finals but can never win them. Nightcliff experienced a horrid run of losses stretching back decades. The defeat at the hands of the Tiwis in the 2011–12 season-decider was their seventh grand final loss since last winning a flag in the 1964–65 season. Nightcliff would up-end that fateful cliché in spectacular fashion when they won a 'three-peat' of flags in seasons 2018–19, 2019–20, 2020–21; the 2020–21 grand final ended in a thrilling draw at regular time before extra-time was added to determine a winner. Yorta Yorta man Chris Baksh orchestrated those premierships as senior coach throughout this period.[6]

It was back to Marrara for this mid-afternoon match and, after last round's defeat, the Redtails were intent to end their time in Darwin on a winning note. The players, now somewhat familiar with the Territory capital and Marrara Oval, were tuning in nicely to the rhythms of Premier League football and growing conditioned to the steamy, sweaty Top End weather as opposed to the dry-desert conditions back home. The majority of those selected for this game had played in the previous three. The Tigers were no pushover. The core group from the March grand final remained. In a high-scoring match, the Redtails were two points down at three-quarter-time before booting four goals to the Tigers' two in the final term to record a stirring 13-point victory. In a football season that began at the start of 2012, Cusack's men ended their four-match trial in October on a happy and winning note.

Overall, the Redtails landed equal-third on the Premier League ladder with a 3–1 win-loss record, ahead on percentage of Waratah in fourth place and just behind St Mary's in second. (See Appendix 1: Scoreboard 1.0 for full teams, scores, results, goals and ladder positions.) Trial buddies Banks were left wanting at 1–3, the Bulldogs' sole victory coming against the enigmatic Wanderers, and they finished eighth.

Although none of this counted toward a premiership, medals or individual trophies, the Redtails' brief time in the tropics was proof positive that this outfit of part-timers certainly had what it took to play as a team in the top level of Northern Territory football. And now, having upheld their end of the bargain, it was the committee's turn to convince Darwin for inclusion.

'WE PUT THE FLAG DOWN!'

Paul Ah Chee is an Arrernte man, a local musician of note, and a Traditional Owner who grew up in Alice Springs at a time when it was a much smaller, more connected town. In 2022, Ah Chee recorded and released a six-track EP called *Nowhere to Hide*, an album that explores his passion for life and place.[7] Another of his passions is seeing young people in his community thrive, and in 2011 he was more than happy to join the Central Australian Football Club as a committee member.

> *Initially, this concept was brought about by that tragedy [Kumantye Palmer's passing], and Rob Clarke — who has a passion for football; he lives and breathes it — said, 'This is not right, this is not good enough'. Then he and Ian McAdam, they got together, formed the Redtails football club and started getting a team together to compete in the NTFL. Rob and Ian said they needed to form a committee and that's when I was approached. We had regular meetings, they were minuted, there was transparency, money started to come in for the program, and it had to be delivered and (financially) acquitted. It was a real commitment, and we were all volunteers; you were on the ground and working hard.*[8]

It wasn't all smooth sailing.

> *Some of these meetings were held on an ad hoc basis and it was always hard to fit everything in, but it was all about trying to expose those young men to a quality experience going forward; this was a vehicle for change. You can't sit around and hope it happens; you have to make it happen.*[9]

As a committee member, Ah Chee was part of the process that approved Shaun Cusack's appointment as first coach.

> *Shaun was the right man for the job. We beat St Mary's, you'll be flat-out beating St Mary's any day! I thought that was amazing, it really showed that the program and the staff, that the leadership in all of it, was telling. We were flying! We put the flag down! After it was all done and the*

dust had settled, my first thoughts were yes, there's some possibilities here and it's possible we could well be entering this team into the NTFL. I thought the foundation, the dedication and the determination should be rewarded; we were feeling optimistic.[10]

SHOW-CAUSE JUST BECAUSE

THE Central Australian Football Club was cause célèbre on media street following their four-game trial period. Players and officials were, at various points, featured on the front and back pages of Northern Territory and national newspapers, on local TV in sports bulletins, and in regular segments on radio.

NT media outlets tracking the Redtails' progress included the *Centralian Advocate* which was a strong... err, advocate for the CAFC, and the Darwin daily tabloid *NT News*, which reported on the club from afar.[1] Both papers ran detailed match previews and reviews, and player, coach and club-official interviews.[2] Territory ABC's digital, radio and television platforms, and local commercial television and radio, kept the public informed on the club's progress at each newsworthy point.

With the CAFC's strong Indigenous component, Indigenous media was also invested in the Redtails' fortunes and they, too, championed the club's cause. This included the Alice Springs-based Imparja broadcaster and Central Australian Aboriginal Media Association with their variety of platforms, as well as the *National Indigenous Times* and *Koori Mail* newspapers, both with an Australia-wide readership. This writer worked for both *Koori Mail* and the *National Indigenous Times* newspapers and covered the Redtails for the *Times* exclusively in Darwin from October 2012 to November 2013. All told, the Central Australian football revolution was enjoying bipartisan support. The script was writing itself.

The Redtails' initial trial run had a remaining game to play out when, in a cheery Monday morning press release, AFLNT trumpeted football's astonishing increase in viewership and spectators, largely on the back of the Central Australians. This came two days after the Redtails Tiwi Bombers game.

> *... a record number of unique visitors to the AFLNT website has been recorded in addition to a 36% increase in newspaper and radio coverage and an 88% increase [in] viewers watching games streamed live on AFLNTv!*
>
> *Saturday's attendance at TIO stadium [for the Redtails v Tiwi Bombers game] was higher than the debut of the Tiwi Bombers in 2005, and the ABC Television broadcast (3pm CST) of next Saturday's Nightcliff v The Central Redtails is expected to attract a huge audience throughout the Territory.*
>
> *The four game trial of the Central Redtails [sic] has been a resounding success with the club proving to be extremely competitive and their televised game next Saturday against last year's grand finalists Nightcliff looks set to be a blockbuster.*[3]

Footy chief Tony Frawley was chuffed, and said so in the AFLNT statement,

> *We are absolutely delighted with how the season is unfolding and ... slightly taken aback by the phenomenal level of interest in this year's competition...*

> *The Redtails is a new and exciting brand which is attracting crowds not only for support but for the unique Central Australian brand of football they play.*
>
> *The club is providing an incredible opportunity for young Indigenous players from Central Australian communities and must be congratulated for doing so.*

Not one to get too carried away, Frawley reminded the Redtails of the hard work ahead.

> *Although super-competitive on the field, the Redtails' greatest challenge is off field, and AFLNT will work closely with the club to ascertain if they can remain viable in the long term. To enter the league full time they must secure a significant amount of funding whilst also negotiating with the Alice Springs Town Council for the use of Traeger Park from November until March.*
>
> *The club must also demonstrate to AFLNT how their inclusion into the league will not impact on the CAFL or NT Thunder and provide us with a draft player movement rule for players that wish to play in the CAFL and the NTFL for the Redtails.*
>
> *There is a lot of work to be done but based on what we have seen thus far the Redtails could well be a NTFL team next season.*[4]

Rewind the tape! '...based on what we have seen thus far the Redtails could well be a NTFL team next season.' Frawley, and Darwin, it seemed, believed.

Frawley reiterated these views on the ABC *7.30 Report (NT edition)* later that week. He spoke about where the Redtails sat in the overall big picture and what the Executive was thinking. There was much to unpack.

ABC TRANSCRIPT

ABC Presenter, Louisa Rebgetz: 'This weekend, the Central Australia Redtails will return to Marrara for their fourth and final trial match in the Northern Territory's top football competition. The Redtails take on Nightcliff, having notched up two wins and one loss in their run in the NTFL. In the next few months they'll learn if they have what it takes to be accepted into the league on a permanent basis. ABC sport reporter Rick Hind asked the AFLNT's Chief Executive, Tony Frawley if the Redtails had met his expectations.'

Tony Frawley: 'Oh I think so. We wanted to make sure that they were competitive and they've really been super-competitive over the three matches they've played and the reason for the trial was we had to see whether they got used to the travelling and the higher level of competition — they've been able to handle that quite well.'

ABC reporter, Rick Hind: 'What prospect do they have of playing full-time next season?'

Frawley: 'We know they can play at the level now and we have to work with the club very closely on their ongoing financial viability. It will cost a lot of money to play a full season in the NTFL. We need access to a ground in Central Australia with lights because they'll have to be played at seven o'clock at night in the NTFL season and, really, we want to protect the brands of Thunder and the Central Australian Football League as well so they're probably the main issues we need to sign off on before they got a licence in the NTFL.'

Hind: 'How much does it cost to fly the Redtails up to Darwin for their games?'

Frawley: 'Yeah it's about $30,000 a flight, but that includes the accommodation as well so it's about $30,000 every time they come up. We flew St Mary's down round 1 to play and it was about $30,000 so it is expensive but it's a very good concept and the community in Alice Springs really want it.'

Hind: 'Where would the Redtails stay in Darwin long-term?'

Frawley: 'They'll stay in the academy. We'll build the academy here next year and there'll be accommodation here at the oval [Marrara Oval] for them and Wadeye and Tiwi Bombers and the like. Clubs that will come in and play NTFL on the weekend will stay there.'

Hind: 'And how are those costs going to be met?'

Frawley: 'Well we'll pick up the costs of the accommodation here because we'll run the academy, but we need to go to corporate Australia, we need to go to government, we need to go to the Alice Springs community and say firstly, do you want it and is it a viable concept? Is it viable, ongoing? And we'll work with all the stakeholders around Central Australia and get a view and see whether they really want the team — I think they do — and then we'll move from there.'

Hind: 'Would you be relying on money from the national AFL?'

Frawley: 'Oh for sure. We've already put into the concept already and certainly we'll look at that. We would see it as a partnership between government, probably corporate and the AFL [Commission and its Executive] to try and fund the team.'

Hind: 'What undertakings have you been given by the new Northern Territory Government?'

Frawley: 'The Chief Minister has been positive about it. We've got the current sports minister, Matt Conlan, based in Central Australia and he's very keen on it, and so we'll work with both levels of government, plus we need to work with the Alice Springs town council as well but certainly the NT Government, the Federal Government will be key drivers of it.'

Hind: 'What does the Central Australian Football League think of having what would be a rep team in the NTFL?'

Frawley: 'Yeah, they're fairly positive. As I said before, we've got to have rules in place — they [the players] can't play 40 matches — they can't come off a full season in the Central Australian league and come in and play a full season of NTFL. At Thunder, we manage that through the Thunder management program so that's one issue we need to sign off on and we need to protect the league — the league's going well down there. We want to make sure that the new team doesn't impact on that too much.'

Hind: 'What do the other teams in Darwin and Palmerston think of this move and the expansion overall since the Tiwi Bombers joined in 2008?'

Frawley: 'I think they've been generally positive. When we've put these concepts to the clubs, they've been very supportive of it. Obviously, cost is a factor for them and we need to pick up those costs but certainly we think the Tiwi Bombers and the Wadeye footy club and now the Central Australian Redtails have been good for the league here. It's created a lot of interest and we need to keep bringing different brands in all the time, to do things differently, and people will come and watch different brands play.[5]

Frawley repeated his concerns on the impact he thought the Redtails would have on the CAFL and NT Thunder. He and the Executive were worried about player burnout. Given the dovetailing seasons of the Top End and Alice Springs, the Central Australians would essentially be playing year-round football.

Thunder, which played in the eastern states' NEAFL during the wintertime, drew most of its players from the summertime NTFL — year-round football, too. Similarly, the summertime NTFL-bound Redtails players would be drawn from the wintertime CAFL. What Frawley wanted to see was evidence on how the CAFC would mitigate potential player burnout. While the CAFL was the CAFC's lifeline, the integrity of the CAFL was paramount, just as the NTFL was in relation to the Thunder. The AFLNT Executive did not want to see the CAFL nor, heaven forbid, the NTFL be relegated to 'secondary' status in the eyes of the players and fans. For this, the Executive had an ace up their sleeves.

PLAYER MANAGEMENT, WELFARE

Top End football demands so much from its players. If it's not the summertime 'wet' season heat and humidity, it's the demands on body and mind in such extreme conditions that no other football league in the country experiences. When NT Thunder began in 2009, AFLNT put in place individualised player management plans for contracted players.[6] These plans held each Thunder player to a reasonable number of games they could play in any one calendar year — January through to December — which was 10 for Thunder and 10 for their original NTFL club (increased to 12 in 2014). This was to mitigate player burnout, given that these players were playing year-round football, but it was also highly problematic.[7]

Let's flesh this out. Pick a club, and a season. OK, the Darwin Buffaloes, and the 2011–12 season. A Darwin Buffaloes player during this football season signs a contract to play for the Thunder. That contract allows him to remain at the Buffaloes. This meant, then, that if our Buffalo played in all the Buffs' 18 regular-season games (October 2011–February 2012) and two or three finals games (February–March 2012) he would have then played 20 or 21 games by the end of the 2011–12 NTFL season. But backtrack to the beginning of the new year, to 1 January 2012, and our Buffaloes' 'football clock' resets to zero games for the new calendar year. So now, by March, once he's done with the Buffaloes' season, he would have already played 9 or 10 games in the 2012 calendar year. He then 'carries' that tally of games with him into the Thunder's 27-week 2012 NEAFL season (May–September), plus travel, in which he can only play 10 more games. Given a good run of form, if our Buffs-Thunder player played in all of Thunder's games this would push him well over the 20 to 22 game threshold for that particular calendar year. But, as a required Buffaloes player for the 2012–13 NTFL season, he would still have three more months of football left to play in the 2012 calendar year (beginning in October).

In raw numbers alone, a combined NTFL–NT Thunder season worked out to around 45 games of football in any one calendar year — an unsustainable amount of games given football's toll on the body over a relatively short period of time. Managing a NTFL–Thunder player's load throughout a 12-month cycle was paramount to their overall wellbeing. It was critical also to the Thunder's fortunes, and to the integrity of the NTFL[i].

But 'management' of the management plan was confusing and somewhat convoluted. It saw some players caught in the middle between club and 'country'. Not that they wanted to play 45 games of football from January through to December, but managing exactly which games they could and *could not* play was the thing. There was even talk of a mid-year NTFL draft, however that might work. It all left some Darwin club presidents hopping mad and some just scratching their heads. Player management plans were an innovative practice unique in Australian football because Territory football was, and is, unique.

---

i The NTFL Premier League home-and-away season is 18 games with a four-week finals series and a two-week break over the Christmas and New Year period — 24 weeks in total.

As the Thunder's former southern division coach, Rob Clarke was familiar with this system, but footy boss Tony Frawley wanted to see it on paper, in practice and in real time if/when the Redtails joined the NTFL on a permanent basis. If done right, the Redtails could provide local footballers another step up in the Territory football food chain. Thunder by then had several Central Australians in the squad and the Centralians' presence could only enhance the Thunder program in the region.[ii]

***

While happy to talk up the rise in numbers of fans at the grounds and an increase in newspaper readers and TV viewers at home, Frawley was looking beyond the football field. Ever the pragmatist, he was asking the club for a show-cause on why it should join the Premier League. The concept demanded it. This was standard corporate best practice: Due Diligence 101. The Board had a brand to protect and was custodian of a unique competition closing in on its 100th year. It would do its stakeholders, constituents and masters in Melbourne a major disservice if it neglected to examine exactly how the club would execute its revolutionary plan.

The Redtails' brand presented a financially attractive add-on for AFLNT, and the NTFL. It was taking semi-professional Premier League football beyond Darwin and into the heart of the country, exposing it to a whole new market. Unlike the crowded Darwin marketplace, the CAFC had an entire town and region to themselves. None of what AFLNT was asking was unreasonable. AFLNT in Darwin answers to AFL House in Melbourne who, like our friends in Moscow and Washington, would rather not be found dabbling in the affairs of nation-states it has no business in. This was Darwin's issue to face alone.

---

ii NT Thunder as a senior men's representative team folded in 2019.

Chief Minister Terry Mills threw conditional support behind the Redtails' permanent entry in the Premier League.[8] While supportive, Mills stopped short at writing out blank cheques. The key issue for the Central Australians was in securing long-term financial support and a readily available venue to play at. Trials were one thing; ongoing and sustainable support for regular-season football was another. The semi-pro clubs in Darwin require sustainable financial investment to operate over a demanding 24-week Premier League season, plus off-season maintenance and housekeeping; even more-so for a club based 1500km away from League HQ planning to undertake a 3000km roundtrip every second week.

If the Redtails' plan to join the Premier League came to fruition, the club's overall annual expenditure was projected to be upwards of five times the initial amount it had raised: $500,000 per annum and rising were some estimates bandied about. Understandably, HQ wanted assurances the CAFC was a self-sustainable enterprise with a multi-year plan, sound financials, evidence of a sound governance and management structure, and proof of community support. Mills was quoted as saying:

> *I think the Redtails have opened up a great possibility. There will be a funding issue and that is a challenge that we are looking at and I support the initiative shown by Central Australia to come into the league.*[9]

The Redtails were also expected to find a solution for regular access to Traeger Park during the summer months. This was a complicated issue bubbling just beneath the surface requiring delicate negotiations with a range of stakeholders. It had put the club in an awkward position. The apparent solution sat with the Alice Springs Town Council. The then mayor of Alice Springs and one-time federal CLP candidate, Damien Ryan, however, put the onus back onto Darwin.

The flying success of the Redtails has been a great start to their NTFL career. I congratulate Rob Clarke, the coaching staff and players on their success. In light of this successful trial and the expansion of AFL in Central Australia, the AFLNT needs to work with the Alice Springs community to find a suitable year-round venue. Traeger Park is a multi-sporting venue and Council needs to be fair to all local sports on allocation of our most functional and popular oval. This places a real challenge on the AFLNT to provide financial support for a suitable venue. With the strength of the Redtails success and the fantastic result of a four-game trial, I look forward to AFLNT being proactive with an investment in Alice Springs.[10]

SURVEY SURPRISE

'Surveys show that surveys never lie.'

NATALIE ANGIER (1991 PULITZER PRIZE WINNER)[1]

ANECDOTALLY, the Central Australian Football Club enjoyed widespread support in Alice Springs, across Central Australia and in pockets of Darwin, and there were more than a few bandwagoners. Fans voted with their feet, and their wallets. Attendance figures in the first month of the 2012–13 NTFL season were on an upward trajectory. This exciting new team came from the desert into the tropics, and everybody loved them.

But cold, hard business decisions rely on more than anecdotes.

In March of 2013 AFLNT announced it would formally consult with key stakeholders to gain a greater understanding of how much localised support there was for the club. This came in the form of a multiple-choice survey that was steered by the late Paul Fitzsimons (see Appendix 2).[2]

The survey was reportedly made available to just over a thousand people: football club presidents, administrative staff, board members, committee members, coaches, assistant coaches, club captains, and sectors within the business community. In total there were 11 questions in the survey, five of which related to financials. Space at the end of the survey was given for respondents to provide their own thoughts on the Redtails overall. Seventy responses were reportedly recorded within the first two days of its release. AFLNT CEO Tony Frawley introduced the survey like this:

> *The survey will ... allow respondents to provide feedback on where the Redtails fit into the overall structure of football in Central Australia. Whilst the survey is just one small element of AFLNT's viability assessment for the Redtails we believe it is an excellent way to gauge the level of support for the concept.*
>
> *The board and AFLNT executive believe that whilst the Redtails concept has merit, we have not yet seen evidence that the required level of community support for the concept exists.* [3]

This came as quite the shock to Rob Clarke, and the man was livid. A mini war of words erupted out from the shadows into the cold light of day. It played out in the local media. In true Rob Clarke fashion, three days after the 5 March announcement, he unloaded to journalist Dale Fletcher who was writing for the 8 March *Centralian Advocate*. Fletcher's first question to Clarke was what he thought of the survey.

> *It was the first I had heard of it when you contacted me. I'm a key stakeholder, and I'm waiting for my survey. Have they asked the players what it means to them? Were they at the St Mary's game? The answers were right there. We were told after that Nightcliff game [the club's fourth and final trial game] that they will do everything in their power to make this happen as it was a fantastic effort. All of the players*

> *and coaching staff after thought We are in! and we talked about it for hours afterwards. We have had letters drawn up for potential sponsors after a meeting with Matt Conlan, Tony Frawley, Michael Long and others on the morning of the [2013 AFL] All-Stars match [8 February in Alice Springs]. Now we hear this has happened and we wonder where we stand. The Redtails [is] one of the best things to happen for local football in the area and we all just want it to continue.*[4]

AFLNT's general manager of community football, Anthony Venes, called for calm and reason.

> *We just wanted to find out what's happening. Every time we go down to Alice we get conflicting messages. We need some sort of concrete [evidence] behind the concept before we can move forward.*[5]

Oh to be a fly on the wall; one of those whispering walls with ears! While Darwin had every right to ascertain the true level of support for the club — given the money, time and resources they had invested to date — it was perhaps the mixed signals HQ was sending that unsettled Clarke and co. Following the Redtails' win over Nightcliff in their final game at Marrara, Frawley and other league executives made their way down to the club's changerooms to personally congratulate the team, team management, which included Clarke, Ian McAdam, coach Shaun Cusack and assistants, and some of the players. Perhaps some at the club felt the football heavyweights' presence was a sort of indicator that the Executive was all-in with Team Redtail. Perhaps something was lost in translation among the noise and excitement following the stirring victory over the Tigers. Perhaps, perhaps.

If lobbing a surprise survey into the fray was enough to rile Rob Clarke, the contents and framing of some of the questions must have annoyed him even more. At play were some interesting by-plays.

Question 9 in the survey asks for a 'Yes' or 'No' response to five scenarios. The third scenario was: *The Redtails should…be managed by the AFLNT* — this was, in effect, asking that Rob Clarke, Ian McAdam and, essentially, Central Australia, cede autonomy of the club to AFLNT; essentially, to wrest control of the entire Redtails operations away from Alice Springs into the hands of Darwin.

In question 10, senior local footballer Charlie Maher was effectively quoted about the challenges he faced spending time away from his young family while playing for NT Thunder in Darwin and in the Eastern States, and how the 'heavy toll on his family life' informed his decision to eventually quit the Territory's flagship team. Maher's words were taken from his acceptance speech for the CAFL's 2012 Minahan Medal as the league's fairest-and-best player. In the survey his words appeared from a 'senior player' without attribution. It was clear in five of the six multiple-choice responses presented in question 10 that this 'anonymous' personal experience with the Thunder and the player's decision to quit was extrapolated to project the difficulties others would experience as Redtails players. Maher was as surprised as anyone when his paraphrased quote appeared anonymously, and somewhat decontextualised to imply a certain level of reluctance by local footballers to buy into the concept generally. But this wasn't the reason Maher quit the Thunder. He later said:

> *I only quit the Thunder because I was coming to the end of my career. For all those young fellas coming through, the Redtails is a goal.*[6]

In a show of solidarity, an Alice Springs sports organisation came out in support of the Redtails. Sally Preece, President of the Rovers Netball Club said:

> *It's the 'Berrimah Line' coming out again isn't it. Everyone in Alice knows how great the Redtails will be for the town.*[7]

Local tour operators were also keen to see the Redtails get up. Scott Fischer, the Assistant Operations Manager of Adventure Tours Australia said:

> *We have already seen the benefits this club has created in Central Australia with little support from certain parties. The impression I'm receiving from this survey is that the NTFL is hoping the CAFC idea will disappear. I believe it is far too late for the Redtails concept to simply go away. Five of the six options are negative, so you know what they want.*[8]

Despite several attempts in the three to four years it took to write this book, requests for the results of the survey went unanswered. While AFLNT receives public funding, they are not a Northern Territory Government organisation; therefore, the football body is not subject to Freedom of Information laws.

CHARTING A NEW FLIGHT PATH

TALKS, tense and terse, continued. The Redtails' commitment to the big picture and a permanent gig in the Premier League was unwavering. The incredible scenes in round 1 and the reaction that followed had them convinced their formula was sound. Others could see it too. In May of 2013, the Redtails took delivery of a $75,000 cheque from NT sports minister Matt Conlan.[1]

But there were mixed signals from Darwin.[2] The '$700,000 per annum' the Redtails would need — as projected in the survey — was $50,000 more than what was told to *NT News*'s long-time football writer, Grey Morris, two months prior to the announcement of the survey, and $200,000 more than what Frawley was quoted as saying two months after that.[3] This was all on the public record. Darwin had also thrown the Central Australians a curve ball with a multiple-choice survey, and the big unknown was what actions, if any, would be taken once the results of the survey were known.

Frawley had to temper the growing expectations of the Central Australians. His view was that, without sustainable funding from either the AFL Executive in Melbourne, the Federal Government and/or by philanthropic means, the Redtails' long-term goal of permanent inclusion in the NTFL would not see the light of day. He asked the Central Australians to provide additional information on how the club would execute phase two of its grand plan. They wanted details. They wanted to see the i's dotted, and the t's crossed — financials, a governance and management structure, security on a home venue, proof of community support. The deadline was 1 June 2013. In official correspondence, Frawley said:

> *Like all clubs who have joined the NTFL or expressed a desire to do so the CAFC will have to put the work in to demonstrate that the club has a solid foundation to build upon both structurally and financially. While we agree that the Redtails concept is an exciting one, we must also protect the integrity and sustainability of the NTFL by ensuring that any new club seeking entry into the league is well prepared and has a well-thought out strategy. Any new club must also be supported by the community and, importantly, have ongoing funding from a variety of sources secured for a number of years. We will not rush the expansion of the NTFL as we have to be sure that any new team can survive and thrive in the long term hence the need for the CAFC to clearly demonstrate their plans for the next 3-5 years.*[4]

Anticipating the writing on the wall — those same walls with ears — the Redtails conceded. The club toned down their demands for immediate and full inclusion in the Premier League and instead sought a compromise: a second trial period. Perhaps having been made aware of the Executive's thought processes earlier, the request was a pre-emptive strike. Ply the decision-makers with grace and play the long game. Whichever way you look at it, the timing was off. Neither party was ready, and permanent entry was not the answer — for now. The compromise both organisations sought and agreed upon was that

Conlan's $75,000, together with other money from sponsor-partners, would go toward another trial period. On 18 June 2013, AFLNT wrote:

> *The AFLNT board has recommended that the Central Australian Redtails be admitted into the TIO NTFL Premier League for season 2013/14 on an eight (8) game trial basis, however admission into the league is subject to a further five (5) years of Federal funding being committed to AFLNT and NT Thunder.*
>
> *"The Redtails may well become an integral part of the overall Central Australian football structure which will enhance the NT Thunder presence and align with AFLNT development programs in the region, however AFLNT is awaiting confirmation of ongoing Federal Government funding to underpin these structures.*
>
> *"Federal funding via the Australian Sports Commission has allowed AFLNT and NT Thunder deliver a myriad of positive outcomes for Centralians in the past five years, most notably the Central Australian Football League (CAFL) has evolved into a well run, financial and competitive league enjoyed by players and spectators alike and it is critical that the progress made continues for the next five years and beyond. We are particularly focused on ensuring that the CAFL continues to thrive," explained Tony Frawley, AFLNT CEO.*
>
> *"We see the Redtails as a very meritorious concept however without federal funding underpinning both a strong AFLNT development presence and a continuation of the NT Thunder program in Central Australia we will not have the necessary structures or resources in Alice Springs to support the admission of the Redtails into the NTFL," said Frawley.*
>
> *"The Redtails are aware of our tireless efforts to secure ongoing funding for the AFLNT and NT Thunder programs*

in Central Australia and we will continue to work with the Redtails administration to map out a feasible future direction for the club."[5]

This second trial period would replicate the Super Tiwis' 2007 campaign in which the Redtails would play all the Premier League teams from rounds 1 to 8 from October to November. Previous trial buddies Banks would be absent from the program this time. The Bulldogs anticipated a return invite but when the club heard back from AFLNT it was too late, too close to the season. The club opted to keep killing it in Division 1. This meant the bye was back.

The Redtails' committee mobilised and took with them again the message to the community they carried 12 months earlier — that of a holistic football and work-study program with dedicated engagement for Central Australian young men wrapped around a competitive football team in the semi-professional NTFL Premier League in Darwin. But this time, for twice the duration of the year before. The Redtails committee relayed the news to the club's supporters.

The Redtails have secured eight trial matches in the 2013–14 NTFL season. [This] has been through the generosity and support of local businesses, national businesses and government who have recognised this as a worthwhile project. Our sponsors have come on board for the on- and off-field outcomes that we strive to achieve as a club.[6]

Ahead of the Redtails, then, loomed a thorough two-month examination — by the fans in the stands, and the suits with the plans.

THE BANK-ABLE BULLDOGS

Banks Football Club — the Bulldogs — is among the best run, most successful of the former TEAFA clubs now absorbed into the AFLNT fold. The Darwin-based club plays out in the NTFL's Premier League Reserves (formerly Division 1) and enjoys a huge following with a strong and vocal support base. The club also has strong links to the football and corporate world in Adelaide.

Banks complemented the Redtails' presence in the 2012–13 NTFL Premier League when they accepted an invitation to play four trial games. While their win-loss record in the trial period was a modest 1–3, AFLNT were keen on the club to go around again the following season. Tony Frawley was certainly an early fan, saying in an AFLNT statement:

> *Other emerging brands and clubs in Division 1 and 2 have also contributed to the early success of the NTFL to date, including premier league trial club Banks.*
>
> *The Banks Football Club have given a very good account of themselves thus far and we are now working with the club to map their future NTFL Premier League aspirations.*[7]

Luke Harris was Banks Bulldogs club president for three seasons, from 2010–11 until 2012–13. He remembers the time well:

> *A few short weeks before the 2012–13 season was to kick off, Banks Bulldogs Football Club was approached by the NTFL to participate in a four-game Premier League trial. Banks did not approach the NTFL, nor have we ever approached the NTFL to play in the Premier League. The League wanted Banks to play in the trial to even out the number of teams playing to offset the potential bye with the Redtails trialling. The committee of the day and club legend Lincoln Jenkin who was the Division 1 coach at the time thought it was a perfect opportunity to challenge ourselves and see how competitive we may be.*
>
> *The four-game trial was a fantastic opportunity to play up and test ourselves but they also highlighted the need for greater*

depth in the club's structure and resources. However, at the end of the 2012–13 season, rather than pushing for Premier League inclusion, the club's committee with input from a number of club identities, made the decision to focus on long-term development. We never formally pursued Premier League status; instead, the club commissioned the 'Bulldog Way', a five-year strategic framework aimed at developing the club into a stronger, more sustainable entity. The 'Bulldog Way' placed a strong emphasis on building a junior pathway, developing a women's team, increasing volunteer support, and improving governance and infrastructure to one day be ready for Premier League inclusion if the Club so decided.

Fast-forward to the end of the 2024–25 season, Banks Bulldogs Football Club now boasts a growing junior program (Under-10s, -12s, and -14s, plus a combined 16s team with Tracy Village Football Club) and a thriving Women's club with teams in both Divisions 1 and 2.

With the NTFL once again approaching the club, there is now a tentative agreement to join the Premier League in the near future.[8]

In 2023, TEAFA powerhouse PINT Football Club was granted a Premier League licence by AFLNT. The Greenants made a strong first impression. AFLNT's aspirations for a 10 to 12 team Premier League, as articulated by Tony Frawley in 2011, remain open.

CRICKET SCHMICKET

SPORT in Alice Springs is plenty and bountiful. The place is a sun-kissed sports-lovers' dream destination, offering a buffet of activity, contest and endeavour that would please the mythical gods of sport. The choices range from basketball to camel racing, from tennis to motorsport, and the annual Masters Games with its variety of disciplines for the over-agers.[1] The national football codes and domestic and international cricket have flirted shamelessly with The Alice over the years and they've come and gone like a lovesick ex that just can't let go.

In 2012, Traeger Park had just come out the other end of a 10-year $4.2 million upgrade set in motion by Alice Springs Town Council (ASTC) and backed by the Clare Martin Labor Government. The work improved the venue's capacity to host crowds in relative comfort for big-ticket games like AFL and NRL matches, the Sheffield Shield and one-day cricket, as well as the Masters Games. That upgrade began in 2003. The money was earmarked primarily for off-field amenities, including upgraded floodlights from 300 lux to 800 lux, upgraded players' and umpires' changerooms and amenities, a first-aid room, a doctor-physio room, seating added in the grandstand, a multipurpose function room, kitchen, corporate rooms, press rooms and a third umpires' room.[2]

The venue is operated by the Alice Springs Town Council and is headquarters for the Alice Springs Cricket Association (ASCA) and AFLNT.

During the local football season, Traeger Park hosts up to five CAFL games each weekend, plus the Community Cup competition, and all finals and grand finals. In September, winter-time football makes way for summer-time cricket. Cricket is played at Traeger Park, Albrecht Oval (within the westside suburb of Larapinta), and six other venues around town, including parklands and school ovals. Traeger Park, however, is cricket's primary venue.

The early months of 2013 was a busy period for the playing surface at Traeger Park.

In February, the venue hosted the AFL's Indigenous All-Stars v Richmond game in front of a near-capacity crowd. It was the first time the event (of the modern era: 1994, 2003–2009) was played outside Darwin. This game was originally slated for February 2011 in Darwin but Cyclone Yasi had come in from the east coast and wreaked havoc in Queensland with heavy rains and localised flooding in the Northern Territory, forcing the AFL to abandon the match altogether. The match was re-scheduled for Alice Springs in 2013. Later that month, Traeger Park played host to the annual national Imparja Cup cricket tournament. The following month, in March, AFL clubs West Coast and Port Adelaide played an official pre-season match there. The grand old girl got a fair workout.

In 2012, there was an overlap between the local cricket and football seasons. The CAFL grand final that year fell on 8 September and the Redtails were fixtured in to play their historic first NTFL trial match at the ground a month later on 6 October, after which the cricketers could move in.

Twelve months later, this scenario was replicated for the Redtails' second trial period but there was a much longer wait-time for the cricketers because the 2013 CAFL season had been pushed back a few weeks due to the Imparja Cup and the two AFL games. The 2013 season, then, became an eight-round season and a four-week finals series. The grand final was played on 31 August, five weeks before the Redtails' first game of its second trial period. This left the cricketers without access to Traeger Park for about six weeks. While there weren't any issues apparent to the football club regarding this arrangement, Redtails co-founder Ian McAdam was acutely aware of the potential for problems to arise over the shared use.

> *There's more sporting teams than there are facilities in Alice Springs. We (sports clubs) juggle ovals, with cricket, too. No sport was saying no; we had no real issues with cricket.*[3]

McAdam's spidey sense would have tingled a little bit stronger when in April of 2013 the local council announced plans for yet more major capital works for Traeger Park, but this time for the playing surface. In a note to the ASTC from the council's works managers, a plan was laid out for a wholesale replacement of the centre-wicket area and the surrounding playing surface. The cost for the entire project was estimated at $85,000. In the brief report, a handful of photos from the cricket centre-wicket area and the playing surface — titled 'Damage after football season' — were helpfully attached. The Alice Springs Town Council issued the following report on 25 March 2013:

> It is recommended that following the 2013 Central Australian Football League season the turf cricket wicket block is replaced and oval renovations conducted concurrently.
>
> Traeger Main has been in operation for over 20 years. The cricket wicket area at Traeger is beginning to show signs of reaching its maximum used by date and needs to be programmed for replacement. The wicket block is taking longer to recover from the football season ... if the cricket wicket area is not replaced, the wicket will become un-manageable. ... In short, we are entering a critical

time in the wicket blocks life where it will need to be replaced.

While the turf wicket area is out of action... the oval surface will also receive a major renovation including scarifying, coring, top dressing and laser levelling at the same time. This is an ideal time to complete a major renovation to ensure the premium playing surface.

Traeger Main is Alice Springs's jewel in the crown for facilities and its ability to attract professional sporting events for the community of Alice Springs including: NAB Cup Matches (Australian Football League), NRL Pre Season Matches, (National Rugby League), Ford Ranger 50 Over Cricket Matches, 2013 Indigenous Australian Football League Match, International Cricket Matches, Masters Games.

With professional sport now monitoring and inspecting ovals prior to matches, the wicket block at Traeger will ultimately deteriorate to a point where Council can no longer grow grass on the centre wicket area. This would mean that the above-mentioned sports would not play matches in Alice Springs and thus having a negative impact on tourism, and subsequently, money into local businesses.

The oval will be unavailable for competition and training for 12 weeks during works program.[4]

Although it was only a recommendation, the '12 weeks' of works program — after the 2013 Central Australian Football League season — would take the planned capital works through to November; the same November the Redtails were scheduled to play their second run of trial games. The timing here was potentially problematic.

Tony Frawley knew about the planned capital works two months prior to the ASTC announcement. He told the *NT News* in January 2013:

> *After the CAFL grand final they're going to do some major reconstructive work on Traeger Park. I'm going to meet with all the stakeholders on the morning of the All-Stars game to discuss exactly where we are at.*[5]

No-one involved can recall if this news was ever shared with the Redtails camp but, given the disjointed nature of communication between Darwin and Alice Springs, it may well not have been.

IN CRICKET'S SHADOW

In many ways, the spectre of cricket loomed large over the Redtails. Cognisant of local needs, the Alice Springs Town Council had long called on successive Territory governments to invest in smaller-scale venues with modern amenities to complement Traeger Park, because local resources could only go so far. A growing and diverse population was adding to the squeeze. The former mayor of Alice Springs, Damien Ryan, had been a strong advocate for a secondary venue in the town.

> *The town needs a new oval. It wouldn't be just for the Redtails, it would be for the whole town. As Alice Springs gets bigger, the town would come under more pressure [but council] just doesn't have the finances; we don't have $10 million to build another oval. It is a huge financial consideration. Now is the time that the AFLNT and AFL need to work with our community to find a suitable year-round venue in Alice Springs and this is going to attract some considerable investment, so I call on the AFL that we need them to become very proactive with an investment in Alice Springs. As the NTFL plays at the opposite time to our season Traeger Park is not a viable*

proposition for games when the Central Australian Redtails become fully involved in the league. So I'm just saying that I feel that football has grown to that point that we really need a big investment from the AFL themselves in a new ground.[6]

IMPARJA CUP RUNNETH OVER

In a puzzling omission, the 13 March 2013 Alice Springs Town Council note outlining the capital works at Traeger Park failed to mention the Imparja Cup as one of the big sporting events in which the venue plays a central role. If Council needed another compelling argument as to why the works were sorely needed, the Imparja Cup was it.

The cricket event was founded in 1994 by Shane and Mervyn Franey from Alice Springs and Ross Williams from Tennant Creek. The trio's original plan was for Aboriginal teams to play an annual cricket match between the two towns. The idea took off. Before long other teams, towns and communities joined in.

Such was its growing popularity that in 1998 NT Cricket took over logistics. In the year 2000 — backed by Cricket Australia (CA) — the states and territories sent representative teams to Alice Springs to play in what became the first national Indigenous cricket tournament. In early 2001, the new-look national tournament was formalised by CA. lutruwita (Tasmania) won the first title. The event picked up and state and territory cricket bodies undertook financial investment plans to ensure its longevity.

Imparja Television broadcast some of the games, and other Indigenous media would cover the event in subsequent years. In 2008, the Imparja Cup added a women's division. In 2016, CA reformatted the event so that the State and Territory division was rebadged as the National Indigenous Cricket Championships (NICC), while the Imparja Cup name was retained for the growing Northern Territory town and community competition.

These tournaments continue to make use of the many ovals and parklands in Alice Springs. The NICC division plays primarily at Traeger

Park, Albrecht Oval and Jim McConville Oval in Gillen on the western side of town. The final is played at Traeger Park (except for that one time in 2019 when it was played at Albrecht Oval).

Graduates of the Imparja Cup-NICC include:

- Ash Gardner – Test, Ashes, Twenty20 and One Day International World Cup-winner
- Hannah Darlington, Anika Learoyd – NSW Blues and Sydney Thunder
- Mikayla Hinkley – Perth Scorchers
- Dan Christian, Brendan Doggett, Josh Lalor, D'Arcy Short (born in Katherine) – Sheffield Shield and Big Bash League
- Scott Boland – Australian Test cricket fast bowler.

The week-long NICC and Imparja Cup tournaments are generally played alongside each other in February each year and have cemented their place in the Alice Springs sporting calendar. In a postscript from October 2024, the NICC was shifted away from Alice Springs for the first time, to Mackay in north Queensland.[7]

The Redtails' camp was mindful of the twin cricket tournaments' place within the community. In fact, many of the footballers were themselves keen cricketers, often playing in the Imparja Cup and/or NICC. Imparja is the accepted version and pronunciation of the word 'impatye', meaning tracks or footprints in the Arrernte language.[8] But if the Redtails' ultimate plan was to become a regular-season club in the NTFL, whose season traversed the entire month of February, how the club, the town council, NT Cricket and AFLNT was to navigate around the NICC, the Imparja Cup and, above all, access to Traeger Park during this period, was anyone's guess.

The Redtails' looming dilemma, however, would soon verge on redundant.

BLOC OF NATIONS

Cricket is beautiful when grace overcomes the brute, where the execution of power via technique and cunning, or the exertion of force with efficiency and style, is a success. It's a flawed beauty to look great and lose. -

NICHOLAS HOGG[1]

AUSSIE rules football and cricket have enjoyed a historical synergy that reaches back to the late 1850s. Tom Wills's original intention in 1859 was to create a foot-ball game that would simply serve to keep cricketer's fit during that game's off-season. What has happened since is a remarkable endeavour of human ingenuity and imagination. Both sports have become masters of their respective domains, and enjoy followers counted in the millions. Their divergent paths in this country, however, have sometimes intersected, most times without repercussion; other times with unfavourable consequences. One of those times was in Alice Springs.

It is perhaps best to start this tale in Melbourne, when Australia and England played in what is officially recognised as the first one-day international cricket match on 5 January 1971. The scheduled Third Test of the 1970–71 Ashes series between the two countries at the Melbourne Cricket Ground (MCG) was abandoned entirely due to incessant rain on all the days it was meant to be played, when Tests back then went for six days.[2] What followed was a serendipitous moment that would forever enrich the sport.

To fill the void for sports-loving Melburnians who had missed out on a long-awaited Ashes Test match, cricket officials hastily arranged a game between the two countries on what would have been the day after day six of the Test. The standalone replacement game would consist of 40 eight-ball overs per side and completed inside daylight hours — revolutionary ground for a traditionally conservative sport. And, well, the gimmick worked. A curious, growing and vocal crowd pushing toward 50,000 people roared the Australians to a five-wicket victory over the 'Old Enemy'.

From unscripted origins, the popularity of limited-overs cricket grew and in a few short years this form of the game would be played the world over. It breathed new life into what was becoming a staid product.

By 1975, the appeal of this format was such that cricket's world body, the International Cricket Conference (later: International Cricket Council) (ICC) organised a World Cup tournament involving the primary cricket-playing nations of the day.[3] This was played in England. The next World Cup was played four years later, again in England. Sport's newest World Cup followed the Olympic model and was held every four years (except for that one-time between the years 1987 to 1992).

From 1983, the ICC had an in-principle understanding that cricket-playing countries or regions which had hosted a World Cup could do so again but only after a 20-year period. This meant that with Australia and New Zealand having co-hosted the 1992 World Cup — the first to be held in the Southern Hemisphere — the two nations were in line to host the World Cup scheduled for 2011. However, that 'in-principle understanding' was never set in stone, and this unwritten rule would be tested by an audacious intervention.

ORBIT OF INFLUENCE

By the early 2000s, a cricket-loving bloc of South Asian nations was tilting the game's orbit of influence away from the Anglosphere and toward the sub-continent. The bloc — India, Pakistan, Sri Lanka and Bangladesh — was, by estimates, home to 1.7 billion souls.[4] A heavyweight delegation from this growing and influential bloc put it to the ICC that the 2011 World Cup destined for the Antipodes would, or should, best be played in South Asia. The delegates presented the ICC with numbers revealing the riches that could be had should this be so. Dutifully, the ICC bean-counters crunched the numbers and it was indeed forecast that a World Cup on the sub-continent would generate somewhere in the vicinity of $2 billion from the broadcast rights alone. In a majority decision, 10–3, the ICC awarded the South Asian bid the right to host the 2011 Cricket World Cup.[5]

Though not entirely chuffed at this turn of events, the Aussies and Kiwis were nevertheless understanding of the game's real-time geo-political shift and what that could do for cricket's overall future and financial health. The Australian and New Zealand cricket bodies made representation to the ICC for compensation, fiscal or otherwise. They got it in the form of the 2015 Cricket World Cup as co-hosts.[6]

All good.

At an ICC meeting sometime later at the organisation's plush headquarters in Dubai, cricket's chuffed conquistadors paused from counting their 30 pieces of silver after chancing upon a real-time problem. What the ICC found was that the time-honoured Australia–England Ashes series was set on an irreversible collision course with the now-relocated 2015 Down Under World Cup.

Not good.

The capital-A 'Ashes' series was the name bestowed upon cricket matches involving Australia and England. It is the game's oldest rivalry. The Ashes is a five-Test series which sits on a four-year cycle. It is hosted in turn by England and Australia. The origin of the term 'Ashes' stems from 1882 when at The Oval in England Australia inflicted a shock and demoralising defeat upon the English from which the charred ashes of the bails from that game were placed inside an urn to signify the apparent death of English cricket, thus the 'Ashes'.[7]

When the Ashes series is played during the English summer, the 'return' series is played 18 months later during the Australian summer — and that has been the cycle since about forever.[8] In keeping with this time-honoured cycle, the Ashes series scheduled for England in 2013 would see the return series played in the Australian summer of 2014–15, except that now this particular summer would be occupied by the relocated 2015 Australia–New Zealand World Cup, scheduled for the early months of that year.

This, simply, would not work.

Presented with a confounding conundrum, the ICC, Cricket Australia and the England & Wales Cricket Board brainstormed their options over a hot pot of Earl Grey tea and a tray of cucumber sandwiches. One option open to them was to hold over the scheduled 2013 Ashes series in England by a year to 2014, so the return series in Australia could be played in 2015–16, thereby avoiding the 2015 World Cup. However, a five-year wait between Ashes series in England — from 2009 to 2014 — was a bridge too far. Another option was to scrap this particular Ashes timeline entirely and start anew from mid-year in England in 2015, then to Australia in 2016–17, but a six-year gap between Ashes series in England — from 2009 to 2015 — would upset the genteel folk at Lord's. An exciting concept emerged as a possible solution: back-to-back Ashes series — 10 consecutive Test matches: five during the English summer, the next five dovetailing into the Australian summer. Australia and England played back-to-back Ashes series in 1974 and 1974–75 so this was not without precedent.

Yeah, but when?

The burning question. Bringing forward the 2013 series in England to 2012 then to Australia in 2012–13 was impossible because of the small matter of the 2012 London Olympic Games. The suits squirming in their seats settled on the only viable option remaining: keep to the 2013 English summer schedule and bring forward the return series to the 2013–14 Australian summer, thus avoiding a clash with the 2015 Aussie-Kiwi World Cup.

Crisis averted.

Well yes, but also no.

With the ICC having earlier locked down the location for the 2015 World Cup, Cricket Australia had already embarked on a recon mission for the big show Down Under. Venues around the country were identified or otherwise earmarked for pool-stage games and finals. One of those venues was Manuka Oval in the nation's capital, Canberra, in the Australian Capital Territory. The Territory Government there leapt at the opportunity to host games in the pool stage of the World Cup. Canberra to that point had yet to host a single Test match, only an occasional one-day international, so this was an opportunity too great to miss.[9] But Manuka's playing surface was deemed unsuitable for international cricket, no less a World Cup. For it to be at an acceptable international standard, the ACT government embarked on a full-scale turf replacement project. This would have Manuka ready for the big show, but it would also put the venue out of commission for the entirety of 2013 and until early the following year.

Sometime later, the ECB was poring over logistics ahead of the English cricket team's 2013–14 five-Test Ashes series and tour to Australia — the return series of this new back-to-back Ashes series — which would begin in late October/early November in 2013 and play through to early in 2014.

Included in the English team's itinerary were several tour matches against various 'Invitational XIs' around the country, as is customary for touring cricket teams. These tour matches generally run for two days. They provide local up-

and-comers and Australian state-level cricketers an opportunity to play against a world-class international team, and a game for the tourists to fine-tune their skills and perhaps try out new batting and bowling combinations. One such tour match scheduled ahead of the Second Test in Adelaide in early December had been slated for Manuka Oval, except that Manuka was now unavailable, as were the majority of Australia's other first-class venues, all booked out for the domestic season ahead — the Sheffield Shield, the 50-over (Ryobi) One-Day Cup, and this new thing called the Big Bash League (Twenty20).

This was a problem.

As host-incumbent, Cricket Australia needed a fix. And quick.

Suddenly, the Northern Territory came into view. Criminally overlooked by a southern-centric cricket administration, the NT this time could be CA's belated saviour. CA approached the NT government with the tantalising prospect of hosting a two-day English tour match before the Second Test in Adelaide. The Territorians were all ears. Ordinarily, a state's or a territory's capital city would host an international sports fixture, but the Northern Territory capital Darwin is anything but ordinary — good-ways.

Darwin sits in the middle of a tropical rainbelt — cyclone-skies, thunderstorm country — and in the summertime it is subject to monsoonal rains and storms that can leave you both awestruck and thunder-struck if you're silly enough to be caught outside. That time of year is not conducive to cricket, only lightning.

The only realistic option in the Northern Territory was the clear skies and flies of the dependably dry Red Centre — Alice Springs, and Traeger Park. The English had 11 days between the First and Second Tests, in Brisbane (24 November) and Adelaide (5 December), respectively.

This was a rare chance for Alice Springs, and great news for local sports-lovers and regional tourism. On 7 May 2013, Cricket Australia and the NT Government agreed to terms. The English were coming to town. Everyone was excited.

An international sporting collision-course was thus averted, and a major diplomatic incident deftly avoided. But there was one organisation that would feel the impact of this cascading series of events, and that was the Central Australian Football Club.

For the Redtails, this was the beginning of a local and logistical nightmare.

To ensure playing surfaces are up to international standards, Cricket Australia's guidelines state that any other 'content' at a specific venue, i.e. sport or other activities, must essentially cease 'within six weeks of the match'. This did not bode well for the Traeger Park-based Redtails.[10]

BOOST FOR ALICE SPRINGS

Alice Springs mayor Damien Ryan was among the first to express delight with the tour match.

> *I'm excited about the announcement of international cricket in Alice Springs and the boost it will bring to the overall economy of our entire community. This announcement will see Alice Springs continue to flourish as a tourist destination, and also allow our community access to a piece of the Ashes tour. We will ensure Traeger Park is of the highest standard and continues to attract major sporting events to our community.*[11]

NT sports minister Matt Conlan was happy to talk up the Ashes-adjacent event coming to Alice Springs. In 2000, Alice Springs hosted the touring West Indies cricket team at Traeger Park. The tourists were captained by Jimmy Adams, with Courtney Walsh and Brian Lara in the side. The Windies played against the Northern Territory Cricket Association Invitation XI in a one-day 50-over match. Lara scored a century.[12]

> *The Ashes is one of the biggest events in Australian sport and for Alice Springs to have a slice of the action in between the first and second Tests of this highly anticipated series is incredibly exciting. It's been 13 years since Traeger Park hosted an international cricket team and I'm delighted this drought will now be broken in November.*[13]

And Cricket Australia was happy to have found a venue somewhere, anywhere, to placate the English.[14]

> *We are excited about... the opportunity to bring elite cricket to the Red Centre. When we were informed that Canberra could not host this year's Chairman's XI fixture, we wanted to bring the match to an iconic part of Australia. Alice Springs, set against the backdrop of the MacDonnell Ranges, is an iconic part of our great country and an ideal setting for the game.*[15]

And the pressing matter of the major capital works scheduled for Traeger Park for September 2013? That could wait.

> *A major oval renovation was scheduled for Traeger Park Main to commence in September 2013. However due to the (NT) Chairman's XI v England cricket match scheduled for November 2013, these renovations have been deferred 12 months and will now be completed September-December 2014.*[16]

NON-COUNCILATORY

Alice Springs Town Council's 12-month handbrake on its 12-week major works program at Traeger Park following confirmation of the English cricket team tour match at the venue is worth a revisit. It raises several points of contention.

If, according to the original March 2013 council note, the condition of the Traeger Park surface was a compelling $85,000 capital-works case, then perhaps its ready availability to the English cricket team suggests the work wasn't as urgent as council suggested. Council's note on the state of the playing surface said 'the wicket block is taking longer to recover from the football season' and it was:

> *beginning to show signs of reaching its maximum used by date and needs to be programmed for replacement ... if the cricket wicket area is not replaced, the wicket will become un-manageable.*[17]

Does this assessment stack up if, suddenly, the surface is now deemed playable for cricket, no less a professional international team, following the end of a busy local football season? Remember also the 2013 CAFL was drastically reduced due to an eight-round 12-week season due to the Imparja Cup and two AFL games in February and March.

Also, if the works could be put off for another 12 months so readily, as per the council's above-mentioned note, was the surface really that bad and/or unmanageable to begin with? Logically, without intervention, the 12-month postponement would further degrade the apparently vulnerable surface to a state well beyond a proposed $85,000 refurb. Ordinarily, and without the tour match, wouldn't the best time for council to begin works on the field be early in December of 2013, immediately following the end of the Redtails' second trial run in October and November, thus minimising disruption to local sport? Darwin's go-ahead for the Redtails' second trial series came one month after the joint Cricket Australia-NT Government announcement.

Had cricket's World Cup kept to its original four-year course, or if the English tour match had found a venue elsewhere, the odds were that Council's planned works would have gone ahead as originally planned. In a sense, this train of events revealed the pecking order at where this new football club sat in sectors within Alice Springs: down on the figurative totem pole of local priorities.

ERASURE

NOTWITHSTANDING the criminal erasure of Djab Wurrung's marngrook by AFL canonists, football will forever be tied to cricket.[1] Aussie rules is the only formalised football code in the world that is played on an oval-shaped field; venue prioritisation and scheduling conflicts with cricket in Australia, therefore, would be inevitable.

It is worth revisiting, then, the football–cricket, cricket–football synergy, an association reaching back to the beginning of Aussie rules in 1858. Before Tom Wills's letter to *Bell's Life* in the hope of forming a 'winter-time foot-ball club' to keep the Victorian colony's cricketers fit during the winter, cricket in the colonies was played on whatever space was available. Invariably, these were expansive fields untouched by the colonialists' voracious appetite for capital and growth. In its early development phase, wintertime football was played on those same roughly drawn circular fields. This was a neat fit, and the game developed its unique aspects within these physical boundaries. As football and cricket grew in popularity, vital infrastructure was built for the needs of both. Infrastructure rose around those shared resources, those expansive fields and circular spaces, rounded off with rope, line markings or a fence, thus becoming oval-shape. The structures built around these spaces, around these ovals, would come in many forms: clubhouses, grandstands, scoreboards, canteens, etc. In time, these structures would form the foundational cornerstones for the profitable use of these venues and, by extension, a guarantee that cricket and football would continue to thrive and co-exist.

There is an argument to be made, however, that modern-era football has provided more toward these resources than cricket, by virtue of a lifelong and increasing uptake by a population smitten with this unique home-grown sport. It is as the great Australian poet Bruce Dawe (1930–2020) put it, 'When children are born in Victoria, they are wrapped in club-colours, laid in beribboned cots, having already begun a lifetime's barracking.'[2]

To be sure, cricket is a global sport with participants and a fanbase numbering in the billions, whereas Aussie rules football at any meaningful level is confined solely to Australia. But it is domestic football, not cricket, that packs out the grounds in this country. It was thus incumbent upon the emerging football industry to be a proactive force in lobbying the various levels of local council and government to co-fund capital works around these shared venues because it had more to gain and more to lose in this space.

The Melbourne Cricket Ground (MCG – capacity 100,000) in Victoria is the world-class venue largely due to football; primarily from the superior attendances of the Victorian Football League / Australian Football League over more than 100 seasons. Former AFL Commissioner Ross Oakley:

> *Our estimate was that football accounted for more than 70% of revenues at the MCG, and yet the calendar of usage of the ground was split 50-50 between cricket and football. In all the research it was very clear that the majority of our supporters saw the MCG as the home of football.*[3]

In South Australia the AFL Commission drove hard for favourable terms around the redevelopment of the Adelaide Oval as the home of the Adelaide and Port Adelaide football clubs — both had previously played at Football Park at outer West Lakes. In Queensland, the Brisbane Cricket Ground — the famous Gabba — is the home venue for the Brisbane Lions AFC. Both Adelaide Oval and the Gabba are central to the Australian cricket story, but in modern times, the first-class facilities they enjoy are largely built on the guarantee of football's consistently high attendance figures.

Carrara Stadium on the Gold Coast was rebuilt for the Gold Coast Suns ahead of their entry into the AFL in 2011. Until the early 1980s, when South Melbourne relocated north to become the Sydney Swans, the Sydney Cricket Ground (SCG) owed much of its development and popularity to the New South Wales Rugby Football League. In 1965, the NSWRL-RFL grand final between St George and South Sydney set the record for the largest attendance at the SCG: 78,056. Today, the SCG-based Swans enjoy the largest seasonal average attendance figures for sport in NSW, which is now the driver of development at the venue.[4]

Unlike the other state leagues, the West Australian Football League (WAFL) was largely unencumbered by the dilly-dallying of its city's cricket establishment, which in Perth was headquartered at the famed Western Australian Cricket Association ground ('the WACA'), home to Sheffield Shield and Test match cricket since the 1890s. Each club in the WAFL had its own home grounds which they also sometimes shared with Perth grade-cricket. The West Australian Football Commission (WAFC) was, for the most part, headquartered at Subiaco Oval.

There is an argument to make that, without the 45,000-seat capacity Subiaco Oval in Perth, the transition of the suburban VFL into the quasi-national AFL from 1987 onward would have failed, or would have been severely hampered. For the VFL-AFL to venture into Western Australia with any meaningful level of sustainability, confidence and/or success, it needed a first-class venue in Perth. Which is why the pitch to the VFL by the consortium that formed the West Coast Eagles Football Club in 1986 earmarking Subiaco Oval as its home-ground venue was successful. Take Subiaco away and there is no doubt there would have been a several-year delay in the VFL becoming the AFL.

'Subi', the oval, was the No. 1 football venue in the west, home to WANFL-WAFL grand finals and, from 1977, State of Origin football. This was the year when Western Australia, and the legendary 'Sandgropers' teams of the era, first blessed the world with the representative football concept. When Western Australia played Victoria at Subiaco Oval in October of that year under these new 'state-of-origin' rules (in which you played for the state you were born in), the concept would find its niche in rugby league; the Australian Rugby League's (ARL) annual New South Wales and Queensland State of Origin series. Crowds averaging 25,000 filled Perth's suburban football venues during the WAFL's heady heydays and over 50,000 fans on average packed in at Subi during finals and grand finals, figures that Perth grade-cricket could only dream of.[5]

Back across town, the WACA was holding on tightly to an agreement it had with the WAFC and WA's two AFL clubs, West Coast (est. 1986) and Fremantle (est. 1994), when they weren't playing at Subiaco Oval. The WACA was desperate for an income stream to maintain its facilities that were outdated, with seats at weird angles and sub-par lighting for night games. It welcomed the Western Reds–Perth Reds Rugby League Football Club (1992–97) as a regular tenant but that association ended when the Reds did; a victim of rugby league's internecine Super League War.[6]

In the mid-1990s, the AFL, the WACA and the West Australian Government hashed out a two-tiered contract whereby West Coast and Fremantle would play a portion of their home games at the cricket venue. But both the Eagles and the Dockers couldn't leave the WACA ground quick enough when their respective contracts expired in 1999 and 2005, after which they shifted all their home games to Subiaco Oval, thus finally ending the WACA's meek hold on WA football.

But then, when Subiaco's facilities could no longer keep up with the growing professionalism of AFL football, and a swelling fanbase that had long turned its back on its state football heritage, lobbyists led by the AFL put forward a solid case to the WA Government to build a new stadium.

In 2018, the state-of-the-art 65,000-capacity Perth Stadium was officially opened, attracting tens of thousands of fans each week to watch West Coast and Fremantle play all their home games throughout the AFL season. It is also where rugby league attracts tens of thousands of fans when it brings its dynamic version of State of Origin football to the west. And as sure as night follows day, cricket, in the form of Tests, Big Bash, Twenty20 and one-day internationals, set up shop soon thereafter. The first cricket Test match played at the new Perth Stadium was in December 2018 between Australia and India.

As one of the major players in global cricket, Australian stadiums are at a world-class standard, perhaps the best in the world. In cricket's birthplace, England, the game has been left to historic and quaint grounds with actual trees in the way and downhill slopes. This holds some charm, to be sure, but the dominant rectangular football code there — soccer — plays in front of massive crowds at high tech ultra-modern stadiums.[7]

***

There is no telling how sub-optimal stadiums in Australia would be today without football. While none of Australia's four professional football codes claim to be its 'national game' — ironically, cricket's rightful boast — Aussie rules football has largely underpinned vital venue infrastructure upon which cricket thrives. Football pulls rank at times, but without ironclad contracts, these instances are few and far between.

In Alice Springs in October 2019, for example, the AFL Executive announced an AFLW game for Traeger Park in March the following year. Closer to the date, Alice Springs Town Council groundkeepers were thus instructed to refrain from trimming the outfield for a softer and safer surface for the visiting footballers. But the flow-on effect on the local cricket season was that batters weren't reaching the boundary with their glorious off-drives and exquisitely timed late-cuts when they otherwise would have.[8]

Still, there exists a hierarchy. So, when situations like the one facing an amateur football club like the Redtails arise, professional sport, international sport, international and national cricket invariably take precedence.

THE 'BUTTERFLY EFFECT'

The term relates more as a metaphor for the principle of Chaos Theory. Technically, the butterfly effect is the 'sensitive dependence on initial conditions'.

EDWARD LORENZ (PARAPHRASED) (FROM 1977 TO 1981, EDWARD LORENZ SERVED AS HEAD OF THE DEPARTMENT OF METEOROLOGY AT MASSACHUSETTS INSTITUTE OF TECHNOLOGY)[1]

THE 'butterfly effect' is not a thing in and of itself — sorry Ashton Kutcher! In the 2004 thriller *The Butterfly Effect* (starring Kutcher as the protagonist) the metaphor is used to demonstrate that a seemingly insignificant event can lead to a significant event or series of events.[2] The Central Australian Football Club, it seemed, would face its own 'butterfly effect'.

While the impact the English tour match at Traeger Park would have on the Redtails had yet to play out, club officials were privately concerned. The question at the front of the mind was whether they would have access to the venue, if at all. And if so, for how long?

The football club was hopeful it could play at least more than one lousy home game there in 2013, to avoid a repeat of 2012. To see how this could work, the schedules were thus:

REDTAILS' 2013–14 NTFL PREMIER LEAGUE TRIAL MATCHES

Round 1 — Saturday 5 October

Round 2 — Saturday 12 October

Round 3 — Saturday 19 October

Round 4 — Saturday 26 October

Round 5 — Saturday 2 November

Round 6 — Saturday 9 November

Round 7 — Saturday 16 November

Round 8 — Saturday 23 November.

English cricket team's 2013 tour match

Friday 29-Saturday 30 November.[3]

Given the 'six weeks' CA needed for all activities to cease at venues it has locked in amounted to 42 days, there was a narrow window in which the Redtails could maintain a meaningful presence at Traeger Park before the curators could move in, take over and begin preparations.

The computational options available to the football club amounted to two games, the caveat being that one of those games be brought forward by one day. Here's the hypothetical options that could have been presented:

- Option 1: Rounds 1 and 2 at Traeger Park allowing for six weeks and five days' preparation time for the curators — with rounds 3, 4, 5, 6, 7 and 8 in Darwin.
- Option 2: Rounds 1 and 3[i] at Traeger Park allowing for six weeks' preparation time for the curators — with rounds 2, 4, 5, 6, 7 and 8 in Darwin.

---

i Brought forward to Friday 18 October.

The CAFC's credibility and legitimacy in the region hinged upon a meaningful local presence. Home games are central to the long-term viability of grassroots sport and clubs. That intangible connection between fan and team builds from the organic process of player-fan engagement that can only come from regular games at home. Local sponsorship, too, is predicated upon a regular show in town. Sponsors pay the way and they would generally like to see a local return on their investment. Playing at home was vital to all of what this football club set out to achieve. Clever marketing can also only do so much. The Redtails' virtual absence from Alice Springs and Central Australia during their initial run in 2012 nullified much of this, despite local support and favourable press.

If anything else could tilt a decision favourable to the Redtails enjoying a meaningful presence at home this time around, it was Alice Springs's glorious weather. The onset of spring is a dry and often pleasant time of the year. According to the weather station at Alice Springs airport 14.5 kilometres from the CBD, the town's long-range forecast for the entirety of November in 2013 was for the absence of rain. Alice Springs's October average temperature is 24°C, while for November it is 27°C. Both months can also experience 40°C days — no chance of rainfall, therefore no possibility of irreparable 'damage after rain' to the Traeger Park playing surface by the footballers.[4]

Despite the forecast, despite growing evidence of meaningful change in the lives of the region's young men, despite all this and a whole lot more, the Redtails' dream of playing more than just one game on their home ground would not be realised. In a thoroughly disappointing outcome for those who had invested so much into the Redtails, the priorities of Cricket Australia and the English cricket team would take precedence. With the council note from March 2013 in mind and on advice from Cricket Australia, the risk to the playing surface was deemed too great to allow the football club more than minimal access. In the end, AFLNT granted the Redtails just the one home game — the first one.

Thus the 'butterfly effect' of a decision made in the ICC's ivory tower by the Persian Gulf in the United Arab Emirates rippled outwards to a local and devastating application. The Redtails were in the right place but there at the wrong time. The subcontinent's rise in cricket saw a World Cup relocated Down Under; the rescheduled Ashes series that followed had gone and stuffed up the plans of this little local Aussie rules footy club. Put simply, the Redtails were collateral damage to world events beyond their scope and control.

The Redtails 2013–14 NTFL Premier League schedule was thus:

• Option 3: Round 1 at Traeger Park allowing for eight weeks-one days' preparation for the curators — with rounds 2, 3, 4, 5, 6, 7 and 8 in Darwin.

THE FIX(TURE) IS IN

The four teams the Redtails did not play in their first trial period —Waratah, Wanderers, Palmerston, Southern Districts — would get a look-in in rounds 1, 5, 6 and 8. The teams they met last season were set for rounds 2, 3, 4 and 7.[5]

- Round 1 vs Waratah at Traeger Park
- Round 2 vs St Mary's at Marrara Oval
- Round 3 vs Nightcliff at Nightcliff Oval
- Round 4 vs Darwin Buffaloes at Palmerston Oval
- Round 5 vs Wanderers at Gardens Oval
- Round 6 vs Southern Districts at Freds Pass
- Round 7 vs Tiwi Bombers at Marrara Oval
- Round 8 vs Palmerston at Marrara Oval.

TOP END — THE SEQUEL

THE 2013 Central Australian Football League season rolled on through the year toward its satisfactory end with the grand final on 31 August. There was heightened interest surrounding the Redtails that year. Announcing the trial in August 2013, AFLNT football operations manager Darryl Griffiths advised that the draw was well balanced and catered to everyone's needs. The inclusion of the Redtails' trial was a big part of the fixture.[1]

While *Redtails — Premier League: Season 1* was an exciting and rollicking adventure, *Redtails — Top End: The Sequel* would peel back the layers and provide a thorough examination of the Central Australian Football Club. It would also test the resolve of an entire organisation.

The club had moved on from the unavailability of Traeger Park, and the fiasco of having just one game of eight scheduled at home. The new season was their focus. A fresh start awaited.

Thirty-seven players had worn the black, white, red and ochre of the CAFC during the team's first trial period in 2012; most of these players would return for the Redtails' 2013 campaign. Some of the first-year Redtails had fielded interest from the Top End clubs and these trials were another chance to display their talents. It was all they could talk about. They saw what playing for the Redtails could do for their own advancement in the game.

Change had come at the club. Shaun Cusack decided against re-nominating for the coaching role. That saw Greg McAdam appointed to the role.

Greg, brother of co-founder Ian McAdam, was a star all-round sportsman and mainstay at the South Alice Springs Football Club in his playing days. From 1977 to 1985, Greg played for North Adelaide in the SANFL and for VFL club St Kilda. He had come with big wraps as a player. Peter Argent, an Adelaide-based South Australian football writer-historian, said SANFL football legend Barrie Robran had named Greg McAdam as 'one of the greatest footballers to ever come out of Alice Springs'. The new coach recalled how excited he was at the journey before him.

> *I came in after they already had that (first) trial period, they were looking for a coach so I said I'll do it. In terms of the pool of players we had, they was all from Central Australia and Tennant Creek and community mob. It wasn't about winning but it was, for a lot of our guys, a taste of this competition, to see what the NTFL was like. The players were all for it. It was 'Central Australia in the NTFL' so the players were really keen, there was a lot of people behind the Redtails and general support around it. (Greg McAdam)*[2]

The Redtails' first game would pit them against Waratah, the Warriors. Like St Mary's, Waratah was an experienced, battle-hardened outfit. The club was a mix of local tradies, labourers and fly-ins who party as hard as they play. With the studious Tiwi Islander Brenton Toy holding the clipboard as coach, the red-and-white Warriors presented a stern test.

Under fire: Redtails midfielder Luke Adams dishes off a handpass to teammate Michaelis McMasters against an opponent from Darwin club Waratah at Traeger Park in Alice Springs. This was Round 1 of the 2013–14 NTFL Premier League (Photo: Charlie Lowson, Saturday 5 October 2013)

Coach Greg McAdam had an extended squad to choose from and in his final 22 were eight debutants. Anticipation ran high. The unbridled excitement at the novelty of the occasion from last year was replaced with a sense of expectation; a sense that this was where the team belonged and nothing short of a win was an acceptable outcome.

Like they had shown in the first game 12 months prior, the hometown team was up for the contest and there was a decent crowd ready to cheer on the boys. The match was a solid encounter with a thrilling last-quarter finish but no fairytale ending. The home team was at the wrong side of the ledger by two points at the final siren.

The might of St Mary's asserted its authority when the Central Australians fronted up at Marrara Oval in round 2. St Mary's singular loss in the 2012–13 season came at the hands of the Redtails and if there was any 'vengeance' to be had then this game was it. The Saints came out marching to 33-point victory.

A heavy 13-goal defeat by Nightcliff a week later was the Redtails' biggest loss, prompting plenty of soul-searching. This game also marked the first appearance of Centralian Matt Campbell, the former AFL North Melbourne player and 2009 Polly Farmer Medal winner. Also featured was Larrakia and Warumungu man Brandan Parfitt for Nightcliff, the son of Darwin Buffaloes great David Parfitt. The young Parfitt would later be drafted by AFL club Geelong and win a premiership with the Cats in 2022.

The Redtails returned to the winners' circle in round 4 when they defeated Darwin Buffaloes in Palmerston, cracking the 20-goal mark for the first time.

Then came the crash, or rather, crashes.

A demoralising loss to Wanderers followed, and another to Southern Districts a week later, games in which the Redtails barely reached double figures in goals. The team had lost its mojo. This was not the Central Australian way, and certainly not an acceptable standard of play by a team from a region with a strong and proud football heritage here to convince Darwin they were the real deal. Maybe it was all just becoming a bit too much? Maybe the weekly travel was beginning to take its toll? Maybe it was Maybelline? Whatever the reason, things weren't looking great for the CAFC.

PRIME-TIME FOOTBALL

When round 7 rolled around, the classy Tiwi Bombers appeared on the horizon. The Tiwis had inflicted the Central Australians' only loss in 2012 in a high-scoring affair that set the football world abuzz.[3] It led AFLNT to trumpet an across-the-board increase in spectators and viewers and readers online.[4] In fact, that game's attendance was higher than when the Super Tiwis played their first trial game in 2007, such was the interest the Centralians were generating. But, as the cliché goes, if a week is a long time in football, then a year is an eternity. Twelve months on, the return match was destined to be a fizzer.

The winged Redtails were facing a third consecutive defeat, while the Tiwis looked more like crepe paper aeroplanes than fearsome Bombers, mustering just two wins in a month of football. Both teams were at the foot of the league ladder with just three wins between them. This game wasn't going to be anything other than an ugly scrap between two stragglers struggling for relevance.

But expectations *always* hit different when exceeded, because from siren to siren this was an incredible exhibition of everything good about Aussie rules football. If you wanted to see what two opposing football sides with an Aboriginal majority of players nurtured in a semi-professional environment were capable of, then this game was it; this was the template from which all else should be cut. The 44 players delivered an incredible spectacle. The skills, the goals, the plays, the individual contests. The lead changed several times over four quarters of frenetic, blistering, one-touch football that saw 42 goals from 67 scoring shots for a combined tally of 277 points. It was a thoroughly entertaining game. This was the highest scoring game in the 2013–14 season, besting the round 11 match between Wanderers and the Tiwi Bombers (which the Wanderers won). The scoreboard told the story in numbers — the Tiwis' 22.11 (143) to the Redtails' 20.14 (134).[5] The reaction in the stands told the story of approval. 'We both walked off to a standing ovation,' a proud Rob Clarke recalled.

Perhaps the sweetest of all ironies, not lost on anyone that day, was Yuendumu's Liam Jurrah playing for the Tiwi Bombers. Jurrah, the Warlpiri star footballer and former AFL player with the Melbourne Demons, played out of his skin and booted six goals for the Bombers to help sink his own Countrymen on the big stage and live on TV.

The shoot-out with the Tiwis was a high point in the Redtails' northern sojourn, despite the result. It was the team's highest total from all its 12 trial games, proving that Central Australian footballers were more than capable of matching their Top End counterparts. It validated coach Greg McAdam's observation that footballers from both regions are on an equal footing but that the difference was mainly at local club level.

> *There is a massive difference between the top clubs in Alice Springs to the bottom clubs in Alice Springs, where you would get just one or two competitive games every few weeks. The difference with both competitions [CAFL and NTFL], the massive difference is in the standard of the competitions, but not a lot of difference in individual [player] standards. I personally don't believe it's the individual skill levels that's any different. The personnel, the players in Alice Springs, in Central Australia, have just as much ability as anyone else in the country. [The trial] wasn't about winning but it was, for a lot of our guys, a taste of this competition, to see what the NTFL was like. The players were all for it. In terms of footy, they will never get that opportunity again, it's hard to physically move from Alice Springs to go to Darwin so the Redtails presented that as a stepping stone.*[6]

A 27-point loss to Palmerston in the Redtails' final game at Marrara Oval was marred by the effects of Tropical Cyclone Alessia. Redtails captain Nathan Mutch wasn't a fan of the conditions.

> *A lot of the boys hadn't played in that sort of wet weather before, it didn't really work in our favour. It was a bit different to playing dry weather football which we do really well.*[7]

The result saw the Central Australians end their 2013–14 campaign with a 1–7 win-loss record; eighth on the nine-team ladder, only just above last-placed Palmerston. (See Appendix 3: Scoreboard 2.0 for full teams, scores, results, goals and ladder positions.)

So close, yet so far: Redtails players show their appreciation to their loyal fans after being narrowly defeated by Darwin club Waratah at Traeger Park in Alice Springs. The Round 1 game of the 2013–14 NTFL Premier League season was the team's first match of their second trial period in the Top End league (and fifth overall). Of the team's 12 trial games (across 2012 and 2013), this was just one of two games the team played at home. (Photo: Charlie Lowson, Saturday 5 October 2013)

JURRAH BOMBSHELL

Liam Jurrah's presence at the Tiwi Bombers in the 2013–14 season saw him reunited with good mate and former Melbourne Demons' teammate, Tiwi man Austin Wonaemirri, who was back home following the end of his AFL career.

Warlpiri man Jurrah had spoken of wanting to challenge himself in football and needing a 'change of scenery'.

He had had a tumultuous time back home when his AFL career ended prematurely after just 36 games (81 goals), court appearances and family feuds among them. 'I just want to get out of Alice Springs and start playing footy again,' he said.[8]

Wonaemirri was the catalyst for Jurrah's recruitment to the Tiwi club.

HARSH, BUT FAIR

The Redtails' second appearance in the Top End was much harder going than their first. Their stunning Premier League debut in 2012 seemed like a lifetime ago. It would be somewhat warranted — if a little harsh — to say that this was a step back in the team's overall on-field performance. While the club often stressed the point that on-field results were not the be-all and end-all, no-one liked to lose. And while no-one cares to hear excuses, and the club certainly hadn't offered any, several mitigating factors pushed the club to its limits.

Ryan Mallard was one of the mature-age players in the Redtails team. He marked his 30th and 31st birthdays over the club's two-year trial period. His personal observation was that the Darwin teams had come well prepared for the Redtails' second showing.

> *The first year was a new concept, [but] the second year they were ready for us. We were making adjustments and tried our best but it just wasn't enough.*

Committee man Paul Ah Chee certainly felt the sting of those losses, even as an observer from the stands. He spoke strongly about the *whys and hows* of the Redtails' dissatisfying 1–7 record.

> *We didn't have much success. It was a pretty big dip to play eight games and not win more than one. In terms of games won, it was a failure, but not the journey we were on. Sometimes you have to face adversity because that's where you find where your real strengths are.*

Mutch was nevertheless proud of the boys. The experience — the journey — was a success for him and the team.

> *We were a little bit unlucky with a few close losses against some good sides. For us to be doing that after playing together for such a short period of time was awesome.*[9]

WHAT FAULT THE OTHER BIG REDTAIL OF THE SKIES?

The CAFL's shortened 2013 season had certainly left the Redtails players lacking in match-fitness and conditioning for the Top End test. A mere 12-week season would do that. Did the Redtails' 1–7 record de-legitimise the CAFC in the eyes of Darwin and the AFLNT Executive? Could this club not cut it in the big time? And were those lofty Premier League aspirations overly ambitious?

While a minimal home season and a demanding two-month cycle of constant travel was a likely contributor to the team's sub-par performances, there was something else that influenced the team's modest showing.

Sometime in 2013, Qantas — the other big redtail of the skies — changed some of its Northern Territory flight schedules. Qantas found that certain routes weren't particularly profitable. One was its direct flight from Sydney to Uluru, which it cut on 3 June along with 15 local jobs at Ayers Rock Airport.[10] The other was Alice Springs to Darwin early on Saturday mornings. Changing this flight to a later time, which is what the airline did, would maintain the profits. But it placed the Redtails in the middle of a logistical nightmare.

The later flight out from Alice Springs meant the players had barely enough preparation time for their mid-afternoon games in Darwin. Having landed with about an hour to spare before their game, the players were left to change into their football gear on the way to the ground, in the team bus. This was the only flight out of town that would allow the club to make its Saturday games. Taking the plane 24 hours earlier on the Friday to avoid this mess was cost-prohibitive, what with an extra day's stay in Darwin, which also meant an extra day off work that could potentially jeopardise the players' jobs. NT football boss Tony Frawley even made overtures to Qantas on behalf of the Redtails to tweak its scheduling, but the airline wouldn't budge. A little country footy club making its trial games on time was of little concern to the big redtail, its shareholders, and a chief executive scrutinising the bottom line.

Even if the Redtails' Saturday games were later and thus more favourable with the new flight schedule, the return leg presented another set of challenges. Qantas's Darwin departure times (and Alice Springs arrival times) on Sundays had left some of the players close to exhaustion. Some from Tennant Creek, more than 500 kilometres north of Alice Springs, and nearby communities, faced several more hours of travel on the road. They were often getting home late on Sunday afternoons. Then they needed to be at work early the next day. Then back in Alice Springs later that week for training. Then ready for the Saturday flights. *Eat. Sleep. Rinse. Repeat.* Some players were reluctant to complain. Some didn't complain at all; they would just quietly decide to make themselves unavailable for selection.

Regular home games were the obvious solution for alleviating the demanding schedule and high player turnover, but factors outside the club's control prevented that from happening. The accumulation of these obstacles was perhaps a sign of things to come.

ROADTRIP FOR REDTAILS

Tony Frawley hit the road in November 2013 as part of a meet-and-greet of the game's major stakeholders, including a series of community consultations in Katherine, Tennant Creek and Alice Springs. Alongside Frawley on this trip were football greats Michael Long and Ted Liddy, as well as members of the AFLNT Executive.

Part of the itinerary in Alice Springs was a meeting with the Redtails camp. This was scheduled for Friday 8 November, the day before the Central Australian team's round 6 game against Southern Districts in Darwin.

Frawley related what he and the Executives wanted from the meeting; answers to lingering questions the Board may have had; grievances, real or imagined, and most likely both, could finally be laid out on the table. Footy's bossman Frawley wanted an update on the Redtails' progress and future plans. Again, while impressed with the work the club was doing in the region, the Board wanted to know more. Frawley said:

> *The Tails have done an excellent job travelling to Darwin each weekend and fielding a reasonably competitive team. We are meeting with the club reps to discuss the club's long term plans and to outline the set of minimum entry requirements AFLNT has devised. The Redtails bring a lot to the town of Alice and to the competition itself but long term viability is critical so we will work with the club to map out a realistic and achievable framework for full inclusion into the TIO NTFL.*[11]

Nothing much was made public from these meetings, so we can only speculate that Darwin had found its answers.

A FALSE DESERT DAWN

There are around 20 different languages spoken in Central Australia but the lingua franca in football-business is English.[12] Even so, translators were sorely needed to understand what was going on with the Redtails if one was to read the English-only press because there were several stories circulating about the team's future that were, simply, incorrect.

A handful of reports and a red-letter 'exclusive' appeared in local media in late 2013 led readers to believe the Redtails inclusion in the NTFL the following season was imminent — that Darwin had hand-delivered a Premier League licence to Rob Clarke himself.

> *AFLNT has given Central Australia [sic] Football Club the green light for full-time participation in the 2014–15 Northern Territory Football League season.*[13]

This was the lead paragraph of a report in the *NT News'* sports section on 20 December 2013. Later that day, just after lunch, local ABC picked up the story and proclaimed:

> *The Central Australian Redtails have won approval to play a full season in the Northern Territory Football League next year.*[14]

But none of any of this was remotely close to being true. It is unclear how the ABC and *NT News* came to these twin conclusions. What *was* true was that before the Redtails could even come close to gaining permanent entry into the NTFL, they first had to solve the issue of regular and unfettered access to Traeger Park or secure another venue of a similar standard in Alice Springs. The club also had to show that it had raised, or could raise, the several hundred thousand dollars it needed to get off the ground. The deadline to do so was April 2014.

ROLL UP! ROLL UP!

AS 2013 ticked over into 2014, St Mary's completed a remarkable season. The powerhouse club played out an undefeated season to win the 2013–14 Premier League premiership, and back-to-back flags after defeating Wanderers by 21 points on 15 March.

Rob Clarke and the Redtails football committee weren't privy to much of what the Executives in Darwin were thinking at the time — on the team's permanent inclusion, on Traeger Park, or both. Still, Clarke still wanted to keep supporters in the loop. Eleven days after the 2013–14 NTFL grand final, on 26 March 2014, clearly frustrated with the situation and in rather forthright terms, he wrote:

> *At this stage, we still have not got a home ground, basically due to some people with no ability to see the big picture. In this whole journey, apart from our members, sponsors, supporters and coaching staff, the Redtails / Right Tracks have had more brick walls put up than doors open. It is very disappointing that people who have the power to back such*

> *a worthy positive program choose to brand it in a negative light. The Redtails are not out to take over other sports; we are willing to help other sports and have done so many times [but] the [various sports'] governing bodies [are] choosing to ignore this fact. We believe doing the right thing, every time all the time, is the only option. We will not give up. The Redtails has achieved so much on and off the field through employment, support, friendship and strong values bringing so many different people from all around our great part of Australia together. I don't know what you all think but we believe there is not much or many things more important.*[1]

Seventeen days later, Clarke, still in the dark, outlined to members and supporters the club's pitch to the AFLNT and to the government. This included the Department of the Prime Minister and Cabinet office (PM&C), and the Chief Minister of the Northern Territory Adam Giles. The Centralians were seeking surety of funding for the 2014–15 season and beyond.

> *The reason for this post is to explain to all of our supporters the reason why there has been no real information, publicly, on what position we find ourselves in. We have presented [to AFLNT] a position statement, [a] letter of support from the office of the Prime Minister of Australia, and other documents to Bess Price, the [NT] community services minister, who we understand has sent a letter of support for our program to the Chief Minister Adam Giles and sports minister Matt Conlan.*[2]

In the same note, Clarke also shared what he felt was a lack of cooperation from Traeger Park's co-tenants, the Alice Springs Cricket Association, alluding that the venue was off-limits to the footballers.

We have been held up in the use of a home ground and have been desperately trying all options, including holding home games in Tennant Creek, as it appears that Traeger Park is a no-go zone for the Redtails. What we can promise everyone is we will not give up. This is an important project for the Red Centre; the good that this program has achieved already, especially bringing people together in our community. Although there are many other important outcomes already provided from the Redtails / Right Tracks concept, this alone surely is worth the support.[3]

'NEVER THE TWAIN SHALL MEET'

It has long been understood that in Alice Springs, football is for the winter, cricket is for the summer, and ne'er the twain shall meet. But the Central Australian Football Club's desire to play in the Top End summertime NTFL turned that notion on its head. A summertime football club wasn't something any of the sports bodies in Alice Springs had reason to think about, because it was never a thing, until now. Even without the exceptional circumstances that brought the English cricket team to Alice Springs, the club's requests for regular access to Traeger Park had become a sticking point.

Local cricket's 13 separate divisions across five grades play at around seven venues across town from October through to February, with Traeger Park the primary host for A-grade and B-grade fixtures. The other venues the local cricket association also play at include Albrecht Oval, Flynn Reserve, Jim McConville Oval, Paul Fitzsimons Oval, Rhonda Diano Oval and Ross Park. Handing the keys to Traeger Park to the footballers during the summer months was a big ask. But it wasn't as though cricket didn't have options, or that locals were flocking to the gate in big numbers. Cricket may well be this country's national sport but in country towns more people play it than watch it.

In Alice Springs, the turnstiles click for footy. But still. A lack of suitable alternatives pushed the Redtails into a corner. Without the town council or the Alice Springs Cricket Association (ASCA) on board, Traeger Park was simply off the table. Mention of Traeger Park was conspicuously absent in the Redtails' formal pitch to AFLNT. Without Traeger Park, a key plank in the club's submission was missing. There really was nowhere else for the club to go.

Despite Clarke's assertion in his 12 April note to members, Tennant Creek was never a realistic option. The Northern Territory's seventh largest town is 500 kilometres north from Alice Springs, 675 kilometres south from Katherine, and not serviced by Qantas that has aircraft capable of carrying two football teams and support staff. If the Darwin clubs were reluctant to jump on direct flights to Alice Springs to play football, imagine the scenes if games were scheduled for Tennant Creek.[4]

Even if the Redtails were granted full and unfettered access to Traeger Park, it would have the deleterious effect of removing the venue from ever hosting Sheffield Shield, Big Bash and/or international cricket-tour matches because the football season would literally never end. Not that the Northern Territory is ever on Cricket Australia's radar, but the venue would forever be off the table as an option for first-class cricket.

The pressure on the Redtails, and Rob Clarke, was clearly growing. Turning closer to home, Clarke alluded to pressures also facing the Territory Government, the same government that held the purse-strings.

> *The NT Government have been extremely busy with the Blain by-election and other obvious issues of late. We were instructed that once this was out of the way a decision on support for the Redtails / Right Tracks program should not be far away. This is fantastic timing as we need in writing to AFLNT proof of financial support, and the use of a home ground, by 21 April 2014.* [5]

The Blain by-election and the 'other obvious issues of late' were the fun part of the rolling circus that was the ruling Country Liberal Party. The entire situation was a doozy.

POLITICAL SHENANIGANS

In early 2013, the then Chief Minister of the Northern Territory, Country Liberal Party MLA Terry Mills, was on a trade mission in Japan spruiking the Territory's resources sector. In Mills's absence, Deputy Chief Minister Adam Giles was elevated to the role of Acting Chief Minister.[6]

The office of Chief Minister and CLP leadership was an ambition Giles had harboured soon after entering NT politics in 2008. Giles, the Member for Braitling, an electorate in Alice Springs, now had a unique opportunity. With the backing of CLP heavyweight Dave Tollner, Giles secured the numbers from a party-room ballot and got his wish. Mills was formally deposed on 13 March 2013 and a day later Adam Graham Giles was sworn in as the 10th Chief Minister of the Northern Territory, and new leader of the CLP — also the first Aboriginal man to hold the twin appointments.[7]

Political acts such as this are nothing new to the Northern Territory. While shopping the Territory's wares in the Land of the Rising Sun, Terry Mills experienced his darkest hour, summarily dethroned in absentia in full view of all. The act split the party down factional lines and Mills resigned which had the effect of leaving vacant the seat of Blain he had held since 1999. That triggered a by-election, and left the party to install an untested candidate, all the while an incredulous electorate was left wondering what the hell was going on.[8] The Country Liberals retained the seat in the subsequent by-election by a narrow margin on a two-party-preferred basis but suffered a 10 per cent swing against at the booths.[9] Football was, understandably, not high on the ruling CLP's list of priorities. Still, promises were made.

An option open to the Redtails would be to hit up the federal treasurer's offices in Canberra. AFLNT had earlier dipped into the bickie tin at AFL House in Melbourne for NT Thunder, whose model on Indigenous engagement aligned with the Redtails, but this would present as a financially untenable duplication of services.

In 2022, Frawley noted that:

> *The AFL had already given us money for NT Thunder and going back to the trough a second time was always going to be difficult. [Federal] Government funding would have been the way; theirs [the Redtails'] was more than just a football program, and in a lot of ways that was the most important part of it all.*[10]

HOPE AGAINST HOPE

In his second correspondence to members in April 2014, Clarke revealed the club had asked for an extension for its submission. At stake also was a guaranteed six-figure sum from the CLP government should the Redtails enter the Premier League for the 2014–15 season.

> *Redtails supporters, the response to the AFLNT's demands have just been sent to the CEO and AFLNT board of directors; we will find out tomorrow if the Redtails will be allowed more time to secure a home ground and the required funding. A power of effort has been used to get this far; let's all hope the people that make the decisions take all [that] into consideration. The good we have achieved together must not stop so no matter what decision is made around the table tomorrow we can guarantee you all that we will never give up.*[11]

The request was later denied.

THESE NUMBERS DON'T RUN

All good things must come to an end.

ADAPTED FROM GEOFFREY CHAUCER (1342/1343–1400)

FOR the Redtails, the end of the football on the field meant it was time for a look at the books, an examination of which would determine the fate of the Central Australian Football Club.

Ross Coburn was in the position of Chair at AFLNT in 2012 and had sat on the Board since 2001.[1] His experience in business and people management, board governance and corporate structure design spans decades. He is a man familiar with the numbers game. As Chair and a Director at AFLNT, Coburn's brief was to be across matters relating to the maintenance and operational stability of the 10 Territory-wide football competitions, including the jewel in its crown, the Premier League division of the NTFL. He was the go-to man at Darwin Football HQ. The question of NTFL expansion, therefore the question of the Central Australian Football Club, was of particular interest to Coburn.

Coburn watched the development of the CAFC from afar. He bore witness to the club's games in Darwin, noted its operations, and remained largely neutral in its affairs, until called upon to give his professional opinion. That time had arrived. Coburn was tasked with going over the Redtails' sales pitch with a ruler, a calculator and a sharp eye early in 2014. The expectation of what he would receive, however, did not match the reality.

The ideology that was driving the Centralian revolution, the club's manifesto, the 'dossier' behind it all was laid bare — and there it was, on a couple of A4 pages, two single-sided printouts. Coburn was not impressed at the time, recalling later:

> *What we saw from the Redtails was rubbery and thrown together. There were a couple of pages, maybe two or three, and that was it; it didn't have any depth to it. We had to push a bit harder in the show-cause. There needed to be a sustainable commitment, something that really drives it. We were nervous about ongoing budgetary funding. A whole season would cost something upwards of $700,000 a year.*[2]

Coburn explained his job was to protect the NTFL *and* the Redtails. In this instance, the Redtails' submission simply did not have enough details, particularly on the financial side of things. All Coburn and the AFLNT could do was ask for more details and make a decision on what the Redtails had presented. 'The Redtails' budgeting wasn't quite there,' he said. 'It just wasn't professionally done, in my opinion. In the end we had to say, *No, it's too hard*.'

Coburn relayed the information to his Chief Executive, Tony Frawely. Word soon reached Rob Clarke, who sought clarification on what was missing from his submission. Clarke said he doesn't care to remember a lot of what he and Tony Frawley spoke about in that conversation, just the main part. 'He [Frawley] goes, *Well it does look amazing… but we're not going to give you a licence; we just don't think it's viable*. And that was that,' Clarke said.

And that, apparently, was that.

According to Coburn the Redtails failed to meet specific criteria critical to a favourable outcome. These included a minimum three-year funding commitment, amounting to around $2.1 million. And security on a home ground, without which AFLNT could not see the venture as a sustainable proposition.

On 23 April 2014, AFLNT made it official with a media release quoting Tony Frawley:

> *As a number of key entry criteria have not been met by the Redtails, the AFLNT Board has not granted a licence for the club to compete in the TIO NTFL Premier League season 2014/15.*
>
> *"The Redtails, despite their best efforts, have not been able to source a home ground for games in Alice Springs, which is the main obstacle for entry into the league as home town support is critical for the concept. The club has also done exceptionally well with its fundraising efforts but have been unable to secure three-year funding commitments which presents a sustainability issue, so the AFLNT Board have not granted the club a licence to compete in the TIO NTFL Premier League next season."*[3]

Later that same day, Frawley spoke to ABC Darwin to explain it all in a bite-sized chunk.

> *There is no AFL approved home ground in Alice Springs for them [the Redtails] to play and the other reason was probably long-term financial viability... We think it's a worthy concept and everyone agrees with that but they were just a long way off our conditions to get them an entry into the competition.*[4]

Clarke told the media of his disappointment but, as ever, remained optimistic.

> *We'll wait for the written response to ourselves and then we'll have a committee meeting in regard to an action plan to move this forward.*
>
> *I just think the community requires this program to be successful, so we're certainly not going to give up.*
>
> *[The AFLNT have] got other agendas that they need to organise and do but you know if you were serious about letting us in or looking at us or letting it proceed, there would have been more direction and a more unified front I suggest when talking to government and councils.*[5]

The dream, the big dream, was all but over. Clarke broke the news to the club's supporters.

> *Disappointingly, as you may or may not have heard, the AFLNT decided not to grant us an extension of time to gain the extra funding and the home ground we require in Alice Springs. This was not surprising to us as AFLNT have given minimal help to this point. To clear up one issue, the Alice Springs Cricket Association — not the cricket clubs — would not entertain the idea of allowing the Redtails to use Traeger Park [up to] eight times during the summer months. It was always our intention to work with cricket so all [cricket] teams could still play on weekends, which is possible to achieve. We also wanted to support cricket in other ways as we have done over the past 12 months. I just felt the admin of cricket wasn't very respectful of other sports, but we respected their decision, we just didn't want to cause any dramas.*[6]

There was more bad news. NT sports minister Matt Conlan, from Alice Springs, was fighting for his political life. He was embroiled in a scandal relating to the ill-fated trade mission to Japan with Terry Mills.[7] In the NT parliament, Conlan was reported to have sworn at Alison Anderson, the Aboriginal and then-powerful MLA, allegedly also using a term considered utterly offensive toward women more broadly.[8]

At an Estimates Committee hearing in June, Labor member for Johnston, Ken Vowles, asked Conlan what funding — if any — would be allocated for the Redtails in the current budget.

> *The only funding that was to be provided – in fact, it probably will not be now – is $100,000 to the Redtails, if they were successful in being granted a licence into the NTFL. So, the answer is no, not at this stage.*[9]

Less than a year later, Conlan resigned from politics.[10] The man, a local ally for the Redtails in Darwin, was now out of the picture.

Clarke wrote to club members outlining in more detail the reasons the bid was ultimately rejected. He remained hopeful.

> *Unfortunately, the Redtails were unable to fulfil the requirements of AFLNT and have consequently failed to secure full-time entry into the 2014–15 NTFL Premier League competition. After ongoing discussions with the Alice Springs Town Council, the club was unable to secure an oval in Alice Springs to hold eight home games. Furthermore, the Central Australian Football Club was also unsuccessful in acquiring the necessary funding to support the side for three years in the NTFL. Looking to the future, the CAFC will continue to strive towards securing a place in the NTFL competition on a full-time basis and is hopeful of eventually achieving this outcome. A meeting was held between the CAFC committee and staff from AFLNT on 28 May in order to determine what steps need to be taken in the near future for the club to become viable.*[11]

In the final wash-up, inaction on the part of successive Territory governments to provide vital sporting infrastructure to a growing population had come home to roost. It left the Redtails, the Committee, the players, Alice Springs, the Central Australian and desert football communities frozen out of the tropical Top End. Clarke was deflated. He said:

> *I was pretty gutted. We put in so much work into it to get to where we had gotten to. We told ourselves,* Let's see if we can do this, *but we got left to do everything ourselves. We always presented well over the journey. There was plenty of local excitement, we drew good crowds.*[12]

By accident or design, the decision to deny the Redtails a Premier League licence barely rated a mention in AFLNT's 2014 Annual Report, save for a brief outline of the Board's rejection of the club's bid, complete with a tactless MS Paint thumbs-down emoji. A final insult to injury — a small paragraph, and a Millennial meme.[13]

IRRARNTE

Irrarnte — the red-tailed black cockatoo. Generally, the irrarnte fly in small flocks and, if they're feeling sociable, sometimes alongside other types of cockatoos. If there's a food source nearby, they will congregate around it in big numbers, sometimes up to 500. Their presence in the skies acts like an early warning system of incoming rain, which they seem so desperate to avoid, despite the life-giving sustenance it provides in the harsh desert environment. The irrarnte is not a wholly migratory bird, they can be selective in their movements, depending on the season and a reliable food source. They prefer to live in open country but have been found in subtropical rainforests.[14]

If football's Irrarnte — the Redtails — could draw on anything remotely positive from the native animal they adopted as a mascot, it was research from the Swiss-based International Union for Conservation of Nature (IUCN), which found that the Australian red-tailed black cockatoo was of 'least concern' in terms of endangerment. That is, they are plentiful in number and not in danger of disappearing anytime soon.[15]

FINGERS POINTING IN ALL DIRECTIONS

WITHIN the space of three years, a small football club from Central Australia achieved something large. In 2011, the freshly minted Redtails set out to harness the power of football for the town of Alice Springs and its people. In the period from 2011 to 2014, the Central Australian Football Club tasked Darwin with a self-examination it was initially unprepared for. The team stared down powerful opponents on the field. They were uncompromising in how they played the game. And the club behind the team worked hard to legitimise the Redtails in Darwin. They never wavered in their resolve to take this club from the desert into the city.

On the field, several Redtails players succeeded in launching semi-professional football careers in Darwin. The trial games provided those players with valuable experience and the confidence to kick on in the Premier League. This included Caleb Hart, who became a key defender at the Nightcliff Football Club; Abe Ankers, who won a senior premiership with Waratah; and Daniel Stafford, whose presence as a powerhouse forward at Darwin Buffaloes has been invaluable in that club's on-field revival.[1 2 3]

When the big moment arrived, however, when it was time to deliver on what they had been saying for nearly three years, the CAFC was found lacking. Everything fell apart at the finish line. This was a devastating blow.

DARWIN'S APPREHENSION

Darwin's rejection of the Redtails would suggest there were serious reservations about the CAFC's grand plan. The unannounced survey early in 2013, and Tony Frawley's guarded public statements throughout much of that year, pointed toward a growing unease of the Redtails' ambitions toward the Top End. It wasn't so much what the club wanted to do, but how they planned on doing it.

Darwin could only work with what was in front of them, and what Ross Coburn saw was not sound. The concept was sound, that wasn't in doubt — as was (and is) the idea of Alice Springs one day in the NTFL — but when the Redtails wanted-in early in 2014 there were key criteria the club could not meet.

The Redtails may have overestimated their readiness for the big time. The consensus from afar was that the people at the club were more 'football people' than they were 'football business' people. A club needs both and in equal measure. The football people at the Redtails had the club's best interests at heart. Money was coming out of their own pockets. They wouldn't tell you, but it was apparent. That level of selflessness is commendable. Football people have the game, the team colours and Dencorub coursing through their veins; the sort who can be counted on when something, anything, needs to be done for the team, for the game, for the boys. Half-time oranges? Check. Ice-cold water? Check. Player regos? Check. It is those people who can be counted on to go above and beyond for a football club. On the flipside, football business people can call on their business acumen sharpened by years in the corporate world, and armed perhaps with a level of calculated thinking the fictional Mentats in Frank Herbert's iconic *Dune* novels would find impressive.

Pitching a multi-layered, multi-faceted concept from 1500 kilometres away to hard-nosed football business people needed to be precise in its execution. *This* was where the Redtails fell down.

If there was anything else to learn from the Redtails' unsuccessful attempt, then perhaps a football analogy is most appropriate. To play football you need an understanding and an appreciation of the rules. To play the game well, you need a sound gameplan and a decent set of skills to execute on that gameplan. Guided by those rules, and with a solid gameplan and skillset, you might win, you also might lose. Whatever the result, you will never be left to wonder what could have been because you came well-equipped to play the game.

Just like footy on the field, boardroom games must be executed to watertight business plans and are measured against high-stakes financial targets. Business likes to leverage visions, dreams and good-news stories — which is what the Redtails presented — where that can strengthen a brand-narrative to attract fans, sell tickets, and increase profit margins. This is the game of football business, and this game also has winners and losers.

Ross Coburn summed it up when reflecting on the Redtails nearly 10 years later, when he said:

> *The Redtails without Rob Clarke wouldn't exist [but] he needed a lot of help. Even though he could be difficult — and we never saw eye-to-eye with everything — what he was doing made sense. Everyone loved the concept, but from an AFLNT perspective, we were mindful of another Katherine scenario; they were in the league before but lasted only a few seasons and that stuck with us. We'd seen the [Redtails] model and saw it work. It was getting young men out from the woodwork who were wanting to play. If Rob didn't get what he wanted for the Redtails then he'd attack it himself, which didn't make it easy for us; we weren't seen as one*

> *unit. We went around Alice Springs to get money, and they'd say, 'Oh, I had Rob Clarke in here the other day talking about this', or they'd tell him, 'Oh, AFLNT were in here the other day talking about this'. That partnership needed to be stronger. I had a few stand-up blues with Rob about that. You can't question his passion [but] we're administering leagues here, and we're dealing with clubs whose main aim is to win grand finals; our aim is to keep clubs in the game. I would have loved for the Redtails to be in the Premier League but it takes a really strong commitment. The Tiwi Bombers are almost failing every year and they haven't got a Rob Clarke. AFLNT have had to work really hard with the Tiwis. We engaged with the other [NTFL] clubs [on the Redtails' permanent inclusion] but at the end of the day it was an AFLNT decision.*[4]

Right or wrong, the Redtails poured all their passion and resources into one part of the game and that came at the ultimate expense of their vision.

Perhaps the club was better served by employing dedicated and skill-specific personnel from the get-go. And tasking them with drafting and executing a strategy, and delivering its pitch to stakeholders and to Darwin. It would have also identified critical risks, specifically the need to secure a home base and address logistical challenges around travel, so tactics could be employed to tackle those risks. With all this in place, the Redtails might have had a greater chance of securing support from Darwin and playing the big game, rather than the game playing them. It would have also freed up time for the football people at the club to focus more on the things they did best.

CREDENCE

CENTRAL Australians have been few and far between in the AFL since the Redtails' formation, reflecting also a steady decline of Aboriginal footballers in the big league in recent years.[1] These facts provide credence to the central tenet that Rob Clarke and Ian McAdam had with the Central Australian Football Club.

Had the football side of the Redtails program achieved its ultimate goal in Darwin, it had the potential to become, if you will, a Central Australian pipeline of talented footballers from the region directly into the AFL. The CAFC was constructing a sound football program that had buy-in from the Alice Springs community and the region's footballers. It was building a window to the world that the AFL and the organisation's talent scouts could come to and see for themselves the multitudinous talent in this part of the country.

Instead, all that remains in the record books is a handful of exceptional talent reaching the big time by exceptional means.[2]

Alice Springs's Ricky Mentha Jnr's path to AFL club Melbourne via the draft in November 2024 perfectly illustrated this point. Ricky's recruitment into the AFL replicated the experience of Central Australian trio Jake Neade, Dom Barry and Curtly Hampton more than 10 years earlier. Like Jake and Dom, Ricky left Central Australia for a town in country Victoria as a teenager (Curtly left home for Adelaide). It was from a chance encounter in Ricky's new town with a new mate that he was invited to play local football. He was later talent-spotted, and from there found a way to the Melbourne Football Club.

Top End Northern Territorian and two-time Indigenous All-Star Matthew Whelan played 150 games for Melbourne from 2000 to 2009. He returned to the club as its Indigenous welfare development manager. Of Ricky Mentha's drafting by the Demons, he said:

> *We were doing the maths and we think Dom Barry or Curtly Hampton was the last player recruited from Alice Springs and that was around 2013, so it has been a while. The talent is obviously there but it is just getting it out of there and the adaption from Alice Springs life to the big city anywhere in Australia. It is certainly exciting for us to finally get someone out of Alice Springs.*[3]

TOUCHING THE SUN

THE heavy cloud hovering like a billowy blanket couldn't hold on to its copious stockpile much longer. An hour past the midday sun, the thundercloud cluster over Marrara Oval finally dumped its payload. It was 10mm, but felt like much more, such was the soaking of the wet-season downpour on this sweaty afternoon in tropical Darwin.

It was 23 January 2021. A Saturday. Out on the field was the Central Australian Football Club, kicking a football in controlled anger in a game that had a measure of meaning. Watching on from the sidelines that day were Rob Clarke, Ian McAdam and Shaun Cusack. The band was back.

The Redtails' return appearance at the Darwin venue marked seven years and two months to the day since the team last played there. But this game wasn't a contest for vital Premier League premiership points, or for a historic finals berth, nor was it another hopeful trial series. Those hopes, those dreams, those aspirations were long gone, lost to the winds of time. This occasion was a one-off representative match against the might of the Big Rivers Football League from Katherine. The CAFC–BRFL representative match was one of three played at Marrara Oval that day. The others were senior men and senior women NTFL sides playing against their counterparts from the Glenelg Football Club from the SANFL. For the record, the Redtails defeated Big Rivers 12.18 (90) to 5.10 (40).

In the Redtails team that day, only Luke Adams and Matt Campbell remained from the side that played in the final Premier League trial match at the same venue on 23 November 2013.

Also in this Redtails team were Gareth Remfrey and Daniel Stafford who, with Luke Adams, were the only players left from the club's historic first game against St Mary's in Alice Springs on 6 October 2012, while Rob Clarke and Ian McAdam, Shaun Cusack (coach) and Alecia Clarke (team manager) remained from the game-day staff.

The invitation to play at Marrara in 2021 was a welcome one, but it came with mixed emotions. The team and the dream that materialised from the Central Desert played at the Top End venue on five occasions during their 12-game trial period from October 2012 to November 2013. Seven years on, the frustrations from the long-drawn-out saga of the Redtails' bid for a Premier League licence had not faded. However, the on-field exploits of the football team made it clear they hadn't been idle in those intervening years.

A 180° PIVOT

The decision to exclude the Redtails from Darwin may have put an end to the Centralians' northern aspirations but it in no way meant the end of the club itself.

In the years following that decision in early 2014, the Alice Springs-based club has become a repurposed outfit. The Redtails did a 180 to pivot southward. They headed to the southern states and found a new purpose. The club has established ties with several SANFL clubs in Adelaide and play pre-season pick-up games in country Victoria. They even played a game overseas — of all places — in Aotearoa-New Zealand.

The CAFC's operations have also expanded to include a junior boys' team, senior women's and junior girls' teams — the Pinktails — and a team called Country Redtails, drawing players into rep footy from remote communities.

The program also has a new name: Redtails Pinktails Right Tracks Program.[1]

These days, this growing band of footballers and journeymen have played in regional representative matches and pre-season games around the country. As Redtails graduates, several individuals have played in a growing score of competitions and clubs in the NTFL and NTFL Women's Premier League, the SANFL and SANFLW, the NT Thunder youth academy programs, at various clubs in Victoria, and at select national under-age events.

In May of 2018, the senior men's Redtails team played in front of an adoring home crowd at Traeger Park against a composite side of their Top End countrymen in a team called the Storm. The occasion that day was a curtain-raiser to an AFL premiership match in front of almost 7000 people that was televised live across the country.[2]

EVERY STEP OF THE WAY

Alecia Clarke was there from the very beginning when her husband Rob Clarke and his good mate Ian McAdam began this Redtails journey. She shared in all the great moments, all the disappointments, all the meetings, all the minutiae, all the emails, all the bills and the cheques and the promises never kept, and all the footy gear that somehow became her new duty to wash each Sunday morning. She remembers it all too well.

> *The one thing I enjoyed being part of the most was seeing the Indigenous and non-Indigenous lads coming together and going away as a team — the camaraderie, the unity, the respect, the genuine care for each other; forgetting all that sideline noise back home. And with all of that, going out on the field, as a team, they became this powerhouse.*[3]

For the first game against St Mary's at Traeger Park, Alecia was altogether occupied sorting the players' gear in the change rooms and at the merchandise stall, so she missed much of the lead-up. Once those duties were done, she could focus a bit more on the game. Of the four-point win over St Mary's, one of the great club football teams in the Northern Territory, Alecia said:

> *It was just euphoric. They were out there playing their hearts out. It came from this pride in where they come from, who they are, saying to everyone,* This is us; we are from Central Australia! *It was this belief in themselves.*

While reflecting on the Redtails' second trial period, Alecia recalled a time that was not great.

> *That whole thing was a huge slog; it was just manic! So [around the same time] Rob had the Adventure Tours' fleet of vehicles to work on and when he and [our son] Daniel and [Redtails midfielder] Luke Adams, who were apprentices, clocked-off, we needed to have the players' gear packed and ready to take to Traeger Park from where we'd get everyone and go to the airport from there. Then if you had some people having to pull out at the last minute, but with the flights already booked, it wasn't easy to change a booking, and the airline didn't give a shit. Then we'd get to Darwin and sometimes we had about an hour — or even just a half-an-hour — to get ready for our games; even then no-one at the NTFL or AFLNT had ice-blocks ready or rehydrated drinks for us. It was like no-one up there wanted us to succeed — all that stuff people don't know or didn't see. That whole eight trial games was just a whirlwind.*

The disappointment and despair from Darwin's rejection was not a feeling shared by all in the Clarke household. Alecia recalled:

> *I was quite relieved, actually. I think I said* Thank god! *The feeling I got was that they didn't want us there and so it just seemed stupid to try and pursue it. If it wasn't an enjoyable experience, why go back and do it again? I didn't see it happening. I just didn't enjoy that whole experience. It was draining on everybody.*

The pivot south and the continued success of the Redtails-(and now)-Pinktails program proved to Alecia Clarke that it was the right move.

> *When we thought where else we could go, we thought SA could be a better option. There is more respect for us down there; they are happy to have us. It was a different feel to Darwin where it seemed no-one really wanted us.*

As crucial as the support roles were at the Redtails, and there were many, to be sure, it was also abundantly clear that without Rob Clarke or Ian McAdam — rather, without Rob Clarke *and* Ian McAdam — there would be no Redtails.

> *None of this could be done if you didn't have the heart for it. Or the devotion and care for it, for each of those players, that Ian and Rob had. (Alecia Clarke)*[4]

REFLECTIONS

Taking his mind back to events of over a decade ago, Rob Clarke is happy with where the club is at today.

> *Just because AFLNT said no, it doesn't mean we can't still exist. Ideally, yes, it would have been good to be an NTFL club but what this has become is more cost-effective. We're seeing excellent social outcomes. I'm comfortable with where it is and in what we've always wanted to achieve.*

> *We're not out there wanting to win premierships so now there's more options to engage in more diverse sports, more social outcomes, keeping kids out of jail and off welfare.*[5]

Co-founder Ian McAdam shared his fellow traveller's thoughts.

> *I'm calling it a blessing in disguise, not allowing us in [to the NTFL]. We've got a good relationship with SA. When we go there, we get that sense of excitement; going north [to Darwin] just felt like we were a hindrance, that's what I felt, but in SA our players get treated like rockstars.*[6]

First-season coach Shaun Cusack saw it also as a lost opportunity.

> *I think it was a bit sad. It is a fantastic concept; it had buy-in from the local community and from the players. It would've been great to have an opportunity to play a full season. If the opportunity was ever to come around again, I think it's a no-brainer. We play in the winter and so for footy people here it is something to do in the off-season. There is plenty of local interest in the NTFL.*[7]

Second-season coach Greg McAdam saw firsthand the good the program had done.

> *From the very beginning of conception, the theory, the philosophy around it was absolutely fantastic.*[8]

Paul Ah Chee, Redtails Committee member, remained unimpressed with what he saw from Darwin, but understood the challenges.

> *It was a difficult time. We were flying up and getting ready an hour before the game. We didn't have good facilities. I just don't think the AFLNT were that committed to the Redtails.*

We didn't fit their masterplan. We could see the writing on the wall. Rob Clarke and Ian McAdam had their eyes wide open and ears close to the ground, so they began to look elsewhere. I think [AFLNT] were caught between a rock and a hard place in having a team from Alice Springs. It's a real challenge to have a team from Central Australia. [The NTFL] is really a Darwin comp; let's face it, that's how it is. But look, I wouldn't change a thing. It built character, that part of the journey for the Redtails. No-one gave us a silver-spoon, we had to work for all of it.[9]

In some quarters, there were rumblings that the Central Australian Football Club and by extension the Redtails Right Tracks program had become a sort of fiefdom for those involved. Ah Chee rejects this notion.

There was no empire-building going on, that's for sure. The pathways for young Aboriginal men who would fall through the cracks, this was for them.

Anthony Venes remained a fan of the Redtails concept. He said if the club had become part of the Premier League in Darwin in 2014 that maybe things today would be quite different.

If there was a Redtails program playing in the NTFL now, Alice [Springs] may not be in the papers for all the wrong reasons. The Redtails program was a good program. Like the Tiwi Bombers, it provided strong social outcomes, which in my view is important for any sporting club.[10]

Ross Coburn said he would like to see the Redtails make another attempt at joining Darwin.

Now that it got itself to where it is, I'd have another crack at it if I was at the AFLNT. You have a really passionate Central Australian in the [AFLNT] chair at the moment in Sean Bowden. I think he'd be very passionate about growing the game there. There is an opportunity to increase the NTFL [Premier League] by two more teams. Either Banks and PINTs[i], or Banks or PINTs or Tracy Village, and the Redtails. It will be good to have 10 sides.[11]

i PINT Football Club, a former TEAFA club, joined the NTFL Premier League ahead of the 2023–24 season; the Premier League as at 2025 is now a nine-team league.

WHAT IMPACT DID RIGHT TRACKS HAVE?

WHILE no longer in the business of chasing premierships, trophies and accolades in regular-season club football, the Redtails Right Tracks Program has maintained its core purpose of guiding young Aboriginal people into gainful employment or study, and physical wellbeing. This, it seems, is the program's true calling.

The work is showing no sign of slowing down.

The 2020–21 Annual Report of the Redtails Pinktails Right Tracks' parental and funding body Central Australian Aboriginal Congress revealed an expansion of the program into several communities, and into other sports.

For example, a softball program was in the early stages of planning for Papunya and Yuendumu. Also, working partnerships have continued with netball clubs in Alice Springs. And the new Country Redtails — an under-20s football team — made its debut in interstate football when they played a team from South Australia at Traeger Park. The country team drew players and coaches from Alparra, Haasts Bluff, Kintore, Ntaria,

Papunya, Plenty Highway, Ti-Tree, Willowra and Yuendumu. The report also wrote:

> *Over the past year the team undertook 20 health sessions with 356 participants of the clubs, covering tobacco, sexual health, domestic violence and alcohol and other drugs. They have assisted 15 participants into full-time employment. The cohort involved in this program have a higher health check rate than that of their comparison group, along with a lower smoking rate.*
>
> *Right Tracks Leadership sessions were delivered to 666 participants with 10 High Performance Leadership sessions conducted with 261 Participants which adds another element to High Performance. There were 47 referrals to Social and Emotional Wellbeing [services].*[1]

STRAIGHTENING PATHS

In 2013, Warlpiri-Anmatjerre man Kenny Morton from small-town Ti-Tree built on the sands of the Central Desert found himself surrounded by a large body of saltwater in the Gulf of Carpentaria.

Morton was at his job at GEMCO's manganese mine in Groote Eylandt, off the east coast of the Northern Territory. To get the job, Morton had to leave his home and the carpentry apprenticeship he was close to completing for the island-home of the Anindilyakwa people. In 2022, Morton had just reached his 10-year milestone at GEMCO's South32 site as a heavy-vehicle operator.

As a fresh-faced 20-year-old in 2007, Morton tied with Henry Labastida for the CAFL Minahan Medal. Morton played for Rovers Football Club that season and he and Labastida from West Football Club polled 13 votes to tie for the league's fairest-and-best medal, the first time this had happened since 1979.[2]

When his mate at Rovers, Rob Clarke, began all this Redtails talk in 2011, Morton was all ears. He played two games for the team in 2012 and three in 2013, wearing the number 24. For those games in 2013, he would travel over the seas from Groote Eylandt, past Arnhemland and into Darwin to join his teammates. Against Wanderers in the round 5 game at Gardens Oval, Morton was the Redtails' standout best-player.

As good as he was at football — and he was a pretty decent player who Clarke reckoned was AFL material — it was the Redtails ethos surrounding off-field personal development that drew Kenny Morton in. When the Redtails Right Tracks program was getting off the ground, Morton was more than happy to jump on board. Here was a program that had structure and meaning, that would welcome those whom society didn't know what to do with. Right Tracks straightened out the path for Kenny Morton — personal stability, meaningful employment, football with purpose. He has stayed true to that path ever since. Of the football program, and of life, he said this:

> *I heard from the guys, and I told myself: I want to be part of this, it's history in the making. The main thing is raising my kids and being a good father and husband; kids go to school, go to college and graduate, achieve their goals; whatever they want to be, they can be it.*[3]

KINGLY CARMODY

Arrernte man Tyson Mpetyane Carmody is a leader of men. He also was an early graduate of the Redtails program. In 2012, he was part of the Redtails' First 22 in that historic game against St Mary's at Traeger Park — 'reliable backman' was the descriptor given for his player bio. The solidly built defender held down his defensive post with aplomb. He was a key plank of the Redtails' back-six defensive structure that kept the formidable Saints at bay in that famous victory.

Carmody later founded Kings Narrative, a space that seeks to rebuild Aboriginal men into authors of their own cultural destinies; where they can 'step outside the negative discourses that prevent them from seeing their true worth.'[4] This work led Carmody toward an NT Australian of the Year nomination.

REGRETS? THERE'S BEEN A FEW

THE Tony Frawley football administration in the Northern Territory was perhaps the most progressive of them all, certainly of the modern era. The strategic overhaul and transformation of football in the NT under his watch from 2005 to 2015 set the game on an upward trajectory from which there has been substantive growth. While Frawley's grand vision of a 10 to 12 team senior men's Premier League may not have eventuated during his time, it is an aspiration that will one day be fulfilled. The feather in Frawley's cap was undoubtedly the Tiwi Bombers, but the arrow in his bow could have been the Central Australian Football Club. As with all things, timing is everything. He said:

> *The Redtails were a professional organisation, much more than the Tiwis were, and they welded together a smart outfit. I reckon this will happen in the future. The Redtails makes it an NT-wide competition. Everyone understands how footy is important to the NT on many levels; not just footy, but on the many levels in how it permeates throughout the*

communities. It is a magnificent vehicle for young Aboriginal fellas, and for women now. There is no doubt the Central Australians would be competitive in the competition.

There are more questions than could reasonably be answered in bringing the Territory's premier football league to the Red Centre on the back of a home-grown football club. It is a concept that needs dedicated attention and substantial buy-in from a myriad of stakeholders. The Redtails' emergence from the desert was a left-field submission that landed near the too-hard basket into which it ultimately fell. Frawley has his regrets:

To be quite honest, I mightn't have focused enough on the Redtails; I probably didn't give it that due process it deserved. That was nobody else's fault. There was a lot to do.

WHEN THOSE STARS ALIGN

THE Right Tracks Tjaiya Rratja Program Central Australian Football Club was a multi-layered response to a preventable tragedy that hit close to home for two big families and a lot of people in Alice Springs. An idea that had been swirling around Rob Clarke's head was given life when a young Arrernte man lost his. What began after a chance encounter during a Saturday afternoon ritual led to a four-year adventure that caught the attention of an entire region, its footballers, and admirers near and far.

The club's quest in seeking a Northern Territory Football League licence was as ambitious as it was far-sighted. But the club's foray into Top End football wasn't predicated upon a favourable win-loss ratio, percentage points, or even ladder positions.

The Redtails' inclusion in the Premier League would have begun the long-overdue process of decentralising the Northern Territory Football League — a somewhat contentious topic in the game's northern suburbs stronghold — or else it would forever remain, essentially, a Darwin football league. That in no way detracts from what is quality-grade football played in the most challenging conditions anywhere in the country. The summertime Premier League is in the unique position to offer something the other state leagues cannot. But this is best left to the game's custodians at Marrara, and in Melbourne.

If the goal was to reach a group of people historically disadvantaged and susceptible to societal prejudice, then the Redtails was ultimately a measured success. But to what extent should sport be responsible for addressing systemic disadvantage? Sport can pick up the pieces of policy failure and societal neglect, but it can only do so much. The football club presented a rare opportunity for young men to build a life as semi-professional athletes and structure in their lives at a time when they might otherwise have none.

While the original plan of Clarke and co. was to go beyond kicking footballs and winning games, doing those things took the Redtails' message far and wide. The Redtails may have failed in their bold plan to revolutionise Territory football this time, but the club's success can be measured in the delivery of its core purpose: to provide a vehicle for positive change for young Aboriginal men in the region.

***

Rob Clarke hasn't forgotten his young friend from Amoonguna whose life was cut short before it could properly begin. The passage of time can change many things: memories, conversations, purpose, people. Clarke hasn't let it change the purpose behind the Redtails. More than a decade later, and with some effort, he said:

> *The passing of Joshy... the passing of Joshy. That was the reason behind it all; that's what started all this.*[1]

The football that the Redtails exist in is a space not dissimilar to their feathered avatar, literally and figuratively. And like the irrarnte, these Redtails moved many miles with the seasons — first north, then south. They once followed the northern rains, leaving the blue skies of open country for the tempestuous tropical Top End in search of sporting fame, fortune and a place to call home. Their presence in those skies signified a purposeful shake-up of Northern Territory football and sporting hope for a region and its young men. Nowadays, they watch the patterns of the southern seasons and take flight that way when conditions permit.

The Redtails' northern revolution may have failed the first time, but that can't be the end of this story, not if the lessons of a decade ago have been learnt. The Top End game will indeed revisit regional expansion with a Premier League vacancy; of this there can be no doubt. Stagnation is the enemy of progress, even in football. So, when that time does come, the Redtails must be ready. And provided there is genuine goodwill between Darwin and Alice Springs, it would make perfect sense for the Central Australian Football Club to be granted that coveted position, to take its rightful place in one of football's true and final frontiers.

If not? So be it. Just let it be known that the Central Australian Football Club — the *Redtails* — did it first; it was the Redtails who first took flight toward the northern skies over and beyond the desert horizon. On that maiden voyage, all those years ago, the Redtails aimed for the sun, found what they were looking for, and left behind a hopeful legacy for others to follow.

EPILOGUE

IN August 2011, 10 months after Kumantye Palmer's untimely death, the Rovers and South Alice Springs football clubs instituted the in-season Josh Palmer Shield match in honour of their young mate, teammate, brother and Countryman. The clubs' ties to Kumantye are through family and football. South has historical ties to Amoonguna, where he is from — Amoonguna was South's original name. Kumantye Palmer was playing at Rovers in 2010 before he died in October of that year.

The shield, and the football match around it, honours his memory in a celebration of his life playing the game he loved. The shield game has been held each year since. In an article for the *Centralian Advocate*, Rob Clarke said:

> *It was one way we as a club could honour such a top young bloke... It was a great tribute with both sides coming together after the match... and the family really liked the day.*[1]

**IN ANNOUNCING THE 2020 MATCH,
AFL CENTRAL AUSTRALIA WROTE:**

The Josh Palmer Shield was started in Round 13 of 2011 to mark the memory of the Roos' fallen teammate who was tragically killed in October 2010.

The original shield game was organised by Rovers President, Rob Clarke, as a way to remember Josh. It has the endorsement of Josh's family.

The game has been a key fixture on the CAFL calendar each year.[2]

**UNDER THE AFLCA ENTRY,
FAMILY AND FRIENDS OF JOSHY PAID THEIR RESPECTS:**

'Always remembered in our hearts' (Roseanne Ellis)

'Always remember we never forget how long does it take cuz (rip)' (Noella Ross)

'Miss you my Lil bunji' (Lachlan Petrick)

'Your always in our hearts lil bro, miss you heaps'
(Jayskee Turner-Kenny)
'Always love an miss you my brother. Never forgotten'
(Laurel Palmer)
'Brother' (Fabian Willis)

After the first shield game, the post-match circular embrace by both teams was a heartwarming scene. It also was a stark reminder that beyond football, beyond sport, beyond all else, life's fragility is ever-present.

APPENDIX 1: SCOREBOARD 1.0

CENTRAL AUSTRALIAN FOOTBALL CLUB – 2012–13 NTFL PREMIER LEAGUE

ROUND 1

- Central Australia vs. St Mary's @ Traeger Park, Alice Springs
- Saturday, 6 October 2012
- Scores
    - Central Australia 13.10 (88) defeated St Mary's 12.12 (84)
    - Progressive scores — Q1: CAFC 4.2 (26) led SMFC 2.2 (14) Q2: SMFC 7.6 (48) led CAFC 6.4 (40) Q3: SMFC 11.10 (76) led CAFC 8.7 (55) Q4: CAFC 13.10 (88) def. SMFC 12.12 (84)
- Goalkickers
    - Central Australia: Daniel Stafford 4, Gareth Remfrey 2, Gibson Turner 2, Abe Ankers 1, G. Jack Miller 1, Charlie Maher 1, Thomas Gorey 1, Ryan Mallard 1.
    - St Mary's: Peter MacFarlane 3, Justin Wilson 2, Henry Labastida 2, Shannon Rioli 2, Leroy Larson 1, Mark McLean1, Karl Lohde 1.
- Best Players
    - Central Australia: Gareth Remfrey, Abe Ankers, Shane Dixon, Luke Adams, Daniel Stafford, Paul Campbell.
    - St Mary's: Justin Wilson, Kevin Tandogac, Karl Lohde, Henry Labastida, Shannon Rioli, Josh Heath.
- Teams
    - Central Australia: #2 Jasper Wheeler #3 Baydon Ngalkin #4 Charlie Maher #6 Abe Ankers #7 Bradley McMasters #8 Paul Campbell #9 Gareth Remfrey #10 Tyson Carmody #11 Jayden Prior #12 G. Jack Miller #13 Thomas Gorey #14 Jack Abrey #17 Ryan Mallard #20 Luke Adams #22 Swaine Hill #31 Darren Young #32 Shane

Dixon #36 Daniel Stafford #37 Bradley Turner #40 Reggie Smith #41 Gibson Turner #42 Caleb Hart. Coach: Shaun Cusack.

 - St Mary's: #1 Justin Wilson #2 Mark McLean #3 Michael Coombes #4 Iggy Vallejo #5 Henry Labastida #6 Leroy Larson #7 Aaron Pollard #9 Karl Lohde #10 Kevin Tandogac #12 Aidan Hill #13 Jack Musgrove #14 John Anstess #15 Jack Long #17 Luke Stapleton #20 Ryan Smith #21 Joshua Lidgerwood #22 Jackson Clark #25 Shannon Rioli #29 Peter MacFarlane #33 Daniel Hill #34 Jonathon Miles #42 Josh Heath. Coach: Jason Cotter.

ROUND 2

- Central Australia vs. Palmerston @ Cazalys Arena
- Saturday, 13 October 2012
- Scores
  - Central Australia 16.11 (107) defeated Palmerston 10.11 (71)
  - Progressive scores — Q1: CAFC 2.2 (14) led PMFC 1.3 (9) Q2: CAFC 9.4 (58) led PMFC 2.4 (16) Q3: CAFC 14.8 (92) led PMFC 9.7 (61) Q4: CAFC 16.11 (107) def. PMFC 10.11 (71)
- Goalkickers
  - Central Australia: Daniel Stafford 6, Thomas Gorey 3, Corey Taylor 2, Charlie Maher 1, Abe Ankers 1, Gareth Remfrey 1, Bradley Turner 1, Gibson Turner 1.
  - Palmerston: Matt Davies 4, Andrew Lovett 2, Sheldon Daye 2, Damien Medwin 1, Alex Johnson 1.
- Best Players
  - Central Australia: Gibson Turner, Jayden Prior, G. Jack Miller, Luke Adams, Daniel Stafford, Abe Ankers.
  - Palmerston: Billy Wells, Matt Davies, Pierce Liddle, Maslyn Braun, Damien Medwin.

- Teams
    - Central Australia: #1 Curtis Haines #3 Baydon Ngalkin #4 Charlie Maher #6 Abe Ankers #9 Gareth Remfrey #11 Jayden Prior #12 G. Jack Miller #13 Thomas Gorey #16 Matt Cunningham #18 Tom Clarke #20 Luke Adams #22 Swaine Hill #24 Kenny Morton #31 Darren Young #32 Shane Dixon #35 Corey Taylor #36 Daniel Stafford #37 Bradley Turner #41 Gibson Turner #42 Caleb Hart #43 Aaron Sharpe. Coach: Shaun Cusack.
    - Palmerston: (numbers # unavailable) Maslyn Braun, Matt Davies, Russell Davey, Sheldon Daye, Luke Farrows, Dylan Gordon, Merl Gurruwiwi, Nick Horsley, Shaun Huy, Matt James, Alex Johnson, Nathan Lawrence, Pierce Liddle, Aaron Lonergan, Marc Mattiazo, Brenton Medbury, Damien Medwin, James Murray, Tavis Perry, James Pile, Zac Stephenson, Billy Wells. Coaches: Russell Jeffrey, Michael McLean.

ROUND 3

- Central Australia vs. Tiwi Bombers @ Marrara Oval
- Saturday, 20 October 2012
- Scores
    - Tiwi Bombers 18.10 (118) defeated Central Australia 13.17 (95)
    - Progressive scores — Q1: TBFC 4.3 (27) led CAFC 0.7 (7) Q2: TBFC 10.4 (64) led CAFC 2.11 (23) Q3: TBFC 14.5 led CAFC 8.16 (64) Q4: TBFC 18.10 (118) def. CAFC 13.17 (95)
- Goalkickers
    - Tiwi Bombers: Roy Kantilla 3, Simon Munkara 3, Paddy Heenan 2, Darcy Barden 2, David Kantilla 2, Michael Dunn 1, Ephrem Tipungwuti 1, Gerrard Cunningham 1, Dion Munkara 1, Cannis Tipuamantimirri 1, Austin Wonaemirri 1.

    - Central Australia: Charlie Maher 3, Jai Pumphrey 2, Daniel Stafford 2, Gibson Turner 2, Reggie Smith 1, Toshie Kunoth 1, Thomas Gorey 1, Ryan Mallard 1.
- Best Players
    - Tiwi Bombers: Simon Munkara, William Barden, Paddy Heenan, Michael Dunn, Darcy Barden, Shane Tipuamantimirri.
    - Central Australia: Darren Young, Toshie Kunoth, Jai Pumphrey, Kenny Morton, Ryan Mallard, Baydon Ngalkin.
- Teams
    - Central Australia — #1 Toshie Kunoth #3 Baydon Ngalkin #4 Charlie Maher #6 Abe Ankers #7 Bradley McMasters #8 Paul Campbell #9 Gareth Remfrey #11 Jayden Prior #13 Thomas Gorey #15 Jai Pumphrey #17 Ryan Mallard #19 Tom Clarke #24 Kenny Morton #29 Dylan Alice #31 Darren Young #36 Daniel Stafford #40 Reggie Smith #41 Gibson Turner #42 Caleb Hart #44 Lloyd Turner #50 Gordon Mallard #51 Dustin Briscoe. Coach: Shaun Cusack.
    - Tiwi Bombers — #2 Jason Puruntatameri #3 Dion Munkara #4 Bradley Palipuamini #5 Simon Munkara #6 Paddy Heenan #7 Ross Tungatalum #9 Roy Kantilla #10 Albert Tipungwuti #12 Austin Wonaeamirri #15 William Barden #17 Cameron Kerinaiua #18 Michael Dunn #19 Ephrem Tipungwuti #20 David Kantilla #21 Cannis Tipuamantimirri #22 Ben McCasker #24 Ben Battams #30 Darcy Barden #31 Gerard Cunningham #35 Donald Mungatopi #36 Michael Fairweather #44 Shane Tipuamantimirri. Coach: Leigh Crossman.

ROUND 4

- Central Australia vs. Nightcliff @ Marrara Oval
- Saturday, 27 October 2012

- Scores
  - Central Australia 17.15 (117) defeated Nightcliff 15.14 (104)
  - Progressive scores — Q1: NFC 5.6 (36) led CAFC 3.2 (20) Q2: NFC 8.11 (59) led CAFC 8.6 (54) Q3: NFC 13.12 (90) led CAFC 13.10 (88) Q4: CAFC 17.15 (117) def. NFC 15.14 (104)
- Goalkickers
  - Central Australia: Baydon Ngalkin 3, Daniel Stafford 3, Ryan Mallard 2, Gibson Turner 2, Thomas Gorey 1, Charlie Maher 1, Bradley McMasters 1, G. Jack Miller 1, Abe Ankers 1, Swaine Hill 1, Bradley Turner 1.
  - Nightcliff: Luke Jarjoura 5, Matthew Rowe 3, Jarrah Maksymow 3, Malcolm Lewis 2, Timothy Jenkins 1, Jesse Haberfield 1.
- Best Players
  - Central Australia: Baydon Ngalkin, Ryan Mallard, Caleb Hart, Charlie Maher, Tom Clarke, Chris Macaskill-Hants.
  - Nightcliff: Joshua Hicks, Jarrah Maksymow, Matthew Rowe, Brandon Hayes, Tim Jenkins, Luke Jarjoura.
- Teams
  - Central Australia: #1 Toshie Kunoth #3 Baydon Ngalkin #4 Charlie Maher #6 Abe Ankers #7 Bradley McMasters #8 Paul Campbell #9 Gareth Remfrey #10 Tyson Carmody #12 G. Jack Miller #13 Thomas Gorey #15 Jai Pumphrey #16 Matt Cunningham #19 Tom Clarke #20 Luke Adams #22 Swaine Hill #28 Ryan Mallard #36 Daniel Stafford #37 Bradley Turner #39 Chris Macaskill-Hants #40 Reggie Smith #41 Gibson Turner 42 #Caleb Hart. Coach: Shaun Cusack.
  - Nightcliff: #1 Brandon Hayes #2 J Woodhouse #3 Marc Reiffel 4# Malcolm Lewis #5 R Hale #6 Adrian Murphy #7 Tim Jenkins #8 Nathan James-Cubillo #9 Joshua Hicks #11 Luke Jajoura #13 Jayden Shaw #15 Jordan Zeitz #17 Anthony Gugliotta #18 Jesse

Haberfield #19 Matthew Rowe #20 Troy Kelm #21 Matthew Metcalfe #23 Jesiah McGarvie #26 Mark Tibbits #27 Anthony Hale #29 Dylan Dempsey #33 Jarrah Maksymow. Coach: Damien Hale.

2012–13 NTFL PREMIER LEAGUE LADDER (AFTER ROUND 4)

Team	Record
1. Tiwi Bombers	4 — 0 — 16pts — 135.37%
2. St Mary's	3 — 1 — 12pts — 280.95%
3. Central Australia	**3 — 1 — 12pts — 107.96%**
4. Waratah	3 — 1 — 12pts — 102.48%
5. Southern Districts	2 — 2 — 08pts — 118.96%
6. Palmerston	2 — 2 — 08pts — 116.23%
7. Nightcliff Tigers	1 — 3 — 04pts — 76.77%
8. Banks Bulldogs	1 — 3 — 04pts — 75.65%
9. Darwin Buffaloes	1 — 3 — 04pts — 51.70%
10. Wanderers	0 — 4 — 00pts — 54.46%

BY THE NUMBERS

37 — the number of players who played in the 2012–13 NTFL four-game trial

8 — the number of players who played in all 4 games: Abe Ankers (Rd 1, 2, 3, 4), Thomas Gorey (Rd 1, 2, 3, 4), Caleb Hart (Rd 1, 2, 3, 4), Charlie Maher (Rd 1, 2, 3, 4), Baydon Ngalkin (Rd 1, 2, 3, 4), Gareth Remfrey (Rd 1, 2, 3, 4), Daniel Stafford (Rd 1, 2, 3, 4), Gibson Turner (Rd 1, 2, 3, 4)

11 — the number of players who played in 3 games: Luke Adams (Rd. 1, 2, 4), Paul Campbell (Rd 1, 3, 4), Tom Clarke (Rd 2, 3, 4), Swaine Hill (Rd 1, 2, 4), Ryan Mallard (Rd 1, 3, 4), Bradley McMasters (Rd 1, 3, 4), G. Jack Miller (Rd 1, 2, 4), Jayden Prior (Rd 1, 2, 3), Reggie Smith (Rd 1, 3, 4), Bradley Turner (Rd. 1, 2, 4), Darren Young (Rd. 1, 2, 3)

6 — the number of players who played in 2 games: Matt Cunningham (Rd 2, 4), Tyson Carmody (Rd 1, 4), Shane Dixon (Rd 1, 2), Toshie Kunoth (Rd 3, 4), Kenny Morton (Rd 2, 3), Jai Pumphrey (Rd 3, 4)
10 — the number of players who played in 1 game: Jack Abrey (Rd 1), Dylan Alice (Rd 3), Dustin Briscoe (Rd 3), Curtis Haines (Rd 2), Gordon Mallard (Rd 3), Chris Macaskill-Hants (Rd 4), Aaron Sharpe (Rd 2), Corey Taylor (Rd 2), Lloyd Turner (Rd 3), Jasper Wheeler (Rd 1).

REDTAILS' SEASON 1.0 GOALKICKING LEADERBOARD:

15 — Daniel Stafford. 7 — Gibson Turner. 6 — Thomas Gorey[1], Charlie Maher. 4 — Ryan Mallard. 3 — Abe Ankers, Baydon Ngalkin, Gareth Remfrey. 2 — G. Jack Miller, Jai Pumphrey, Corey Taylor, Bradley Turner. 1 — Toshie Kunoth, Bradley McMasters, Reggie Smith.

1 Thomas Gorey kicked the Redtails' first-ever goal in a competitive match.

APPENDIX 2: REDTAILS SURVEY QUESTIONNAIRE

1. How well do you understand the Central Australian Football Club / Redtails concept:
    - Extremely well
    - Very well
    - Quite well
    - Poorly
    - Not at All
2. How would you support the Central Australian Football Club:
    - Attending all matches played at Traeger Park
    - Active volunteer at home games
    - Active volunteer at trainings
    - Follow through the media only
    - Follow through word-of-mouth only
    - Not at all
3. Would you support the Central Australian Redtails financially as a:
    - Major sponsor
    - Minor sponsor
    - Player sponsor
    - Financial member
    - Purchaser of club attire (shirts/jumpers/caps)
    - Not at all
4. It is estimated that the cost of the Central Australian Redtails will be in the vicinity of $700,000 per annum. In your opinion is this:
    - A worthwhile amount for a great concept
    - Too much money to spend on one team
    - Money that could be better spent elsewhere
    - I don't have an opinion on this

5. How do you expect the annual cost of the Central Australian Redtails to be funded?
   - That the AFL Northern Territory would fund the full amount
   - That the Northern Territory government would fund the full amount
   - That the local community of Alice Springs would fund the full amount
6. That a combination of the AFLNT, NTG and Alice Springs community would fund the full amount
   - I don't have an opinion either way
7. Based on the $700,000 per annum estimated cost to run the Central Australian Redtails what would you expect the long-term viability to be:
   - One to two seasons
   - Two to three seasons
   - Three to four seasons
   - Five-plus seasons
   - Not make it through season one
   - Not get off the ground
   - No Comment
8. The AFLNT currently provide clubs in the NTFL competition with financial assistance towards their administration. In your opinion should the AFLNT:
   - Provide financial assistance to the Redtails the same as they do to other NTFL clubs
   - Provide more funds to the Redtails because they are an expansion club
   - Provide more funds to a struggling club so that they can be more competitive in the Premier League
   - Provide more funds to the CAFL so that it can grow and expand further
   - Provide more funds to the other regions in the Northern Territory
   - Do not have an opinion on this

9. Rank from 1 to 6 what you feel to be the most critical impact on Central Australian Football as a result of the Redtails playing in the NTFL:
   - Reduced access to Traeger Park for the CAFL
   - Player restrictions as a result of Player Management Rule
   - 12 month of the year involvement as a volunteer
   - Possibility of Thunder matches removed from Alice Springs
   - Diminished sponsorship of CAFL Clubs or Competition
   - I do not believe there will be any impact

10. Do you agree with the following statements in regards to the Central Australian Redtails:
    - The Redtails should play 9 games at Traeger Park and 9 games in Darwin - Yes/ No / N/A
    - The Redtails should play all of their home games at Traeger Park ahead of other Centralian Sports - Yes / No / N/A
    - The Redtails should represent the region of Central Australia and be managed by the AFLNT staff based in Central Australia - Yes / No / N/A
    - The management of players who continually play over a 12 month period is critical - Yes / No / N/A
    - Travelling to Darwin on a fortnightly basis will be a problem for Redtails players - Yes / No / N/A

11. Based on a senior player's comments at the 2012 Minahan Medal, noting the travel commitment to Thunder as a player took a heavy toll on his family life, answer Yes or No to the following questions:
    - Travelling to Darwin every fortnight will take a physical toll on players? Yes / No
    - Community based players who have to travel into town each weekend will find it difficult? Yes / No

- Families will be impacted on as players will be away overnight on weekends? Yes / No
- Players will be fatigued playing across two seasons (NTFL Oct-March / CAFL April to Sept)? Yes / No
- Players would choose to play either NTFL (Redtails) or CAFL? Yes / No
- I do not believe that there would be any impact on the players welfare. Yes / No

12. In your opinion what is the best governance/management structure for the Redtails:
    - Current Administrative group
    - Club managed by AFL Central Australia
    - Club Managed by AFL Northern Territory
    - I don't have an opinion

13. Final comments:

AFLNT 2013 (5 March), 'Survey commissioned to evaluate support for Redtails', https://www.aflnt.com.au/news/2013/survey-commissioned-toevaluate-support-for-redtails

APPENDIX 3: SCOREBOARD 2.0

CENTRAL AUSTRALIAN FOOTBALL CLUB — 2013–14 NTFL PREMIER LEAGUE

ROUND 1

- Central Australia vs. Waratah @ Traeger Park
- Saturday, 5 October 2013
- Scores — Waratah 12.11 (83) defeated Central Australia 12.9 (81)
- Progressive scores — Q1: CAFC 3.2 (20) led WFC 1.5 (11) Q2: CAFC 8.2 (50) led WFC 5.8 (38) Q3: CAFC 12.7 (79) led WFC 8.11 (59) Q4: WFC 12.11 (83) def. CAFC 12.9 (81)
- Goalkickers
    - Waratah: Davin Hall 4, Ryan Cocks 3, William Hetherington 1, Jake Farrell 1, Jamie Mccarthy 1, Jacob Schaper 1, Sam Nickless 1.
    - Central Australia: Gibson Turner 3, Thomas Gorey 2, G. Jack Miller 2, Nathan Mutch 1, Reggie Smith 1, Michaelis McMasters 1, Chris Cooper 1, Abe Ankers 1.
- Best Players
    - Waratah: Jake Farrell, Ryan Cocks, Hayden McDonald, Davin Hall, James Wray, Luke Harder.
    - Central Australia: Nathan Mutch, Michaelis McMasters, Jayden Prior, Caleb Hart, Gibson Turner, Seth Matson.
- Teams
    - Central Australia: #5 Luke Adams #10 Troy Lawton #11 Toshie Kunoth #12 G. Jack Miller #13 Thomas Gorey #15 Luke Farrows #18 William Foster #19 Jayden Prior #20 Gibson Turner #21 Mathew Axten #22 Abe Ankers #23 Michaelis McMasters #25 Caleb Hart #27 Bradley Turner #28 Thomas Gillett #29 Nathan Mutch #31 Darren Young #33 Chris Cooper #40 Reggie Smith #42 Andrew Baker #44 Tom Clarke #48 Seth Matson. Coach: Greg McAdam.

   - Waratah: #1 Jacob Schaper #2 Davin Hall #3 Will Hetherington #4 Jayden Clayfield #5 James Wray #7 Jamie Mccarthy #8 Julian Brown #9 Brett Rowley #10 Kyle Press #11 David O'Sullivan #13 Daniel Simpson #14 Jake Smart #15 Jake Farrell #16 Josh Westerberg #18 Sam Nickless #20 Ryan Cocks #21 Josh Barton #23 Josh Chaplin #24 Tom Marsh #25 Justin Beugelaar #27 Luke Harder #28 Hayden McDonald. Coach: Brenton Toy.

ROUND 2

- Central Australia vs. St Mary's @ Marrara Oval
- Saturday, 12 October 2013
- Scores — St Mary's 13.15 (93) defeated Central Australia 9.6 (60)
- Progressive scores — Q1: SMFC 6.5 (41) led CAFC 1.1 (7) Q2: SMFC 10.7 (67) led CAFC 5.5 (35) Q3: SMFC 11.13 (79) led CAFC 7.5 (47) Q4: SMFC 13.15 (93) def. CAFC 9.6 (60)
- Goalkickers
   - St Mary's: Lucas White 3, Henry Kerinaiua 2, Nicky Yarran 2, Leroy Larson 2, Justin Wilson 1, Jack Musgrove 1, Ryan Clark 1, Karl Lohde 1.
   - Central Australia: Aaron Sharpe 2, Daniel Stafford 2, Gibson Turner 2, Thomas Gorey 2, Andrew Baker 1.
- Best Players
   - St Mary's: Karl Lohde, Nicky Yarran, John Anstess, Henry Kerinaiua.
   - Central Australia: Thomas Gorey, Caleb Hart, Gibson Turner, Paul Campbell, Nathan Mutch, Andrew Baker.
- Teams
   - Central Australia: #1 Curtis Haines #5 Luke Adams #6 Jayson Brown #8 Paul Campbell #9 Faron James #10 Troy Lawton #13 Thomas Gorey #17 Ryan Mallard #20 Gibson Turner #21 Mathew Axten #25 Caleb Hart #26 Rhbair Woods #27 Bradley Turner #29

Nathan Mutch #30 Dylan Alice #32 Matt Cunningham #33 Chris Cooper #36 Daniel Stafford #37 Aaron Sharpe #40 Reggie Smith #42 Andrew Baker #48 Seth Matson. Coach: Greg McAdam.

- St Mary's: (numbers # unavailable) John Anstess, Jackson Clark, Ryan Clark, Raphael Clarke, Michael Dunn, Josh Heath, Henry Labastida, Leroy Larson, Josh Lidgerwood, Karl Lohde, Ben Long, Jack Long, Russell McAdam, Jono Miles, Jack Musgrave, Luke Stapleton, Justin Wilson, Lucas White, Nicky Yarran. Interchange from: Justin Cooper, Jarred Ilett, Henry Kerinaiua, Brett Kroger, Shaq McKenzie, Sebastian Rioli Jnr. Coach: Rick Nolan.

ROUND 3

- Central Australia vs. Nightcliff @ Nightcliff Oval
- Saturday, 19 October 2013
- Scores — Nightcliff 21.20 (146) defeated Central Australia 10.6 (66)
- Progressive scores — Q1: NFC 6.11 (47) led CAFC 0.1 (1) Q2: NFC 12.15 (87) led CAFC 5.3 (33) Q3: NFC 16.18 (114) led 9.4 (58) Q4: NFC 21.20 (146) def. CAFC 10.6 (66)
- Goalkickers
  - Nightcliff: Brant Chambers 5, Brandan Parfitt 4, Daniel Dzufer 3, Nathan Brown 2, Anthony Hale 2, Toby Stribling 2, Lachlan McKenzie 1, Seb Guilhaus 1, Ashley Duncan 1.
  - Central Australia: Gibson Turner 4, Michaelis McMasters 2, Kenny Morton 1, Matt Campbell 1, Kevin Renehan 1, Lauchlan Lake 1.
- Best Players
  - Nightcliff: Toby Stribling, Ashley Duncan, Brandan Parfitt, Trevor Baust, Seb Guilhaus.
  - Central Australia: Gibson Turner, Charlie Maher, Matt Campbell, Caleb Hart, Jayden Prior, Reggie Smith.

- Teams
    - Central Australia: #2 Kevin Renehan #3 Matt Campbell #4 Charlie Maher #8 Paul Campbell #9 Faron James #12 G. Jack Miller #17 Ryan Mallard #19 Jayden Prior #20 Gibson Turner #21 Mathew Axten #23 Michaelis McMasters #24 Kenny Morton #25 Caleb Hart #26 Rhbair Woods #29 Nathan Mutch #30 Dylan Alice #32 Matt Cunningham #38 Aiden Hill #40 Reggie Smith #43 Lauchlan Lake #48 Seth Matson #50 Lloyd Turner. Coach: Greg McAdam.
    - Nightcliff: #1 Darren Guelfi #2 Brandan Parfitt #3 Jonathan Peris #4 Tim Jenkins #6 Adrian Murphy #7 Joseph Collinson #8 Brant Chambers #10 Seb Guilhaus #12 Raphael Sampi #14 Nathan Brown #15 Toby Stribling #16 Jayden Kickett #17 Anthony Gugliotta #18 Ashley Duncan #19 Julian Lockwood #20 Lachlan McKenzie #22 Daniel Dzufer #23 Jesiah McGarvie #25 Deon Gordon #27 Anthony Hale #41 Trevor Baust #51 Jonathon Coghlan. Coach: Damien Hale.

ROUND 4

- Central Australia vs. Darwin Buffaloes @ Cazalys Arena
- Saturday, 26 October 2013
- Scores — Central Australia 20.8 (128) defeated Darwin Buffaloes 12.6 (78)
- Progressive scores: Q1: DBFC 7.2 (44) led CAFC 4.2 (26) Q2: CAFC 10.4 (64) led DBFC 8.3 (51) Q3: CAFC 13.4 (82) led DBFC 11.5 (71) Q4: CAFC 20.8 (128) def. DBFC 12.6 (78)
- Goalkickers
    - Central Australia: Daniel Stafford 6, Chris Cooper 3, Andrew Baker 3, Charlie Maher 3, Reggie Smith 2, Matt Campbell 1, Paul Campbell 1, Aaron Sharpe 1.

 - Darwin: Shaun Wilson 2, Steven Anderson 2, Jarrod Stokes 2, Dion Gordon 1, Robert Beswick 1, Luke Clark 1, Phillip Wills 1, Travis O'Donohue 1, Luke Moore 1.
- Best Players
 - Central Australia: Andrew Baker, Caleb Hart, Will Foster, Chris Cooper, Nathan Mutch, Matt Campbell.
 - Darwin: Phillip Wills, Liam Philpott, Dylan Fuller, Jarrod Stokes, Tim Eldridge.
- Teams
 - Central Australia: #3 Matt Campbell #4 Charlie Maher #6 Jayson Brown #8 Paul Campbell #10 Troy Lawton #11 Toshie Kunoth #16 Adam Davis #18 William Foster #20 Gibson Turner #23 Michaelis McMasters #25 Caleb Hart #29 Nathan Mutch #32 Matt Cunningham #33 Chris Cooper #34 Antonio Riley #36 Daniel Stafford #37 Aaron Sharpe #40 Reggie Smith #42 Andrew Baker #44 Tom Clarke #46 Thomas Ambrose #48 Seth Matson. Coach: Greg McAdam.
 - Darwin: (numbers # unavailaible) Steven Anderson, Robert Beswick, Jalen Clark, Luke Clark, Juan Darwin, Tim Eldridge, Dylan Fuller, Dion Gordon, Michael Hagan, Thomas McDowell, Luke Moore, Travis O'Donohue, Liam Philpott, Jarrod Stokes, Kelvin Williams, Shaun Wilson, Phillip Wills. Coach: Mark Motlop.

ROUND 5

- Central Australia vs. Wanderers @ Gardens Oval
- Saturday, 2 November 2013
- Scores — Wanderers 16.11 (107) defeated Central Australia 9.6 (60)
- Progressive scores — Q1: WFC 4.3 (27) led CAFC 3.2 (20) Q2: WFC 8.5 (53) led 5.5 (35) Q3: WFC 10.7 (67) led CAFC 7.5 (47) Q4: WFC 16.11 (107) def. CAFC 9.6 (60)

- Goalkickers
    - Wanderers: Shane Thorne 5, Eddie Sansbury 2, Brad Vassal 2, Chris Dunne 2, Daniel Motlop 1, Aaron Motlop 1, Robert Howard 1, Sam Arthur 1, Keelan Fejo 1.
    - Central Australia: Daniel Stafford 3, Faron James 2, Thomas Gorey 2, Caleb Hart 1, William Foster 1.
- Best Players
    - Wanderers: Eddie Sansbury, Shane Thorne, Keelan Fejo, Brad Vassal, Aaron Motlop.
    - Central Australia: Kenny Morton, Antonio Riley, Tom Clarke, Matt Campbell, Jayden Prior, Matt Cunningham.
- Teams
    - Central Australia: #3 Matt Campbell #4 Charlie Maher #6 Jayson Brown #9 Faron James #11 Toshie Kunoth #13 Thomas Gorey #16 Adam Davis #18 William Foster #19 Jayden Prior #20 Gibson Turner #24 Kenny Morton #25 Caleb Hart #29 Nathan Mutch #32 Matt Cunningham #33 Chris Cooper #34 Antonio Riley #36 Daniel Stafford #38 Aiden Hill #39 Chris Macaskill-Hants #40 Reggie Smith #44 Tom Clarke #46 Thomas Ambrose #50 Lloyd Turner. Coach: Greg McAdam.
    - Wanderers: #1 Chris Dunne #3 Robert Howard #4 Aaron Motlop #5 Simon Bates #6 Nook Mansell #7 Shane Thorne #8 Jarred Erlandson #9 Keelan Fejo #10 Alex Erlandson #12 Zelio Casimiro #13 Eddie Sansbury #14 Brad Vassal #15 Braedon McLean #16 Neil Vea Vea #17 Brett Totham #18 Mitch Taylor #19 Daniel Motlop #21 Daniel Weetra #22 Liam Patrick #24 Sam Arthur #25 Joel Cubillo #28 Justin Wilson-King. Coach: Paul Motlop.

ROUND 6

- Central Australia vs. Southern Districts @ Freds Pass
- Saturday, 9 November 2013
- Scores — Southern Districts 18.7 (115) defeated Central Australia 4.14 (38)
- Progressive scores — Q1 SDFC 8.3 (51) led CAFC 1.3 (9) Q2: SDFC 12.5 (77) led CAFC 1.6 (12) Q3: SDFC 15.6 (96) led CAFC 2.11 (23) Q4: SDFC 18.7 (115) def. CAFC 4.14 (38)
- Goalkickers
    - Southern Districts: Damien Cupido 8, Troy Taylor 4, Matt Cannard 2, Dean Staunton 2, Shane Hodges 1, Henry Armour 1.
    - Central Australia: Gibson Turner 2, Tim Kelly 1, Thomas Gorey 1.
- Best Players
    - Southern Districts: Jake Roe-Duggan, Lionel Ogden, Henry Armour, Dylan McLachlan, Ben Dowdell, Thomas Fittock.
    - Central Australia: Caleb Hart, Michaelis McMasters, Matt Campbell, Aiden Hill, Murray Liddle, Lloyd Turner.
- Teams
    - Central Australia: #2 Kevin Renehan #3 Matt Campbell #6 Jayson Brown #8 Paul Campbell #10 Troy Lawton #13 Thomas Gorey #14 Travis King #19 Jayden Prior #20 Gibson Turner #21 Mathew Axten #23 Michaelis McMasters #24 Kenny Morton #25 Caleb Hart #26 Nicholas Corbett #27 Murray Liddle #35 Tim Kelly #38 Aiden Hill #42 Andrew Baker #44 Tom Clarke #45 Franklyn Anderson #47 Tyrell Egan #49 Franky Gorey #50 Lloyd Turner. Coach: Greg McAdam.
    - Southern Districts: #1 Dean Staunton #2 Richard Tambling #4 Ben Ah Mat #5 Dylan McLachlan #6 Matt Cannard #9 Henry Armour #10 Lionel Ogden #11 Thomas Gleeson #12 Zane Carter #15 Keegan Dingo #18 Shane Hodges #19 Damien Cupido 22

#Ryan Lovegrove-Hudson #23 Dane McGennisken #24 Aaron Craufurd #25 Troy Taylor #26 Aaron Gepp #27 Will Farrar #28 Jake Roe-Duggan #29 Nathan Roach #32 Thomas Fittock #35 Ben Dowdell. Coach: Shannon Rusca.

ROUND 7

- Central Australia vs. Tiwi Bombers @ Marrara Oval
- Saturday, 16 November 2013
- Scores — Tiwi Bombers 22.11 (143) defeated Central Australia 20.14 (134)
- Progressive scores — Q1: CAFC 4.3 (27) led TBFC 4.2 (26) Q2: CAFC 10.8 (68) led TBFC 9.3 (57) Q3: TBFC 19.9 (123) led CAFC 15.10 (100) Q4: TBFC 22.11 (143) def. CAFC 20.14 (134)
- Goalkickers
    - Tiwi Bombers: Liam Jurrah 6, Roy Kantilla 5, Ross Tungatalum 3, Gerrard Cunningham 2, Dion Munkara 2, Mark Parmbuk 1, Jerome Tipuamantimirri 1, Kenny Puruntatameri 1, John Kelantumama 1.
    - Central Australia: Lindsay Turner 3, Matt Campbell 3, Gibson Turner 3, Daniel Stafford 2, Toshie Kunoth 2, Travis King 1, Abe Ankers 1, Bradley Turner 1, Faron James 1, Thomas Gorey 1, Nathan Mutch 1, Jayden Prior 1.
- Best Players
    - Tiwi Bombers: Adam Tipungwuti, Liam Jurrah, Nyaburu Kelly, Roy Kantilla, Tim Bongetti, Ross Tungatalum.
    - Central Australia: Gibson Turner, Matt Campbell, Lindsay Turner, Abe Ankers.
- Teams
    - Central Australia: #3 Matt Campbell #8 Paul Campbell #9 Faron James #11 Toshie Kunoth #13 Thomas Gorey #14 Travis King

#16 Adam Davis #19 Jayden Prior #20 Gibson Turner #22 Abe Ankers #25 Caleb Hart #26 Lindsay Turner #27 Bradley Turner #29 Nathan Mutch #30 Dylan Alice #34 Antonio Riley #35 Tim Kelly #36 Daniel Stafford #41 Dale Campbell #47 Tyrell Egan #48 Seth Matson #51 Dylan Briscoe. Coach: Greg McAdam.
  - Tiwi Bombers: #1 Samson Mungatopi #2 Jason Puruntatameri #3 Dion Munkara #6 Aalastair Darcy #7 Ross Tungatalum #8 Nyaburu Kelly #9 Roy Kantilla #12 John Kelantumama #18 Kevin Portaminni #21 Jonus Babui #24 Liam Jurrah #27 Tim Bongetti #29 Kenny Puruntatameri #31 Gerard Cunningham #33 Rupert Pupangamirri #35 Donald Mungatopi #36 Bronson Mungatopi #37 Mark Parmbuk #40 Chris Warlipinni #41 Adam Tipungwuti #45 Jerome Tipuamantimirri #49 Michael Fairweather. Coach: Willie Rioli Snr.

ROUND 8

- Central Australia vs. Palmertston @ Marrara Oval
- Saturday, 23 November 2013
- Scores — Palmerston 13.6 (84) defeated Central Australia 8.9 (57)
- Progressive scores — Q1 PMFC 5.1 (31) led CAFC 0.3 (3) Q2: PMFC 6.4 (40) led CAFC 2.4 (16) Q3: PMFC 10.6 (66) led CAFC 6.5 (41) Q4: PMFC 13.6 (84) def. 8.9 (57)
- Goalkickers
  - Palmerston: Cameron Cloke 6, Pierce Liddle 2, Aaron Lonergan 1, Lochlan Dhurrkay 1, Blake Grant 1, Kriston Hunter 1, David Liston 1, Keidan Holt-Tubbs 1.
  - Central Australia: Lindsay Turner 2, Troy Lawton 1, Thomas Gorey 1, William Foster 1, Gibson Turner 1, Nathan Mutch 1.
- Best Players
  - Palmerston: Gavin Dhurrkay, Cameron Cloke, Pierce Liddle, Aaron Lonergan, Lochlan Dhurrkay, Callan Wilson.

    - Central Australia: William Foster, Chris Macaskill-Hants, Nathan Mutch, Abe Ankers, Adam Davis, Matt Campbell.
- Teams
    - Central Australia: #3 Matt Campbell #5 Luke Adams #8 Paul Campbell #9 Faron James #10 Troy Lawton #13 Thomas Gorey #16 Adam Davis #18 William Foster #19 Jayden Prior #20 Gibson Turner #22 Abe Ankers #23 Michaelis McMasters #25 Caleb Hart #26 Lindsay Turner #29 Nathan Mutch #30 Dylan Alice #34 Antonio Riley #38 Aiden Hill# 39 Chris Macaskill-Hants #40 Nicholas Tracker #42 Andrew Baker #51 Dylan Briscoe. Coach: Greg McAdam.
    - Palmerston: #1 Gavin Dhurrkay #2 Jack Shannahan #4 Justin Emery #5 Alex Johnson #6 Pierce Liddle #9 Lochlan Dhurrkay #10 Keidan Holt-Tubbs #11 Steven Smith #12 Blake Grant #13 David Liston #15 J Jukes #16 Kristen Hunter #17 Nathan Hartley #18 William Carlyle #19 Aaron Lonergan #20 Callan Wilson #21 Jamie Damaso #22 Warren Berto #28 Cameron Cloke #29 Julian Jeffrey #32 Amaziah Gameraidj #34 Curtly Reid. Coach: Dean Rioli.

2013–14 NTFL PREMIER LEAGUE LADDER (AFTER ROUND 8)

Team	Record
1. St Mary's	8 — 0 — 32pts — 212.42%
2. Wanderers	7 — 1 — 28pts — 129.67%
3. Nightcliff Tigers	5— 3 — 20pts — 130.35%
4. Waratah	5— 3 — 20pts — 93.89%
5. Southern Districts	3 — 4 — 14pts — 115.90%
6. Tiwi Bombers	3 — 4 — 14pts — 94.44%
7. Darwin Buffaloes	2 — 6 — 08pts — 70.83%
8. Central Australia	**1 — 7 — 04pts — 73.50%**
9. Palmerston	1 — 7 — 04pts — 53.58

BY THE NUMBERS:

33 — the number of players who played in the 2013–14 8-game trial

2 — the number of players who played in all 8 games: Caleb Hart (Rd 1, 2, 3, 4, 5, 6, 7, 8), Gibson Turner (Rd 1, 2, 3, 4, 5, 6, 7, 8)

1 — the number of players who played in 7 games: Nathan Mutch (Rd 1, 2, 3, 4, 5, 7, 8)

3 — the number of players who played in 6 games: Matt Campbell (Rd 3, 4, 5, 6, 7, 8), Thomas Gorey (Rd 1, 2, 5, 6, 7, 8), Jayden Prior (Rd 1, 3, 5, 6, 7, 8)

7 — the number of players who played in 5 games: Andrew Baker (Rd 1, 2, 4, 6, 8), Paul Campbell (Rd 2, 3, 4, 6, 8), Faron James (Rd 2, 3, 5, 7, 8), Troy Lawton (Rd 1, 2, 4, 6, 8), Seth Matson (Rd 1, 2, 3, 4, 7), Michaelis McMasters (Rd 1, 3, 4, 6, 8), Reggie Smith (Rd 1, 2, 3, 4, 5)

12 — the number of players who played in 4 games: Dylan Alice (Rd 2, 3, 7, 8), Mathew Axten (Rd 1, 2, 3, 6), Jayson Brown (Rd 2, 4, 5, 6), Tom Clarke (Rd 1, 4, 5, 6), Chris Cooper (Rd 1, 2, 4, 5), Matt Cunningham (Rd 2, 3, 4, 5), Adam Davis (Rd 4, 5, 7, 8), William Foster (Rd 1, 4, 5, 8), Aiden Hill (Rd 3, 5, 6, 8), Toshie Kunoth (Rd 1, 4, 5, 7), Antonio Riley (Rd 4, 5, 7, 8), Daniel Stafford (Rd 2, 4, 5, 7)

6 — the number of players who played in 3 games: Luke Adams (Rd 1, 2, 8), Abe Ankers (Rd 1, 7, 8), Charlie Maher (Rd 3, 4, 5), Kenny Morton (Rd 3, 5, 6), Bradley Turner (Rd 1, 2, 7), Lloyd Turner (Rd 3, 5, 6)

12 — the number players who played in 2 games: Thomas Ambrose (Rd 4, 5), Dylan Briscoe (Rd 7, 8), Tyrell Egan (Rd 6, 7), Tim Kelly (Rd 6, 7), Travis King (Rd 6, 7), Chris Macaskill-Hants (Rd 5, 8), Ryan Mallard (Rd 2, 3), G. Jack Miller (Rd 1, 3), Kevin Renehan (Rd 3, 6), Aaron Sharpe (Rd 2, 4), Lindsay Turner (Rd 7, 8), Rhbair Woods (Rd 2, 3)

11 — the number of players who played in 1 game: Franklyn Anderson (Rd 6), Dale Campbell (Rd 7), Nicholas Corbett (Rd 6), Luke Farrows (Rd 1), Thomas Gillett (Rd 1), Franky Gorey (Rd 6), Curtis Haines (Rd 2), Lauchlan Lake (Rd 3), Murray Liddle (Rd 6), Nicholas Tracker (Rd 8), Darren Young (Rd 1).

REDTAILS' SEASON 2.0 GOAL-KICKING LEADERBOARD

15 — Gibson Turner. 13 — Daniel Stafford. 9 — Thomas Gorey. 5 — Matt Campbell, Lindsay Turner. 4 — Andrew Baker, Chris Cooper. 3 — Faron James, Michaelis McMasters, Charlie Maher, Aaron Sharpe. 2 — Abe Ankers, William Foster, Toshie Kunoth, G. Jack Miller, Nathan Mutch. 1 — Paul Campbell, William Foster, Caleb Hart, Travis King, Lauchlan Lake, Troy Lawton, Kenny Morton, Jayden Prior, Kevin Renehan, Bradley Turner.

Scoreboards 1.0 and 2.0 — teams, scores, goals, goal-kickers best players, ladder positions, game tallies — compiled from *SportingPulse*, *NT News*, *Centralian Advocate*, and other varied resources — Author.

APPENDIX 4: AFLNT

In its entirety AFLNT oversees the operations of the following competitions: Barkly Australian Football League in Tennant Creek; Big River Australian Football League in Katherine; Central Australian Football League in Alice Springs; Gove Australian Football League in north-east Arnhemland; Northern Territory Football League in Darwin; Tiwi Islands Football League on the Tiwi Islands.[1]

APPENDIX 5: GOLD COAST SPORTS GRAVEYARD

Failed Gold Coast-based national sports clubs: Aussie Rules: Brisbane Bears (VFL–AFL, 1987–1992 (moved to Brisbane); Baseball: Daikyo Dolphins–Gold Coast Clippers (Australian Baseball League, 1989–1994); Basketball: Gold Coast Cougars-Rollers (NBL, 1990–1996, licence revoked), Gold Coast Blaze (NBL, 2007–2012); Ice Hockey: Brisbane Blue Tongues (2008-2013); Rugby League: Gold Coast–Tweed Giants, Gold Coast Seagulls (NSWRL–ARL, 1988–1995), Gold Coast Gladiators (ARL, 1996 pre-season only, licence revoked); Gold Coast Chargers (ARL–NRL, 1996–1998); Rugby Union: East Coast Aces (Australian Rugby Championship, 2007, competition folded); Soccer: Gold Coast United (A-League, 2009–2012, licence revoked).[2]

---

1 AFL Northern Territory 2025, 'AFL Northern Territory (AFLNT) is the peak body for Australian Rules Football in the Northern Territory', accessed 18 March 2025, https://www.aflnt.com.au/competitions#:~:text=This%20includes%20the%20famous%20wet-season%20competition%20run%20out,Alice%20Springs%2C%20the%20Central%20Australian%20Football%20League%20%28CAFL%29.

2 Prain, M 2015 (9 July), 'The Gold Coast: our sporting graveyard', *The News Daily*, accessed 18 March 2025, https://www.thenewdaily.com.au/sport/sport-focus/2015/07/09/gold-coast-australias-sporting-graveyard

ENDNOTES

CHAPTER 1: SOMETHING GOOD MUST COME OF THIS

1 Alice Springs Town Council 2024, 'Visitor Info', https://www.alicesprings.nt.gov.au/residents/community/arts/alice-springs-public-art-map/history.aspx

2 'The Central Australia region, located at the geographic centre of Australia, is mostly covered by desert land, spanning over 600,000 square kilometres, or 40% of the Northern Territory' – Territory Resources, Central Australia, https://northernterritoryresources.com.au/my-region/central-australia

3 Department of Health 2020, *Mortality in the Northern Territory 1967-2014, Northern Territory Government, Darwin,* https://health.nt.gov.au/__data/assets/pdf_file/0005/924260/Mortality-in-the-Northern-Territory-1967-2014-Fact-Sheet.pdf

4 Tangentyere Council: 'Town Camps' — https://www.tangentyere.org.au/town-camps; Department of Territory Families, Housing and Communities 2024, 'About town camps', https://tfhc.nt.gov.au/housing-and-homelessness/town-camps-and-community-living-areas/about-town-camps

5 Clarke, R 2024 (12 November). Personal interview with the author.

6 Trove n.d., 'Centralian Advocate 9Alice Springs, NT: 1847-1964)', accessed 3 March 2025, https://trove.nla.gov.au/newspaper/title/63

7 ABS (Australian Bureau of Statistics) 2011, 'Alice Springs', https://www.abs.gov.au/census/find-census-data/quickstats/2011/LGA70200

8 Rosewarne, C, P Vaarzon-Morel, S Bell, E Carter, M Liddle, J Liddle 2007, 'The Historical Context of Developing an Aboriginal Community-Controlled Health Service: A Social History of the First Ten Years of the Central Australian Aboriginal Congress', *Health and History* 9(2):114-143.

9 Griffen-Foley, B (ed.) 2014, A Companion to the Australian media. Australian Scholarly Publishing, Melbourne.

10 Australian Law Reform Commission: Recognition Of Aboriginal Customary Laws (ALRC Report 31), https://www.alrc.gov.au/publication/recognition-of-aboriginal-customary-laws-alrc-report-31/

11 Batty, P 2018, 'Freda and Me: The Birth of CAAMA, Imparja and Indigenous media in Australia', Wakefield Press, www.wakefieldpress.com.au/blog/2018/10/freda-birth-caama-imparja-indigenous-media-australia/

12 Library & Archives NT 2010 (9 November), The Centralian Advocate, Centralian Advocate Collection, v. 64 no. 47. https://hdl.handle.net/10070/653198

CHAPTER 2: THEY MIGHT BE GIANTS

1 Pearson, N 2016 (8 December), 'The Soft Bigotry Of Low Expectations', *You're York Partnership, accessed 2024,* https://capeyorkpartnership.org.au/noel-pearson-the-soft-bigotry-of-low-expectations/

2 Sherrin Kangaroo Brand 2025, 'About Sherrin', accessed 2024, www.sherrin.com.au/about-sherrin

3 Barkly Regional Council 2025, 'Elliott & LA Meetings', accessed 2024, www.barkly.nt.gov.au/communities/elliott

4 City of Ballarat 2022 (8 April), 'Ballarat Population', accessed 2024 https://data.ballarat.vic.gov.au/explore/dataset/ballarat-population/table/?sort=-year

5 National Museum of Australia n.d., 'Eureka Stockade', *National Museum Australia*, accessed 3 March 2025, https://www.nma.gov.au/defining-moments/resources/eureka-stockade

6 Electrical Trades Union 2024, 'A History of Unionism in Australia', accessed 2024, www.etuwa.com.au/union-history

7 AFL (Australian Football League) 2024, 'Coats Talent League', accessed 2024, www.afl.com.au/talent-league

8 Giants 2025, *Foundation Years*, accessed 14 March 2025, https://www.gwsgiants.com.au/club/history/foundation-years

9 AFLNT (Australian Football League Northern Territory) 2022 (2 November), 'AFLNT NT footy set to thrive with continuation of strong participation', accessed 2024, www.aflnt.com.au/news/2022/nt-footy-set-to-thrive-with-continuation-of-strong-participation

10 Burgan, M 2010 (17 October), 'Dees win Shanghai thriller', *Melbourne Demon Spirit, accessed 2024,* www.melbournefc.com.au/news/126374/dees-win-shanghai-thriller

11 Gill, S 2023 (7 December), 'Victoria State of Origin team: The incredible honour roll of Big V players and their match history', *Code Sports, accessed 2024,* www.codesports.com.au%2Fafl%2Fvictoria-state-of-origin-team-the-incredible-honour-roll-of-big-v-players-and-their-match-history%2Fnews-story%2F447820d92c955254e341c549e1f92605&memtype=anonymous&mode=premium

12 Bush, G 2000 (10 July) 43rd Pres. of the United States, www.washingtonpost.com/wp-srv/onpolitics/elections/bushtext071000.html

13 Pearson, N 2016 (8 December), 'The Soft Bigotry Of Low Expectations', *You're York Partnership, accessed 2024,* https://capeyorkpartnership.org.au/noel-pearson-the-soft-bigotry-of-low-expectations/

CHAPTER 3: FORKS IN THE ROAD

1 'Yin & Yang in Chinese' n.d. accessed 2025, https://goeastmandarin.com/yin-yang-in-chinese/
2 Clarke, R 2022 (5 May), Personal interview with the author.
3 ABS (Australian Bureau of Statistics) 2010, 'Prisoners in Australia' in 4517.0, accessed 2024, www.abs.gov.au/AUSSTATS/abs@.nsf/DetailsPage/4517.02010?OpenDocument
4 Clarke, R 2022 (5 May), Personal interview with the author.
5 Monument Australia 2010, *Alfred Traeger*, accessed 14 March 2025, https://monumentaustralia.org.au/themes/people/industry/display/80017-alfred-traeger-traeger-park
6 Royal Flying Doctor Service 2019 (27 September), 'How Alfred Traeger gave the outback its voice', accessed 2024, www.flyingdoctor.org.au/qld/news/how-alfred-traeger-gave-outback-its-voice/
7 Austadiums 2025, 'NAB Challenge: Adelaide d West Coast', accessed 2024, www.austadiums.com/sport/event/6562
8 Austadiums 2025, 'TIO Traeger Park', accessed 2024, www.austadiums.com/stadiums/traeger-park-oval
9 Austadiums 2025, 'MCG', accessed 2024, www.austadiums.com/stadiums/mcg
10 ABC News 2006 (17 July), 'Ex-AFL star humbled by grandstand naming', accessed 2024, https://www.abc.net.au/news/2006-07-17/ex-afl-star-humbled-by-grandstand-naming/1802766
11 Perkins, R 2008, First Australians: No other law – 'The Altyerre is their life and their law', Ep. 4, Blackfella Films, Australia.
12 Britannica n.d., 'MacDonnell Ranges', accessed 2024, www.britannica.com/place/MacDonnell-Ranges

CHAPTER 4: ADAPTING TO COLONISATION

1 Sheppard, L. K., S. B. Rynne, J. M. Willis 2021, 'Sport as a cultural offset in Aboriginal Australia?', *Annals of Leisure Research 24 (1)*, doi: 10.1080/11745398.2019.1635895 Reproduced with permission through PLSclear.
2 Warrane; Berewalgal, definitions: https://www.sydneybarani.com.au/sites/sydney-cove-warrane/
3 Aboriginal Heritage Office n.d., 'A Brief Aboriginal History', https://www.aboriginalheritage.org/history/history/
4 Magdoff, H, R Webster 2025 (27 February), *Portugal's seaborn empire*, Britannica, accessed 14 March 2025, https://www.britannica.com/topic/Western-colonialism/Portugals-seaborne-empire
5 Manifest Destiny 2010 (5 April), 'Manifest Destiny', accessed 14 March 2025, https://www.history.com/topics/19th-century/manifest-destiny
6 Australian Sports Commission 2008, *Yulunga: Traditional Indigenous Games*, https://www.sportaus.gov.au/__data/assets/pdf_file/0006/705462/Yulunga_Games.pdf
7 Mifsud, Jason, (Gunditjmara man) 2022 (27 January). Personal correspondence with the author.
8 Howitt, A 1889, 'Notes on Australian message sticks and messengers', The *Journal of the Anthropological Institute of Great Britain and Ireland* 18: 314–332.
9 Huff, E 2010 (30 September), 'Thomas Wentworth Wills and Cullin-la-ringo Station', *Queensland Historical Atlas, accessed 2024,* https://www.qhatlas.com.au/content/thomas-wentworth-wills-and-cullin-la-ringo-station; Jackson, R 2021 (18 September) 'Research discovery suggests AFL pioneer Tom Wills participated in massacres of Indigenous people', *ABC News, accessed 2024,* https://www.abc.net.au/news/2021-09-18/suggests-afl-pioneer-tom-wills-participated-indigenous-massacres/100463708
10 Huff, E 2010 (30 September), 'Thomas Wentworth Wills and Cullin-la-ringo Station', *Queensland Historical Atlas*, accessed 14 March 2025, https://www.qhatlas.com.au/content/thomas-wentworth-wills-and-cullin-la-ringo-station
11 Stunzner, I 2016 (10 October), 'Wills family remembers 155-year-old massacre that marked turning point in Australian history', *ABC News*, accessed 14 March 2025, https://www.abc.net.au/news/2016-10-10/wills-massacre-marked-turning-point-australian-history/7919894
12 Wills, T. 1858 (10 July), 'Winter Practice', https://trove.nla.gov.au/newspaper/article/201371696
13 Collins, B 2019 (17 May), 'When Australian Football was born, these were the first 10 rules', https://www.afl.com.au/news/133990/when-australian-football-was-born-these-were-the-first-10-rules
14 Mark, D 2019 (14 June), 'AFL's position on Indigenous history of Aussie Rules leaves game's historians baffled', https://www.abc.net.au/news/2019-06-14/afl-latest-stance-proves-history-of-aussie-rules-is-in-debate/11202802
15 Hibbins, G 2008, 'Wills and the Aboriginal Game: A Seductive Myth' in *The Australian Game of Football since 1858, GSP Books, p. 45*
16 Poulter, J. 2007 (September), 'Marn-Grook's contextual link to Aussie Rules', https://websites.mygameday.app/assoc_page.cgi?c=1-5545-0-0-0&sID=220493
17 Sports Industry AU n.d, *AFL Revenue 2012-2023*, accessed 14 March 2025, https://footyindustry.com/index.php/afl-aflw/afl-revenue-2012-2023/
18 PROCOLOMATION 1927 (4 February), *Commonwealth of*

Australia Gazette (National: 1901 – 1973), accessed 6 March 2025, p 374, https://trove.nla.gov.au/newspaper/article/232518783

19 Wilkins, P n.d., *Alice Springs - A Brief History, accessed 14 March 2025*, https://www.wilmap.com.au/nt/nttowns/as_history.html

20 Northern Territory n.d., Alice Springs in WWII, accessed 14 March 2025, https://northernterritory.com/articles/alice-springs-in-wwii

21 Historical Australian Towns n.d., *Alice Springs, NT; Australia's Red Centre*, accessed 14 March 2025, https://historicalaustraliantowns.blogspot.com/2019/09/alice-springs-australias-red-centre.html

22 Stephen, M 2015 (31 May), *Colour Bar: Remembering and Forgetting Northern Territory Football 1916-1955, pp 173, 177-180, Historical Society of the Northern Territory, Uniprint NT, Charles Darwin University.*

23 AFL n.d., 'TIO CAFL', https://play.afl/northern-territory/competitions/tio-cafl

24 Coombe, R 2022, The Centre of Australian Football – 25 Years (1997-2022) of AFL in Central Australia – From the Commentary Box, CDU Print

25 Sheppard, L. K., S. B. Rynne, J. M. Willis 2021, 'Sport as a cultural offset in Aboriginal Australia?', *Annals of Leisure Research 24 (1)*, doi: 10.1080/11745398.2019.1635895

26 Osmond, G 2019 (1 July), 'Decolonizing Dialogues: Sport, Resistance, and Australian Aboriginal Settlements', Journal of Sport History 46 (2): 288–301, doi: 10.5406/jsporthistory.46.2.0288

27 Campbell, L. Jupurrurla Kelly, F. & Jupurrurla White, N. 2007, *Aboriginal Rules* [film], Warlpiri Media Association, Yuendumu.

28 Clarke, R 2012. Archived Redtails social media post.

CHAPTER 5: BUILDING A BLUEPRINT

1 Fletcher, D 2011 (25 September), 'Thunder soars to take prized double', *Sunday Territorian, p 60, accessed 6 March 2025*, https://territorystories.nt.gov.au/10070/648135/0/59

2 (CAAC) Central Australian Aboriginal Congress 2022, 'About us', accessed 6 March 2025, https://www.caac.org.au/about-us/

3 McAdam, I 2021 (31 October). Personal interview with the author.

4 (CAAC) Central Australian Aboriginal Congress 2022, 'Redtails Pinktails Right Tracks program', accessed 6 March 2025, https://www.caac.org.au/programs/redtails-pinktails-right-tracks-program/

CHAPTER 6: SHOW ME THE MONEY

1 National Museum of Australia 2023 (4 December), '*Aboriginal Land Rights Act*', https://www.nma.gov.au/defining-moments/resources/aboriginal-land-rights-act#:~:text=In%20December%201976%20the%20federal,traditional%20ownership%20could%20be%20proven

2 Northern Land Council n.d., 'About Us', https://www.nlc.org.au/about-us#OURGOVERNINGLAWS

3 Entsch, W 2022 (31 January), 'Inquiry into the Opportunities and Challenges of the Engagement of Traditional Owners in the Economic Development of Northern Australia', Parliament pf Australia, accessed 6 March 2025, https://www.aph.gov.au/Parliamentary_Business/Committees/Joint/Former_Committees/Northern_Australia_46P/TraditionalOwners46P/Report/section?id=committees%2Freportjnt%2F024836%2F78314

4 West Australian Football Commission n.d., 'Rio Tinto partners with WA Football Indigenous Programs', https://www.wafootball.com.au/news/20788/rio-tinto-partners-with-wa-football-indigenous-programs

5 Borschmann, G 2020 (5 June), 'Report reveals Rio Tinto knew the significance of 46,000-year-old rock caves six years before it blasted them', ABC News, accessed 6 March 2025, https://www.abc.net.au/news/2020-06-05/rio-tinto-knew-6-years-ago-about-46000yo-rock-caves-it-blasted/12319334

6 Santos 2024, 'Our Story', Santos, accessed 6 March 2025, https://ourstory.santos.com/

7 Santos 2018 (31 December), 'Annual Report 2018', accessed 6 March 2025, chrome-extension://efaidnbmnnni bpcajpcglclefindmkaj/https://www.santos.com/wp-content/uploads/2020/02/2018-annual-report.pdf

8 Merriam-Webster.com Dictionary 2025, 'Santo', *Merriam-Webster, accessed 6 March 2025*, https://www.merriam-webster.com/dictionary/santo

9 Kurmelovs, R 2021 (10 November), 'Fossil fuel advertising in sport 'the new cigarette sponsorship', ex-Wallabies captain David Pocock says', *The Guardian*, accessed 6 March 2025, https://www.theguardian.com/business/2021/nov/10/fossil-fuel-advertising-in-sport-the-new-cigarette-sponsorship-says-ex-wallabies-captain-david-pocock

10 Davidson, H 2015 (29 July), 'Artists call on Darwin festival to reject Santos sponsorship over fracking', *The Guardian*, accessed 6 March 2025, https://www.theguardian.com/australia-news/2015/jul/29/artists-call-on-darwin-festival-to-reject-santos-sponsorship-over-fracking

11 Small, S 2014 (8 December), 'Anti-CSG group Lock the Gate angry Santos logo being used on Qld police cars', https://www.abc.net.au/news/2014-12-

08/anti-csg-group-angry-at-santos-logo-used-on-qld-police-cars/5953030

12 Safi, M 2014 (8 December), 'Queensland police defend use of vehicles branded with Santos logo', *The Guardian*, accessed 6 March 2025, https://www.theguardian.com/australia-news/2014/dec/08/queensland-police-defend-use-of-vehicles-branded-with-santos-logo

13 The Greens 2023 (12 April), 'Uncle Major 'Moogy' Sumner demands apology from SANTOS for misleading use of his image', https://greens.org.au/news/media-release/uncle-major-moogy-sumner-demands-apology-santos-misleading-use-his-image

14 Tlozek, E & D Keane 2023 (12 April), 'Santos apologises for using image of Aboriginal elder Major 'Moogy' Sumner in corporate video', *ABC News*, accessed 6 March 2025, https://www.abc.net.au/news/2023-04-12/santos-urged-to-apologise-for-using-image-of-aboriginal-elder/102213092

15 Doman, M & T Baddeley 2013 (29 November), A Letter to the Committee on the Northern Territory's Energy Future, accessed 6 March 2025, chrome-extension://efaidnbmnnnibpcaj pcglclefindmkaj/https://parliament.nt.gov.au/__data/assets/pdf_file/0011/363656/Submission_No22_Santos_Ltd_3_December_2013.pdf

16 Amoonguna Football Club changed its name to South Alice Springs in 1971.

17 Essendon Football Club Past Players 2023, *Long, Michael*, accessed 14 March 2025, https://essendonfcpastplayers.com.au/past-player-profiles/listing/long-michael/

18 Qantas n.d., 'Our History', https://www.qantas.com/au/en/about-us/our-company/our-history.html

19 Clarke, R 2021 (6 October). Personal interview with the author.

CHAPTER 7: BIG SKY COUNTRY

1 Alice Springs Town Council n.d., 'Visitor History', https://alicesprings.nt.gov.au/about-alice-springs/more/a-brief-history

2 Australian Bureau of Statistics 2016, 'Alice Springs' (People, demographics & education), https://www.abs.gov.au/census/find-census-data/quickstats/2016/LGA70200

3 Kraft, W 2021 (6 October). Personal interview with the author.

CHAPTER 8: FOOTBALL'S SEISMIC SHIFTS

1 Gramenz, Emilie 2018 (29 May), 'The invisible border separating the haves and have-nots of the Territory', https://www.abc.net.au/news/2018-05-29/berrimah-line-invisible-money-border-separating-haves-have-nots/9800858

2 Frawley, T 2021 (19 November). Personal interview with the author.

3 AFLNT 2010 (23 April), 'NTFL-TEAFA merger given tick of approval', https://www.aflnt.com.au/news/2010/ntfl-teafa-merger-given-tick-of-approval

4 AFLNT 2011 (2 September), 'AFLNT absorbs AFLCA into its operations', https://www.aflnt.com.au/news/2011/aflnt-absorb-aflca-into-its-operation

5 Moncrieff, D 2003 (18 June), 'Sisters can play!', *Koori Mail*, p 71.

6 AFL Northern Territory 2012 (12 July), *Michael Long secures his dream with $1.5M*, accessed 14 March 2025, https://www.aflnt.com.au/news/2012/michael-long-secures-his-dream-with-15m

7 Australian Government n.d., 'Appendix E - Aboriginals Benefit Account Annual Report 2022–23', https://www.transparency.gov.au/publications/prime-minister-and-cabinet/national-indigenous-australians-agency/national-indigenous-australians-agency-annual-report-2022-23/section-6%3A-appendices-/appendix-e---aboriginals-benefit-account-annual-report-2022%E2%80%9323

8 AFL 2015 (14 March), *Michael Long Learning and Leadership Centre launched*, accessed 14 March 2025, https://www.afl.com.au/news/199689/michael-long-learning-and-leadership-centre-launched

9 ABC News 2014 (24 November), 'Northern Territory Government confirms sale for $424m after months of speculation, protests and petitions', https://www.abc.net.au/news/2014-11-24/nt-government-confirms-$424m-tio-sale/5912838

10 ESPN cricinfo n.d., 'TIO Stadium', https://www.espncricinfo.com/australia/content/ground/56390.html

11 Stephen, M, Historical Society of the Northern Territory 2015 (31 May), *Colour Bar: Remembering and Forgetting Northern Territory Football, 1916-1955, Uniprint NT, Charles Darwin University*, https://books.google.com.au/books/about/Colour_Bar.html?id=PPFyrgEACAAJ&redir_esc=y

12 Kakadu National Park n.d., 'Seasons', https://parksaustralia.gov.au/kakadu/discover/nature/seasons/

CHAPTER 9: 'THE CODE WARS' – A CONDENSED HISTORY

1 Back Story Podcast 2022, 'Dr Hunter Fujak – Author of *Code Wars*', https://soundcloud.com/user-644544597/dr-hunter-fujak-author-of-code-wars

2 Rugby AU 2024, *About Us: Our History, Australian Rugby – Its Origins and Evolution*, accessed 14 March 2025, https://australia.rugby/about/about-us/history

3 Fagan, S 2006, 'Excerpt: Centenary of Rugby League',

NRL Operations, accessed 14 March 2025, https://www.nrl.com/operations/history-of-rugby-league/

4 AFL and NRL Revenue – 2012-2023, https://footyindustry.com/index.php/between-the-codes/afl-and-nrl-revenue-2012-2023/

5 Monument Australia n.d., 'Brisbane Line', https://monumentaustralia.org.au/themes/conflict/ww2/display/91052-brisbane-line; The Maher Cup 2015 (11 August), 'Drawing the Barassi (Jim Keyes) Line', https://mahercup.com.au/blog/2015/08/11/jim-keys-line/

6 Smith, M n.d., 'Everything you need to know about the Gold Coast Titans', *Best in AU*, accessed 14 March 2025, https://bestinau.com.au/gold-coast-titans-nrl/

7 2023 AFL and NRL Memberships, https://footyindustry.com/index.php/afl-aflw/state-of-the-game-2023-afl-attendance-social-media-support-participation-memberships-and-tv-ratings/; https://footyindustry.com/index.php/rugby-league/state-of-the-game-2023-nrl-nrlw-tv-ratings-attendances-social-media-memberships-and-finance/

8 The Australian 2010 (5 June), *Who's afraid of the AFL, asks Titans boss Michael Searle, https://forums.leagueunlimited.com/threads/whos-afraid-of-the-afl-asks-titans-boss-michael-searle.361780/*

9 Gold Coast Bulletin 2008 (14 October), *Palmer lobbing bombs at GC17, https://webcf.waybackmachine.org/web/20081016065606/http://www.goldcoast.com.au:80/article/2008/10/14/17419_gold-coast-soccer.html*

10 Bowen, M. and Ryan, P 2013 (25 January), Millionaires' club explodes, https://www.afl.com.au/news/450377/millionaires-club-explodes

11 Barrett, D 2014 (30 July), 'Hunt, Folau poaching a failed experiment', https://www.afl.com.au/news/442958/hunt-folau-poaching-a-failed-experiment

12 ibid.

13 Craig, M 2011 (20 May), 'Throwing Cat Among Pigeons', *The Northern Star, accessed 25 March 2025, p 44.*

14 The AFL and the World Cup Bid, 2014 (4 May), FootyIndustry.com – http://www.footyindustry.com/?page_id=186

15 The Guardian 2017 (28 June), 'FIFA report claims FFA made 'improper payments' in 2022 World Cup bid', https://www.theguardian.com/sport/2017/jun/28/fifa-report-claims-ffa-made-improper-payments-in-2022-world-cup-bid

16 The Greens 2024 (10 October), 'Labor & Liberal weak on Murdoch as media reform stalled', https://greens.org.au/news/media-release/labor-liberal-weak-murdoch-media-reform-stalled

CHAPTER 10: PUTTING THE HARD WORD ON DARWIN

1 Clarke, R 2021 (26 August). Personal interview with the author.

2 AFLNT 2011 (27 October), 'Central Australia bid for NTFL licence', https://www.aflnt.com.au/news/2011/central-australia-bid-for-ntfl-license

3 Lee, D & Barfoot M 1995, *Northern Territory Football League: A history of Australian football in Darwin and the Northern Territory from 1916 to 1995, Northern Territory Football League, page 116*

4 Venes, A 2021 (11 December). Personal interview with the author.

5 ibid.

6 Thomson, W 2011 (15 November), 'Local club support', *Centralian Advocate*, page 32 https://territorystories.nt.gov.au/10070/643693/0/31

7 ibid.

8 AFLNT 2012 (19 June), 'NTFL & Palmerston future plans take shape', https://www.aflnt.com.au/news/2012/ntfl-palmerston-future-plans-take-shape

9 Clarke, R 2021 (26 August). Personal interview with the author.

10 Venes, A 2021 (11 December). Personal interview with the author.

11 Frawley, T 2021 (19 November). Personal interview with the author.

12 AFLNT 2012 (14 August), '2012-13 TIO NTFL Fixture, Redtails & Bulldogs on show', https://www.aflnt.com.au/news/2012/2012-13-tio-ntfl-fixture-redtails-bulldogs-on-show

13 Wilson, Kerry 2017, Nimbin

CHAPTER 11: KEY PERSONNEL

1 Cusack, S 2021 (7 November). Personal interview with the author.

2 AFL Northern Territory 2022 (8 June), 'Santa Teresa Oval wins the AFL Community Facilities Award for the NT', accessed 5 March 2025, https://www.aflnt.com.au/news/2022/santa-teresa-oval-wins-the-afl-community-facilities-award-for-the-nt#:~:text=Santa%20Teresa%20Oval%20wins%20the%20AFL%20community%20facilities%20award%20for%20the%20NT

3 Northern Territory Football n.d., 'AFL Central Australia', accessed 5 March 2025, https://ntfootball.tripod.com/id12.html

4 New York State Department of Health 2013 (May), 'Population, Land Area, and Population Density by County, New York State – 2011', accessed 5 March 2025, https://www.health.ny.gov/statistics/vital_statistics/2011/table02.htm

5 Bout, M 2010 (8 November), 'Indigenous runners complete first NY marathon', *ABC News*, accessed 5 March 2025, https://www.abc.net.au/news/2010-11-08/indigenous-runners-complete-first-ny-marathon/2327724

6 New York Road Runners Race Results n.d., 'NYRR Race Results 1970-Present', https://results.nyrr.org/home

7 New York Road Runners Race Results n.d., 'Reggie Smith', accessed 5 March 2025, https://results.nyrr.org/runner/1928/result/108

CHAPTER 12: REDTAILS' FIRST 22

1 AFL Northern Territory 2025, *Grand Final results from 1917*, accessed 14 March 2025, https://www.aflnt.com.au/competitionstio-ntflntfl-history/mens-premier-league-premierships

2 AFL Northern Territory 2025, *Grand Final results from 1917*, accessed 14 March 2025, https://www.aflnt.com.au/competitionstio-ntflntfl-history/mens-premier-league-premierships

CHAPTER 13: TELEVISING THE REVOLUTION

1 Cusack, S 2021 (7 November). Personal interview with the author.

2 Campbell, M., R Coombe, C King 2012 (6 October). Transcript from the commentary box, accessed 25 March 2025, https://www.youtube.com/watch?v=r9YMkkp3oGU

3 Campbell, M., R Coombe, C King 2012 (6 October). Transcript from the commentary box, accessed 25 March 2025, https://www.youtube.com/watch?v=r9YMkkp3oGU

4 Coombe, R 2022, The Centre of Australian Football – 25 Years (1997-2022) of AFL in Central Australia – From the Commentary Box, CDU Print.

CHAPTER 14: A HAPPY AFTERGLOW

1 Goetze, E & J Fenwick 2022 (12 February), 'Renewed push to reinstate Northern Territory Football League games in Alice Springs', *ABC News*, accessed 15 March 2025, https://www.abc.net.au/news/2022-02-12/calls-to-reinstate-ntfl-matches-in-alice-springs/100810182

2 Cusack, S 2021 (7 November). Personal interview with the author.

3 Mallard, R 2021 (7 May). Personal interview with the author.

4 Coombe, R 2022 (7 May). Personal interview with the author.

5 'Classifieds' 2015 (27 March), 'Geoffrey Jack Miller (Jnr)', *The Centralian Advocate*, accessed 2024, https://digitalntl.nt.gov.au/10070/520370/0/36

6 Gorman, S 2020 (1 August), 'We got the keys to the city: AFL great Peter Matera on WA in the 90s', *AFL, accessed 18 March 2025, https://www.afl.com.au/news/477026/peter-matera-deadly-files-write-off*

7 History of Australian music from 1960 until 2000 2013 (21 November), *Chocolate Starfish, accessed 5 March 2025, https://historyofaussiemusic.blogspot.com/2013/11/chocolate-starship.html#:~:text=Their%20debut%20album%2C%20%27Chocolate%20Starfish%27%2C%20appeared%20in%20April,40%20on%20the%20ARIA%20End%20of%20Year%20Charts.*

8 Adam Thompson 2025, *Musikarma*, accessed 15 March 2025, https://www.adamthompson.com/charity/

9 Thompson, A 2023 (9 March). Personal interview with the author. 9 March 2023

CHAPTER 15: SCORES ON THE BOARD

1 The Canberra Times 1994 (13 February), 'Aboriginal All-Stars fly too high for the Magpies', accessed 15 March 2025, https://trove.nla.gov.au/newspaper/article/134301472

2 AFL Northern Territory 2025, *Southern Districts*, accessed 15 March 2025, https://www.aflnt.com.au/competitionstio-ntflclubs/southern-districts-crocs

3 ABC News 2007 (23 February), 'McCasker's funeral draws crowd of mourners', accessed 15 March 2025, https://www.abc.net.au/news/2007-02-23/mccaskers-funeral-draws-crowd-of-mourners/2201882

4 Daz Footy 2020 (19 April), 'NTFL V Fremantle 1995 Full Game', accessed 15 March 2025, https://www.youtube.com/watch?v=WSBhxj2pa6E

5 AFL Northern Territory 2025, *Grand Final results from 1917*, accessed 15 March 2025, https://www.aflnt.com.au/competitionstio-ntflntfl-history/mens-premier-league-premierships

6 Moncrieff, D 2021 (7 April), 'How Baksh turned Nightcliff into a Top End powerhouse', *Koori Mail, pp 52-53.*

7 Ah Chee, P (2022), *Nowhere to Hide (EP), Ngala Music*

8 Ah Chee, P 2022 (1 December). Personal interview with the author.

9 Ah Chee, P 2022 (1 December). Personal interview with the author.

10 Ah Chee, P 2022 (1 December). Personal interview with the author.

CHAPTER 16: SHOW CAUSE JUST BECAUSE

1 Fletcher, D 2013 (4 June), 'Plenty of backing for the Central challenge', *The Centralian Advocate*, accessed 15 March 2025, p 45, http://territorystories.nt.gov.au/10070/585405/0/43

2 Stewart, A 2013 (31 May), 'Redtails push case for second trial', *ABC News*, accessed 15 March 2025, https://www.abc.net.au/news/2013-05-31/redtails-push-case-for-second-trial-season/4725990

3 AFLNT 2012 (22 October), 'NTFL season generating unprecedented interest', https://www.aflnt.com.au/news/2012/

ntfl-season-generating-unprecedented-interest
4 ibid.
5 Hind, R 2012 (26 October), 'Central Australia Redtails' bid for a spot in the big league', ABC News, https://www.abc.net.au/news/2012-10-26/central-australia-redtails-bid-for-a-spot-in-the/4336748?nw=0
6 Morris, G 2017 (26 July), 'Territory Thunder's player management rule and contract negotiations under threat', *NT News*, accessed 15 March 2025, https://www.ntnews.com.au/sport/local-afl/territory-thunders-player-management-rule-and-contract-negotiations-under-threat/news-story/83452909f1ae7d9f7f77d629925a095f
7 Morris, F 2014 (3 December), 'NTFL club get a Thunder boost', *NT News*, accessed 15 March 2025, https://www.ntnews.com.au/sport/local-afl/ntfl-clubs-get-a-thunder-boost/news-story/f573d879593f864|de7389136da6efae2
8 Herbert, C & G Liston 2012 (29 October), 'Mills offers qualified support for Redtails' NTFL bid', ABC News, https://www.abc.net.au/news/2012-10-29/mills-offers-qualified-support-for-redtails-ntfl/4339432
9 ibid.
10 Alice Springs Town Council 2012 (29 October), 'Mayor congratulates Central Australian Redtails on successful games', https://alicesprings.nt.gov.au/council/media/media-releases/2012/redtails-trial-success

CHAPTER 17: SURVEY SURPRISE

1 Angier N 1999, *Woman: An Intimate Geography*, Houghton Mifflin Company, New York.
2 AliceNow 2013 (15 March), 'The Redtails survey', https://web.archive.org/web/20130410021820/http://alicenow.com.au/news/article/the-redtails-survey
3 AFLNT 2013 (5 March), 'Survey commissioned to evaluate support for Redtails', https://www.aflnt.com.au/news/2013/survey-commissioned-to-evaluate-support-for-redtails
4 Fletcher, D 2013 (8 March), 'Redtails survey surprise, *Centralian Advocate, p 43, accessed 5 March 2025*, https://territorystories.nt.gov.au/10070/594808/0/42
5 Fletcher, D 2013 (15 March), 'Designed to fail', *Centralian Advocate, pp 54-56*, https://territorystories.nt.gov.au/10070/593106/0/55
6 Fletcher, D 2013 (15 March), 'Confusion as responses come in to 'negative' survey', *Centralian Advocate, p 54, accessed 5 March 2025*, https://territorystories.nt.gov.au/10070/593106/0/53
7 ibid.
8 ibid.

CHAPTER 18: CHARTING A NEW FLIGHT PATH

1 Senate Estimates Committee proceedings, 25 June 2013 – https://parliament.nt.gov.au/__data/assets/pdf_file/0011/387344/ESTIMATES-DAY-4-25-JUNE-2013.pdf
2 Territory Stories 2013 (8 March), 'Redtails survey surprise', Centralian Advocate 2013 (8 March), p 43, https://digitalntl.nt.gov.au/10070/594808/0/42
3 Morris, G 2013 (30 January), 'Money for Redtails', NT News, p 45, https://digitalntl.nt.gov.au/10070/598539/0/44; Morris, G 2013 (29 May), ' Redtails "more than footy"', *NT News, p 53*, https://digitalntl.nt.gov.au/10070/586794/0/52
4 Hull, W 2013 (17 March), 'Central Australian Redtails – More Information, Please', World Footy News, https://www.worldfootynews.com/article.php/20130318134506416
5 AFLNT 2013 (18 June), 'Redtails earn a new conditional trial', https://www.aflnt.com.au/news/2013/redtails-earn-a-new-conditional-trial-total-player-points-system-gets-nod
6 Clarke, R 2013 (June). Archived Redtails social media post.
7 AFLNT 2012 (22 October), 'NTFL season generating unprecedented interest', https://www.aflnt.com.au/news/2012/ntfl-season-generating-unprecedented-interest
8 Harris, L 2025 (20 March), Personal interview with the author.

CHAPTER 19: CRICKET SCHMICKET

1 Alice Springs Masters Games 2025, 'About', accessed 5 March 2025, https://www.alicespringsmastersgames.com.au/enter-now
2 McArdle, J 2014 (25 March), 'Redtail's dream hampered by renovations of Traeger Park', *NT News, accessed 15 March 2025*, https://www.ntnews.com.au/news/alice-springs/redtails-dream-hampered-by-renovations-of-traeger-park/news-story/88913214c7b12341567ae6084f7960e6
3 McAdam, I 2022 (5 May). Personal interview with the author.
4 Allen, S 2013 (25 March), 'Updated Traeger Park cricket wicket replacement report', ASTC, https://assets-astc.s3-ap-southeast-2.amazonaws.com/files/files/meetings/12._Agenda_14.4.1_-_Updated_Traeger_Park_Cricket_Wicket_Replacement.pdf
5 Morris, G, 2013 (30 January), 'Money key for Redtails, *NT News, p 45*, https://digitalntl.nt.gov.au/10070/598539/0/44
6 Herbert, C & G Liston 2012 (29 October), 'Mills offers qualified support for Redtails' NTFL bid', *ABC News*, https://www.abc.net.au/news/2012-10-29/mills-offers-qualified-support-for-redtails-ntfl/4339432
7 Morse, C 2024 (30 October), 'Cricket NT disappointed in National Indigenous Cricket

Championships departure from "spiritual home of Indigenous cricket"', *National Indigenous Times*, accessed 5 March 2025, https://nit.com.au/30-10-2024/14563/cricket-nt-disappointed-in-national-indigenous-cricket-championships-departure-from-spiritual-home-of-indigenous-cricket
8 NFSA n.d., 'Imparja: Indigenous Broadcasting', https:/ /dl.nfsa.gov.au/mod ule/687/#:~:text='Imparja%20is%20the %20anglicised%20spelling, region.'%20(Imparja%20 Television)/

CHAPTER 20: BLOC OF NATIONS

1 Hogg N 2016, 'On beauty', *The Cricket Monthly*, accessed 2024, https://www.thecricketmonthly.com/story/1058018/on-beauty#:~:text=Sport%2C%20and%20especially%20cricket%2C%20I,to%20look%20great%20and%20lose
2 Sharma, S 2017 (9 February), 'The Story of First Ever ODI', *Cricket n more*, accessed 15 March 2025, https://www.cricketnmore.com/cricket-special/australia-vs-england-first-odi-in-1971-at-melbourne-23737
3 The women did it first, https://en.wikipedia.org/wiki/1973_Women%27s_Cricket_World_Cup
4 Worldometer n.d., 'Southern Asia Population (LIVE), https://www.worldometers.info/world-population/southern-asia-population/
5 ESPN-Cricinfo 2006 (30 April), 'Asia to host 2011 World Cup', https://www.espncricinfo.com/story/asia-to-host-2011-world-cup-245789
6 NZC 2006 (1 May), 'NZ-Australia to host 2015 World Cup', accessed 15 March 2025, https://www.nzc.nz/news-items/archive/nz-australia-to-host-2015-world-cup
7 The Institute of Australian Culture 2012 (12 July), *The Ashes [cricket, Australia vs. England], accessed 15 March 2025,* https://www.australianculture.org/the-ashes/
8 ESPN cricinfo n.d., 'Records in The Ashes', https://stats.espncricinfo.com/ci/engine/records/team/series_results.html?id=1;type=trophy
9 ESPN cricinfo n.d., 'Manuka Oval', https://www.espncricinfo.com/australia/content/ground/56370.html
10 Field of Play, Venue guidelines for Australian cricket, Tier 2 venues, Cricket Australia, 2017-2018, page 7
11 Alice Springs Town Council 2013 (7 May), 'International Cricket at Traeger Park', https://alicesprings.nt.gov.au/council/media/media-releases/2013/international-cricket-traeger-park
12 NDTV Sports 2013 (7 May), 'Australia to host England in Ashes tour game in Alice Springs', https://sports.ndtv.com/the-ashes-2013/australia-to-host-ashes-tour-match-in-the-alice-1537043
13 ESPN cricinfo n.d., 'Alice Springs to host Ashes tour match', accessed 2024, https://www.espncricinfo.com/story/alice-springs-to-host-ashes-tour-match-634434
14 The Guardian 2013 (7 May), 'England to play Ashes tour match in the Australian outback', https://www.theguardian.com/sport/2013/may/07/england-ashes-outback-cricket
15 Passmore, R n.d., 'Traeger Park Oval Renovations', https://assets-astc.s3-ap-southeast-2.amazonaws.com/files/files/meetings/16.%20TS%20Agenda%20Item%209.4%20-%20Traeger%20Oval%20renovations.PDF
16 Allen, S 2013 (25 March), 'Updated Traeger Park cricket wicket replacement report', ASTC, https://assets-astc.s3-ap-southeast-2.amazonaws.com/files/files/meetings/12._Agenda_14.4.1_-_Updated_Traeger_Park_Cricket_Wicket_Replacement.pdf

CHAPTER 21: ERASURE

1 Hocking, J & N Reidy 2016 (Winter), 'Marngrook, Tom Wills and the continuing denial of Indigenous history', https://meanjin.com.au/essays/marngrook-tom-wills-and-the-continuing-denial-of-indigenous-history/
2 Dawe, B 1968, 'Life Cycle' in *An Eye for a Tooth*, Cheshire, Melbourne Victoria.
3 Oakley, R, J Green & G Slattery 2014, *The Phoenix Rises*, Slattery Media Group, Australia.
4 SCG Attendances n.d., 'S.C.G, Attendances (1952-2024)', accessed 2024, https://afltables.com/afl/crowds/vn_scg.html; SCG Attendances n.d., 'S.C.G, Attendances', accessed 2024, https://afltables.com/rl/crowds/s.c.g._vn.html
5 WAFL Footy Facts n.d., 'All Teams-Attendance Records', https://waflfootyfacts.net/team/all/attendances.php
6 Mascord, S 2021, Two Tribes: The Untold Story of Rugby League's Divided Year and the Birth of the NRL, Lightning Source Inc, Australia.
7 ESPEN cricinfo n.d., 'St Lawrence Ground', accessed 2024, https://www.espncricinfo.com/england/content/ground/56869.html#:~:text=The%20St%20Lawrence%20Ground%20was,from%20their%20deckchairs%20or%20cars; SportsAdda 2014 (1 June), 'Sloping down the hill at the home of cricket', accessed 2024, https://www.sportsadda.com/cricket/features/lords-cricket-ground-slope-england
8 Raymond, J 2020 (28 February), 'Traeger Park too slow for players', *Centralian Advocate, accessed 2024,* https://territorystories.nt.gov.au/10070/788762/0/51

CHAPTER 22: THE 'BUTTERFLY EFFECT'

1 Ambika, G 2015, 'Ed Lorenz: Father of the "Butterfly Effect"', *Reason, 20: 198-205, https://doi.org/10.1007/s12045-015-0170-y*
2 Bess, E, J Gruber 2004, *The Butterfly Effect*, New Line Cinema, United States of America.
3 The Guardian 2013 (7 May), 'England to play Ashes tour match in the Australian outback', *The Guardian*, accessed 3 March 2025, https://www.theguardian.com/sport/2013/may/07/england-ashes-outback-cricket
4 'Post Weather in Alice Springs, Northern Territory, Australia' November 2013, accessed 3 March 2025, https://www.timeanddate.com/weather/australia/alice-springs/historic?month=11&year=2013
5 2013-14 NTFL Premier League season fixtures, https://websites.mygameday.app/comp_info.cgi?c=0-2860-0-272172-0&pool=1&round=1&a=FIXTURE

CHAPTER 23: TOP END – THE SEQUEL

1 AFLNT 2013 (27 August), '2013-14 TIO NTFL Draw Officially Released', *AFL Northern Territory*, accessed 2024, https://www.aflnt.com.au/news/2013/2013-14-tio-ntfl-draw-officially-released
2 McAdam, G 2021 (6 October). Personal interview with the author.
3 ABC News 2012 (21 October), 'Tiwi Bombers hand Central Redtails their first defeat', *ABC News*, accessed 3 March 2025, https://www.abc.net.au/news/2012-10-21/tiwi-bombers-hand-central-redtails-their-first/4325772
4 AFLNT 2012 (22 October), 'NTFL Season Generating Unprecedented Interest', *AFL Northern Territory*, accessed 3 March 2025, https://www.aflnt.com.au/news/2012/ntfl-season-generating-unprecedented-interest
5 Alice Springs News 2013 (18 November), 'Redtails in high-scoring thriller', *Alice Springs News*, accessed 3 March 2025, https://alicespringsnews.com.au/2013/11/18/redtails-in-high-scoring-thriller/
6 McAdam, G 2021 (6 October). Personal interview with the author.
7 McArdle, J 2013 (26 November), 'Cyclone Alessia played havoc for Central Australia's Redtails', NT News, https://www.ntnews.com.au/news/centralian-advocate/cyclone-alessia-played-havoc-for-central-australias-redtails/news-story/6da3c7bdc69de17d0666ccabec63899d
8 Essendon FC 2013 (9 November), 'Jurrah joins Tiwi Bombers', https://www.essendonfc.com.au/news/142764/jurrah-joins-tiwi-bombers
9 NT News/Centralian Advocate 2013 (26 November), *Cyclone Alessia played havoc for Central Australia's Redtails*, https://www.ntnews.com.au/news/centralian-advocate/cyclone-alessia-played-havoc-for-central-australias-redtails/news-story/6da3c7bdc69de17d0666ccabec63899d
10 Weiss, K 2013 (23 April), 'QANTAS stops flights', *AliceNow*, https://web.archive.org/web/20130501091928/http://alicenow.com.au/news/article/qantas-stops-flights
11 AFLNT 2013 (6 November), 'Road Trip for future direction of AFLNT', https://www.aflnt.com.au/news/2013/road-trip-for-future-direction-of-aflnt
12 Central Land Council 2021, 'Aboriginal Languages of Central Australia', https://www.clc.org.au/aboriginal-languages-of-central-australia/
13 McArdle, J 2013 (20 December), 'Redtails make the grade', *NT News*, https://digitalntl.nt.gov.au/10070/565408/0/47;
14 Liston, G 2013 (20 December), 'Central Australian Redtails achieve goal of full place in Top End's tough NTFL competition', *ABC News*, https://www.abc.net.au/news/2013-12-20/ntfl-redtails-full-season-entry-announced/5169704

CHAPTER 24: ROLL UP! ROLL UP!

1 Clarke, R 2014 (26 March), Archived Redtails social media post.
2 Clarke, R 2014 (12 April), Archived Redtails social media post.
3 Clarke, R 2014 (12 April), Archived Redtails social media post.
4 Australian Bureau of Statistics (ABS) 2021, 'Tennant Creek', https://www.abs.gov.au/census/find-census-data/quickstats/2021/SAL70251
5 Clarke, R 2014 (12 April), Archived Redtails social media post.
6 SBS News 2013 (13 March), 'NT leadership shock makes history', *SBS News*, accessed 2024, https://www.sbs.com.au/news/article/nt-leadership-shock-makes-history/d7akht3mo
7 Harrison, D 2013 (13 March), 'Giles named NT's new leader', *The Sydney Morning Herald*, accessed 2024, https://www.smh.com.au/politics/federal/giles-named-nts-new-leader-20130313-2g0c2.html
8 ABC News 2016 (7 August), 'Ex-CLP leader Terry Mills quits party, slams Adam Giles leadership', *ABC News*, accessed 2024, https://www.abc.net.au/news/2016-08-07/mills-quits-clp-re-enters-nt-politics/7698268
9 The Poll Bludger n.d., *Blain*, accessed 15 March 2025, https://www.pollbludger.net/nt2020/Blain.htm
10 Frawley, T 2022 (10 June), Personal interview with the author.
11 Clarke, R 2014 (12 April), Archived Redtails social media post.

CHAPTER 25: THESE NUMBERS DON'T RUN

1 Chaucer, G (1380s), Troilus and Criseyde, https://www.gutenberg.org/files/257/257-h/257-h.htm#link2H_4_0005
2 AFL Northern Territory 2013, 'AFL Northern Territory Annual Report' chrome-extension://efaidnbmnnni bpcajpcglclefindmkaj/https://play.afl/sites/default/files/2024-09/2013_AFLNT_Annual_Report.pdf
2 Coburn, R 2021 (1 December), Personal interview with the author.
3 Hull, W 2014 (24 April), *Central Australian Redtails' future delayed, accessed 2024,* https://worldfootynews.com/article.php/20140423144212630?query=Redtails
4 Liston, G 2014 (23 April), 'Redtails denied AFLNT comp entry this year', ABC News, https://www.abc.net.au/news/2014-04-23/redtails-wont-play-in-afl-nt-comp-this-year/5406774
5 ABC News 2014 (23 April), *Redtails denied AFLNT comp entry this year,* https://www.abc.net.au/news/2014-04-23/redtails-wont-play-in-afl-nt-comp-this-year/5406774
6 Clarke, R 2014 (5 May), Archived Redtails social media post.
7 Smee, B 2015 (2 May), 'Former Minister for Tourism Matt Conlan was left holding a $5k bill at a Japanese "cabaret club"', *NT News*, accessed 2024, https://www.ntnews.com.au/news/northern-territory/former-minister-for-tourism-matt-conlan-was-left-holding-a-5k-bill-at-a-japanese-cabaret-club/news-story/a72123824257fd|9a3d0ca4656a2fdcf4
8 The Guardian 2014 (13 March), 'NT minister under pressure to resign over alleged verbal abuse of colleague', *The Guardian*, accessed 2024, https://www.theguardian.com/world/2014/mar/13/nt-minister-under-pressure-to-resign-over-alleged-verbal-abuse-of-colleague
9 Estimates Committee Proceedings, 12 June 2014, page 160, par. 1 and 2, https://parliament.nt.gov.au/__data/assets/pdf_file/0009/387333/ESTIMATES-DAY-3-12-JUNE-2014.pdf
10 ABC News 2015 (10 February), 'NT Transport Minister Matt Conlan resigns from frontbench *to spend time with family*', ABC Radio Darwin, accessed 2024, https://www.abc.net.au/news/2015-02-10/matt-conlan-resigns-from-front-bench-nt-government/6082408
11 Clarke, R 2014 (4 July), Archived Redtails social media post.
12 Clarke, R 2021 (26 August). Personal interview with the author.
13 AFLNT 2014, AFLT Annual Report, page 19, https://www.aflnt.com.au/sites/default/files/2014_AFLNT_Annual_Report.pdf
14 Animalia 2021, 'Red-Tailed (Black) Cockatoo', https://animalia.bio/red-tailed-black-cockatoo%20
15 https://www.iucnredlist.org/species/22684744/93044811#assessment-information

CHAPTER 26: FINGERS POINTING IN ALL DIRECTIONS

1 Play HQ 2025, *Caleb Hart*, accessed 16 March 2025, https://www.playhq.com/public/profile/f04fa184-9d26-45f4-95fd-546552f1434d/statistics
2 Play HQ 2025, *Abraham Ankers*, accessed 16 March 2025, https://www.playhq.com/public/profile/b5d19366-f934-4acf-95bd-5cb4887336c3/statistics?tenant=afl
3 Play HQ 2025, *Daniel Stafford*, accessed 16 March 2025, https://www.playhq.com/public/profile/7eaac5a5-4c99-416a-aba4-97ae5f7a864d/statistics?tenant=afl
4 Coburn, R. Personal interview with the author. 1 December 2021

CHAPTER 27: CREDENCE

1 Taylor, C, A Peters 2024 (19 November), 'It's clear footy has an Indigenous participation problem, and the AFL draft is only part of the solution', *The Conversation*, https://theconversation.com/its-clear-footy-has-an-indigenous-participation-problem-and-the-afl-draft-is-only-part-of-the-solution-228779#:~:text=It's%20an%20issue%20the%20AFL,high%20of%20109%20in%202020
2 Draftguru n.d., 'Alice Springs', https://www.draftguru.com.au
3 AFL 2024 (12 December), 'If you can see it, you can be it': Alice's newest hero aims to inspire', https://www.afl.com.au/news/1263026

CHAPTER 28: TOUCHING THE SUN

1 (CAAC) Central Australian Aboriginal Congress 2022, 'Redtails Pinktails Right Tracks program', accessed 2024, https://www.caac.org.au/programs/redtails-pinktails-right-tracks-program/
2 Demonwiki (n.d.), 'The history of the Melbourne Football Club', accessed 2024, http://demonwiki.org/Round+10+2018
3 Clarke, A 2024 (14 December), Personal interview with the author.
4 ibid.
5 Clarke, R 2024 (21 June). Personal interview with the author.
6 McAdam, I 2021 (31 October), Personal interview with the author.
7 Cusack, S 2021 (7 November). Personal interview with the author.
8 McAdam, G 2021 (6 October). Personal interview with the author.
9 Ah Chee, P 2022 (1 December), Personal interview with the author.
10 Venes, A 2021 (11 December), Personal interview with the author.

11 Coburn, R 2021 (1 December), Personal interview with the author.

CHAPTER 29: WHAT IMPACT RIGHT TRACKS?

1 Central Australian Aboriginal Congress 2021, *Central Australian Aboriginal Congress Annual Report 2020-2021, accessed 2024*, www.caac.org.au/wp-content/uploads/2022/06/2020-2021-Annual-Report_web.pdf
2 CAFL Minahan Medallists, n.d., accessed 15 March 2025, chrome-extension://efaidnbmnnnibpcajpcglclefindmkaj/https://play.afl/sites/default/files/2024-10/CAFL%20Minahan%20Medallists.pdf
3 Chlanda, E 2016 (10 May), 'Footy plus a job is a formula for life', *Alice Springs News, accessed 2024, https://alicespringsnews.com.au/2016/05/10/footy-plus-a-job-is-a-formula-for-life/*
4 Kings Narrative 2021, 'About Kings Narrative', accessed 16 March 2025, https://www.kingsnarrative.com.au/about-us/

CHAPTER 31: WHEN THOSE STARS ALIGN

1 Clarke, R 2024 (21 June). Personal interview with the author.

EPILOGUE

1 Fletcher, D 2011 (16 August), 'Rovers win for mate Josh', *Centralian Advocate, p 34.*
2 AFL Central Australia 2020 (15 July), 'The Josh Palmer Shield makes a return this afternoon when Rovers play South at TIO Traeger Park', Facebook, accessed 2024, https://www.facebook.com/AFLCA/posts/the-josh-palmer-shield-makes-a-return-this-afternoon-when-rovers-play-south-at-t/3066738926709014/

ACRONYMS

ABA Aboriginals Benefit Account
ABC Australian Broadcasting Corporation
ACT Australian Capital Territory
AFLNT Australian Football League Northern Territory
AFLCA Australian Football League Central Australia
AFL Australian Football League
AFLW Australian Football League Women's competition
AFLQ Australian Football League Queensland
AGM annual general meeting
AIS Australian Institute of Sport
AL A-Leagues (soccer)
ARIA Australian Recording Industry Association
ARL Australian Rugby League
ASCA Alice Springs Cricket Association
ASTC Alice Springs Town Council
ATSIC Aboriginal and Torres Strait Islander Commission
BAFL Barkly Australian Football League
CA Cricket Australia
CAAC Central Australian Aboriginal Congress
CAFA Central Australian Football Association
CAFC Central Australian Football Club
CAFL Central Australian Football League
CLP Country Liberal Party
DPC Desert Peoples Centre
FIFA Fédération Internationale de Football Association
GWS Greater Western Sydney
ICC International Cricket Conference/Council
MCG Melbourne Cricket Ground
MLA Member of the Legislative Assembly (NT)
MoU memorandum of understanding
NT Northern Territory
NEAFL North East Australian Football League
NFL National Football League (USA)
NICC National Indigenous Cricket Championships
NRL National Rugby League
NTFC Northern Territory Football Club
NTFL Northern Territory Football League
NSW New South Wales
NSWRL New South Wales Rugby League
NTFA Northern Territory Football Association (now TEAFA)
PINT (Postal Institute of the Northern Territory) Club (Greenants)
QAFL Queensland Australian Football League
RFL Rugby Football League (UK)
SANFL South Australian National Football League
SCG Sydney Cricket Ground
SR Super Rugby
TEAFA Top End Australian Football Association
TSL Tasmanian State League
VFA Victorian Football Association
VFL Victorian Football League
WA Western Australia
WACA Western Australia Cricket Ground
WAFC Western Australia Football Commission
WAFL Western Australian Football League
WANFL Western Australian National Football League

INDEX

C

ACKNOWLEDGEMENTS

None of anything that is written in this book could have been done alone. There were so many people who provided support and advice during the research phase and the actual writing of this book that it is impossible to name and thank every single one.

I particularly want to make mention of Rob Clarke, Alecia Clarke and Ian McAdam. This deadly trio, key to the Redtails' formation and ongoing operation, gave much of their time and energy to attend to my countless calls and emails, and in several one-on-one interviews in Alice Springs. Their recollection, insight and willingness to share was invaluable in piecing this story together.

I want to thank several people who also were involved at the club at the time of its formation: committee members Paul Ah Chee and Wayne 'Krafty' Kraft, who were happy to provide their rationale for wanting to get involved with the Redtails; coaches Shaun Cusack (2012) and Greg McAdam (2013), who were comfortable in revealing their 'trade secrets' as coaches, and perspectives on Central Australian football; and Redtails' 'First 22' squad member Ryan Mallard, whose firsthand account as a player was invaluable.

Outside the club, I want to thank Central Australian football guru and author Randall 'Stan' Coombe, and former Banks Bulldogs club president Luke Harris for their insights. And a huge thanks to former AFLNT office-holders Tony Frawley, Ross Coburn and Anthony Venes.

Organisations pivotal to the Redtails' early success deserve a mention, such as the Central Australian Aboriginal Congress, the Desert Peoples Centre, Centrecorp Foundation, Red Centre Technologies and AsBuild NT.

I want to make clear that, while individuals and organisations mentioned above played key roles and were central characters in this book and the Redtails story overall, my book wasn't written *for* them; this was written *about* them. Their only input was their answers to the questions I asked.

I also thank the custodians of language: the Arrernte and Gadigal, also Bundjalung peoples, whose words and ancestral links I weave into this story and to our shared histories.

On a personal level, there are several people who made this all possible. The first among them is my partner, Rebecca Stewart — my soulmate who found delight in my writing, this story and my wild passion for football. Her investment in the Redtails story matched mine. Becc spent countless hours into the night poring over the manuscript and new chapters as I completed them. Possessing a super-sharp mind, her pointed advice provided me with much-needed perspective. She also got me through those brief moments of self-doubt we all experience, and through a critical period at the end of 2024. Becc, I remain forever grateful.

Also, my cousin Denzyl Moncrieff, who reminded me often how happy he was that the storytelling tradition of our people (albeit in book format) would continue within our family; my large Yamaji family (of which number I have literally lost count), all of whom I love with everything that I am; and my dear friends Emma Delahunty, Anne Morris and Richie Singh for their input and support, and Marnicka Young for her early support and encouragement.

To my children, Bailey, Sachin, Jesse, Trey and Lucy: your presence in my life is something I cherish.

Huge thanks to the publishing arm of AIATSIS, Aboriginal Studies Press, who took a punt on my manuscript, the result of which sits in your hands now. Thank you to everyone who helped with fact-checking and language questions, and for giving me permission to use images and lyrics. A special mention also to the late Colin Tatz, whose dedication and work in the Aboriginal sports space from the late 1980s and 1990s will forever remain pivotal to the path I have been on since the late 1990s.

Writing is such a solo, introspective effort: the focus must be maintained; personal morale could only improve if I got that part right. So I want to thank anyone who I've ever (unintentionally) ignored in the course of writing this book — loved ones, lost ones, random passersby, the coffee lady… also Belle, Toby, Charles and Grommy, the best four-legged companions a man could ask for. So to all, in my ignorance of your nearby presence in those moments, I will say this: it wasn't you, it was me!

SARAH MARY JONES AND KUMANTYE PALMER – A TRIBUTE

There are two people I want to acknowledge, both of whom have arrived at the Great Eventuality that comes for us all, only for them it was way before time — one was a dear friend; the other I hadn't met but felt as if I did.

Early in 2021, I told my friend Sarah Mary Jones about this football club in Alice Springs, the backstory to their formation, and what they had done since. And then, more as a question, I said to her that 'being their 10th year next year, maybe I can write a book about them?' Sarah immediately lit up and was adamant that I should do this. Over the next few weeks, and whenever the Redtails was brought up, all I could ever hear from her were variations of: 'You should write it' 'You can do this!' 'You love football, you write about it all the time; you'll be great!' 'You totally should do it!' And so I did. Sarah would check in on its progress and I would show her what I had written to that point, to which she would offer advice and further encouragement. To me, it is important I relate this because without Sarah in those first few weeks and months of 2021, I don't think I would have tackled this with that early enthusiasm. The 'seed' for this book was there, sitting unplanted, but it took Sarah to plant, water and nurture it during its infancy. Earlier, in 2020, Sarah found small lumps in her breast. These were found to be cancerous, but to outward appearances you wouldn't know it for much of the next two years. Despite ongoing treatment, those lumps would grow and eventually become untreatable. In October 2023, Sarah succumbed. She was only 45.

Kumantye Palmer was a young man from Amoonguna near Alice Springs. I never met him. His time on this Earth was short. He was only 21 when he died, in October 2010. His loss is still felt by his family and community, the footy clubs he played for, his team-mates, and by his mate, Redtails co-founder, Rob Clarke and Rob's family. Kumantye's senseless death was the catalyst for what Rob Clarke and Ian McAdam would do in the weeks, months and years that followed. Throughout the writing of this book, the young man was very much present and he loomed large.

I would trade this book in a heartbeat if it meant the return of Sarah Mary Jones and Kumantye Palmer. This book is dedicated to their memory.

ABOUT THE AUTHOR

Darren Moncrieff is a Wadjarri-Tharrgari man and a longtime sportswriter from Western Australia. He had a front-row seat to the Redtails phenomenon as the sportswriter for the *National Indigenous Times* covering the Northern Territory, and as an Aussie rules footballer in the NTFL in Darwin at the same time as the Redtails' presence in the Top End.

A lifelong footy fan, Darren has played Aussie rules football for almost 40 years, reluctantly hanging up his boots only a few years ago. He has written about Aboriginal and Torres Strait Islander issues and extensively on Indigenous sport since the late 1990s.

His first job in media was as sports reporter-editor at *Yamaji News* in 1997. *Yamaji News* was a small Aboriginal newspaper based in Geraldton in WA's mid-west, covering the Yamaji area of his people. Darren's Wadjarri and Tharrgari bloodline comes from his gami (grandfather), Tony Moncrieff, and gantharri (grandmother), Alice Moncrieff, respectively. In shorthand, that means he is Yamaji. He was born in Boorloo-Perth and grew up entirely with his mother's family in Kuwinyardu-Carnarvon in WA's north-west.

Darren has held the roles of sports editor and sports reporter for *Yamaji News, Koori Mail, National Indigenous Times* and *Torres News*.

From early 2021 to mid-2023, Darren formulated, researched, wrote and completed this book within the serene hills, big trees and flowing streams on Country belonging to the Bundjalung Nation of the Widjabul Wiyabul clan group in the ancestral lands of Nimbinjee, in the surrounds of Nimbin, in Northern NSW.

www.ingramcontent.com/pod-product-compliance
Lightning Source LLC
LaVergne TN
LVHW050955080826
845145LV00006B/1504

* 9 7 8 0 8 5 5 7 5 2 0 6 4 *